Bidding and Estimating Procedures for Construction

D01417Ø1

Bidding and Estimating Procedures for Construction

G.L. Mansfield

Reston Publishing Company, Inc., Reston, Virginia
A Prentice-Hall Company

Library of Congress Cataloging in Publication Data

Mansfield, G. L. (G. Leo)
Bidding and estimating procedures for construction.

Includes index.
1. Building—Contracts and specifications.
2. Building—Estimates. I. Title.
TH425.M35 1983 692'.5 82-23019
ISBN 0-8359-0474-1

© 1983 by
Reston Publishing Company, Inc.
A Prentice-Hall Company
Reston, Virginia

All rights reserved. No part of this book
may be reproduced in any way, or by any means,
without permission in writing from the publishers.

10 9 8 7 6 5 4 3 2 1

Printed in the United States of America

In loving memory of Alexandra Marie Swan

Contents

Preface *xi*

Metric Conversion Factors *xiii*

Introduction *1*

1 ***Preliminary Procedures*** 4

1.1 The Bid Call 4
1.2 Recording the Bid Documents 6
1.3 Checking the Bid Documents 8
1.4 Checklist of Trades 10
1.5 Bid-Info Reports 12
1.6 Soliciting Bids from Subcontractors 14
1.7 Recap 18

2 ***Prebid Communication*** 19

2.1 Initial Communication 19
2.2 Drawings 21
2.3 Reading the Specification 22
2.4 Specification Sections Relating to Subtrades 26

2.5 "Work by Others" Clauses 28
2.6 Items Relative to Normal Trade Practice 29
2.7 Approved Trade Contractors or Manufacturers 30
2.8 Making and Recording Queries 31
2.9 Addenda 34
2.10 Review 35

3 Take-off: General Comments 37

3.1 Basic Principles of Quantity Surveying 37
3.2 Methods of Measurement 40
3.3 Net and Gross Quantities 41
3.4 Take-off Sheets 44
3.5 General Contractor's Trades 44
3.6 Drawings 45

4 Take-off: Sitework 54

4.1 General 54
4.2 Soil Report 56
4.3 Compaction 57
4.4 Measurements: General Principles 58
4.5 Schedule of Items and Measurements: Excavation 59
4.6 Fill and Backfill: General 61
4.7 Schedule of Items and Measurements: Fill and Miscellaneous Earthwork Items 62
4.8 Perimeter Piling and Shoring 63
4.9 Underpinning 64
4.10 Dewatering 65
4.11 Demolition 66
4.12 Schedule of Items and Measurements: Demolition 67
4.13 Take-off Example 68

5 Take-off: Concrete and Formwork 76

5.1 Concrete: General 76
5.2 Schedule of Items and Measurements—Concrete 78
5.3 Formwork: General Remarks 83
5.4 Schedule of Items and Measurements—Formwork 85
5.5 Take-off Example 89

6 *Take-off: Masonry* 101

6.1 General 101
6.2 Schedule of Items and Measurements: Masonry 102
6.3 Masonry Equipment 106
6.4 Conversion Factors: General 106
6.5 Concrete Block Masonry 108
6.6 Structural Clay Tile Masonry 110
6.7 Structural Glazed Tile 111
6.8 Fireproofing Tile for Structural Steel Beams 111
6.9 Mortar 111
6.10 Masonry Ties and Anchors 112
6.11 Review 112
6.12 Take-off Example 113

7 *Take-off: Rough and Finished Carpentry, Miscellaneous Items* 121

7.1 Rough Carpentry 121
7.2 Measuring Rough Carpentry Work 123
7.3 Schedule of Items and Measurements: Rough Carpentry 124
7.4 Finish Carpentry 126
7.5 Schedule of Items and Measurements: Finish Carpentry 128
7.6 Doors and Frames 129
7.7 Miscellaneous Metals 130
7.8 Specialities 132
7.9 Miscellaneous Contractor's Work 132
7.10 Schedule of Items and Measurements: Miscellaneous Trades 133
7.11 Take-off Example 136

8 *Pricing the Estimate: Basic Principles* 140

8.1 General 140
8.2 Material Prices 141
8.3 Labor Units 143
8.4 Equipment 152
8.5 Subcontractors' Unit Prices 153
8.6 Examples of Pricing 154

9 **Pricing the Estimate: Examples** 156

9.1 General 156
9.2 Labor Rates 156
9.3 Composite Labor Rates 158
9.4 Schedules of Man-hour Factors 159

10 **Estimating Site Overhead Costs** 187

10.1 Definitions 187
10.2 Schedule 189
10.3 Site Visit 189
10.4 Categorizing Site Overhead Items 191
10.5 Category 1: Project Supervision 193
10.6 Category 2: Offices and Administrative Requirements 194
10.7 Category 3: Site Access, Protection, and Security 195
10.8 Category 4: Temporary Utilities 198
10.9 Category 5: Construction Facilities and Services 203
10.10 Category 6: Hoisting, Materials and Personnel 208
10.11 Category 7: Small Tools and Equipment 211
10.12 Category 8: Permits, Insurances, and Bonds 212
10.13 Review 213

11 **Closing the Bid** 215

11.1 General 215
11.2 Bid-Closing Checklist 216
11.3 The Bid Form 217
11.4 Telephone Bids 220
11.5 Bid Depository Quotations 223
11.6 Prebid Subtrade Proposals 224
11.7 Subtrade Quotation Analysis 229
11.8 Sales Tax 231
11.9 Main Estimate Summary 232
11.10 Unit Prices 234
11.11 Bid Delivery 234
11.12 Brief "Recap" 235

Appendix Et Alia 237

Postbid Activities 237
Bid Analysis 238
Mechanical and Electrical Trades 239

Index *241*

Preface

Many people—family, friends, colleagues, business associates and others—voluntarily helped me in the preparation and writing of this book. I would first like to identify and express my thanks to those who made the major contributions. My wife, Bee, labored many hours checking through the manuscript for errors and discrepancies; any mistakes detected in the text will surely exist in those portions that were not subjected to her vigilant scrutiny. Stan Dean meticulously read and offered valuable suggestions on the early drafts of the various chapters and the quantity take-off examples; he did most of this during a period when he suffered considerable physical pain and discomfort.

My thanks also to Peter Mansfield, O.L.S., for taking time to prepare the site plan, and to Hilary Oosterhof who steered her father onto the right path with the compilation of the index.

I wish also to acknowledge and express my appreciation to the following organizations:

The Canadian Institute of Quantity Surveyors for permission to quote from the "Method of Measurement of Construction Works" and other publications of that Institute.

The Canadian Construction Association Documents Committee for allowing me to quote pertinent clauses from CCDC 12 1979 for a Stipulated Sum Contract. (Note: effective June 15th 1982, this document has been revised and published as CCDC 2 1982).

The American Institute of Architects for granting permission to quote a clause from AIA Document A201 1976 edition.

Construction Specifications Canada and the Construction Specification Institute

Inc. (U.S.A.) for permission to quote from and make reference to sections from Masterformat.
The Clay Brick Association of Canada for allowing me to repeat certain calculation factors for brickwork and mortar from their "Technical Notes on Brick Construction." I strongly recommend these well-prepared and detailed technical sheets to students of quantity surveying and estimating.

There were many other people who formed a voluntary back-up team and contributed assistance in numerous and varying ways: checking calculations, reviewing and advising on construction operations, wrapping manuscripts, typing labels, and many other things. Also, there were the "morale boosters" who quickly dispelled the author's periodic despondencies with cheery greetings of "So,—how's the book coming along?".

These people have not been individually named here, but they are certainly not forgotten. My deep and sincere thanks to every one of them.

G. L. MANSFIELD

Metric Conversion Factors

Length

1 millimeter (mm)	=	0.039 inch	1 inch	=	25.4 mm
1 meter (m)	=	3.28 feet	1 foot	=	0.304 m
1 kilometer (km)	=	0.621 mile	1 mile	=	1.621 km

Area

1 square meter (m^2)	=	10.764 square feet	1 square foot	=	0.093 m^2
1 hectare (ha)	=	2.471 acres	1 acre	=	0.405 ha

Volume

1 cubic meter (m^3)	=	1.308 cubic yards	1 cubic yard	=	0.765 m^3
1 liter (L)	=	0.219 gallon	1 gallon	=	4.546 L

Mass

1 kilogram (kg)	=	2.204 pounds	1 pound	=	0.454 kg
1 tonne (t)	=	1.102 ton (2,000 lbs)	1 ton	=	0.907 t

NOTE: Above factors are rounded off to a maximum of three (3) decimal places.

Bidding and Estimating Procedures for Construction

Introduction

As the title implies, this is a book on the subject of estimating construction costs, but it is one written with a particular emphasis on the preparation of a "stipulated sum" bid by a general contractor. The aim of the book is:

1. to review all the normal bid-preparation activities that take place in a contractor's estimating section, from the initial receipt of the drawings and specifications to the final hour of bid-submission to the building owner, and
2. to recommend and outline practices and methods to handle these functions.

Included amongst these activities would be the recording of the bid documents; organizing and planning the estimate format; reading the specifications; quantity 'take-off'; pricing; analyzing subcontractors' quotations; assessing the cost of on-site overhead; and closing the bid. These operations are not confined solely to a general contracting organization; trade contractors—who usually become subcontractors to the prime contractors—also employ estimators and quantity surveyors who undertake similar responsibilities and provide the same expertise.

"What's so special about a 'stipulated sum' contract?" someone will ask. "Surely quantity surveying and estimating skills are equally essential to other types of construction contracts—construction management for example, or a unit price contract, or a Guaranteed Maximum Price contract? Also, what about cost feasibility studies for owners and architects? Surely these functions demand as much construction costing expertise as a stipulated sum bid?"

Agreed!

However, it is my opinion—an opinion no doubt influenced by the many years I have worked in general contractors' offices!—that the preparation of

an estimate for a firm or "fixed" price type of contract is always a challenging exercise for a construction estimator. Contractors are usually allowed a short period of time in which to establish a monetary amount to which they will be committed for a *long* period of time—many months or years. During that short, usually hectic, bid-preparation period much planning and organization has to be accomplished and expertise and experience are put to the test; everything must be done quickly and done right, or as right as is humanly possible. It also should be done methodically.

The estimator in a contracting organization—general contractor or single-trade contractor—has a *professional obligation* to his or her employer to provide with proper care and judgment a realistic estimate of cost; he or she must ensure that this estimate faithfully represents all the information provided in the bid documents—the drawings and specifications, and addenda thereto. Nothing should be intentionally ignored or distorted for the sake of satisfying the contractor with a low bid. I am not inferring with that last statement that an estimator or quantity surveyor should be disinterested in his or her company's performance; everyone likes to be successful or be on a winning team, but company loyalty should never sway an estimator from examining and assessing the facts as they appear in the documents. Speculation, strategy, probability factors, market assessment—all these are as common to the construction industry as to other business enterprises; but they should always be recognized as forming part of the *bidding function* rather than the *estimating function*.

This book addresses itself to reviewing procedures and methods that would assist an estimator to prepare an estimate in a professional manner. The examples of quantity "take-off" and pricing are limited to those trades traditionally performed by a general contractor with his own labor force (although many of these are now subcontracted to specialist contractors); excavation and general earthwork operations; concrete and formwork; masonry; and rough and finished carpentry work.

This is *not* an estimating reference book which an estimator can "flip" through to find unit costs of plastering, or painting, or plumbing or heating installations or other specialist trade work. There are many excellent books available which cover those and similar items, and some of these books are listed at the end of this Introduction.

For whom, then, has this book been written?

The person I visualized when I started writing would be a young person presently taking, or had recently completed, a two- or three-year construction technology course at a community college, university, or polytechnical institute—a course which placed a certain emphasis on quantity surveying and estimating techniques. I would hope this book might prove a useful source of reference or add further dimension or perspective to what had been taught and studied; or be equally useful to someone starting his or her career in the construction industry, particularly as a junior or trainee estimator.

Who else might find it useful?

Well, a construction company manager might dip into these pages for some background on estimating and bidding functions; also someone starting a new construction company—an ex-superintendent or engineer perhaps—might learn a few pointers about organizing an estimating division. Even a few veteran estimators—my peers in fact!—might gain a little satisfaction from either seeing some of their own methods endorsed or feel even more satisfied with their own methods where they differ from those recommended in these pages!

The quantity take-off examples are provided to demonstrate some of the fundamental quantity surveying techniques; although, I fully agree that time-limitations would restrict the indulgence in such meticulous recording and "side-noting" of the dimensions. However, it is beneficial to all of us—trainees and experienced estimators alike—to be occasionally reminded about the basic rules of good quantity surveying practices.

The quantities and examples of priced estimates evolve (somewhat loosely) around a university or college building to be used as a research center. The drawings of this building were prepared to show only the pertinent details necessary for a demonstration of quantity take-off; in some instances, items appear on the quantity sheets or in the estimate summaries for which no drawings or details are provided.

A brief word should be said about the Metric or S.I. (Système Internationale) units noted on the Schedules of Items and Measurements. These units are intended to show the recommended units of measurement for work measured in the Metric system; they *do not represent the exact equivalent in metric for an Imperial unit of measurement*. For example, the recommended unit of measurement for an item stated in Imperial as "square foot" is usually stated in metric as "square meter" or m^2, recognizing that a square meter (10.764 square feet) is closer in actual size dimensions to a square yard! Also, the metric dimensions shown on the drawings are "hard metric" conversions, indicating what these dimensions would be if the project were *designed in Metric*.

And lastly, following are some of the text or reference books I would recommend to both trainee and experienced construction estimators:

Frank R. Dagostino, *Estimating in Building Construction*, Reston Publishing Company, Inc., 1973.

Norman Foster, *Construction Estimates from Takeoff to Bid*, 2nd ed., McGraw-Hill, 1973.

Michael F. Kenny, *Concrete Estimating Handbook*, Van Nos Reinhold, 1975.

Robert S. Means, *Building Construction Cost Data*, Robert Snow Means Company, Inc., 1978.

Robert L. Peurifoy, *Estimating Construction Costs*, 3rd ed., McGraw-Hill, 1975.

Frank R. Walker, *The Building Estimator's Reference Book with Vest-Pocket Estimator*, 19th ed., Frank R. Walker Company, 1977.

Yardsticks for Costing, joint venture publication of Southam Business Publications and Construction Data Systems Ltd, 1978.

1
Preliminary Procedures

1.1 The Bid Call

The methods by which a general contractor is informed about a potential bid will generally depend on whether it is an open bid for work to be financed wholly or partially by public funds, and will therefore be called by some branch of government (federal, provincial, state, or municipal) or a public authority such as a school or hospital board, or whether it will be a "closed" bid called by private individuals, companies, or organizations.

Public bids are usually advertised in national or regional newspapers or trade journals, although it is not unusual for such public announcements to be supplemented by printed or mimeographed "flyers" mailed out to general contractors. It is also not uncommon for architectural offices to delegate someone to telephone all known contractors in a given area or locality and draw their attention to the publicized bid call.

Figure 1.1 illustrates a typical advertisement for a public bid. It will be noticed that this particular example announces that the bids will be opened publicly; but it should be observed that it is the rule rather than the exception for bids for public funded projects to be opened and the results read out publicly, which is not necessarily always (or need be) stated in the bid call advertisement. Estimators should check early in the bidding period with the architects if there are any doubts about this.

Invitations to bid on nonpublic work are sometimes mailed in individual letter form to a number of selected contractors; however, a common practice is for the initial contact to be made by telephone to ascertain the contractor's interest and intention, and then to confirm the invitation (and the contractor's acquiescence!) by letter. Figure 1.2 shows an example of such a letter.

PORT CRAGFIELD,
Ontario

Sealed stipulated sum bids clearly marked "Bids for Johnson Heights High School" will be received until 3:00 p.m. local time,

TUESDAY, AUGUST 12th, 1980

at the offices of the Port Cragfield Board of Education, at which time and place the bids will be opened publicly. General contractors may obtain drawings and specifications from the office of the architects, Peck and Hugg Partnership, 1 East Street, Port Cragfield on the deposit of a certified check in the amount of $100.00, refundable when the documents are returned in good condition.

Bids must be accompanied by a bid bond equal to 10% of the bid amount.

Lowest or any bid not necessarily accepted.

Peck and Hugg Partnership

Figure 1.1.

The selection of contractors to be invited to bid on certain projects is often made by the process of prequalification. Printed forms are made available to general contractors, and a date and time announced (usually advertised in a trade journal or paper) for the completion and return of their forms to the architect's office. The information requested usually pertains to a contractor's financial background, previous experience in similar projects, and details of the designated supervisory staff. A standard prequalification document is published by the Canadian Construction Association, which requires only the most pertinent information about the contractor's organization and experience. Some owners and/or architects prepare their own prequalification documents with similar requirements, but occasionally contractors are confronted with menacing fact-finding dossiers that attempt to extract every morsel of confidential information about their companies!

The wording of bid calls (public and private) is usually restricted to information regarding the name of the project, the date and time of the bid closing, the monetary deposit required for the bid documents, the type and amount of the bid security (certified check or bid bond), and where the documents can be examined. Also, a statement might be made regarding the period the bid must remain open before actual award of a contract. When the documents are received, they should be checked to ensure that any repeated information agrees with the bid call. (For example, the bid call might state the bid will remain open for a period up to 30 days before a contract is awarded, whereas the specifications might state 60 days. Such a discrepancy should be queried immediately with architects.)

DODGSON AND CARROLL, ARCHITECTS

April 21, 1982

Gellem Construction Company
23 North St. W.
Centreville, Ontario

Attention: Mr. S. Gellem

Dear Sirs:

Re: New Research Wing,
Jackson University

Further to our telephone discussion of this date, wherein you expressed interest in submitting a bid for the above-noted project, we are pleased to confirm the inclusion of your firm's name on the list of selected bidders.

The drawings will be available at our offices April 24, 1982.

There will be two (2) sets of drawings and specifications available to you. A deposit of $100.00 per set in the form of a certified check made payable to Dodgson & Carroll is requested. This amount will be refunded upon the return of the bid documents.

The bid closing date is May 27, 1982.

Yours truly,

L. Carroll

Figure 1.2.

The phrase "the lowest or any bid not necessarily accepted" is common to all bid invitations, whether public or private.

1.2 Recording the Bid Documents

Contractors are usually allowed two sets of drawings and specifications for bidding purposes, for which they are normally required to provide some form of monetary deposit, usually a certified check. However, some architectural firms only permit the issuance of one set of documents for the deposit and require the contractor to pay the *cost of printing* of any additional sets required. A deposit will still be required on this extra set, redeemable upon return of the documents to the architect's office. (Architects request these extra drawings be returned as a protection of design copyright.)

It is important to properly record the receipt of the bid documents as soon as they are received in the contractor's office. A *separate record* for each project being bid is recommended, rather than keeping a general office register that records all drawings received in the estimating department. This record for a specific project will not only be used for the initial receipt of the documents, but it will also be used to keep track of the distribution to subcontractors during the bidding period.

Contractors' estimators are accustomed to being perpetually trapped in the "squeeze" between the utilization of the drawings and specifications for their own bid preparation work (quantity surveys, specification reading, scheduling, and so on), while at the same time responding to the pressures from the many subtrade contractors who also require these documents to prepare their own estimates. When two sets of documents are made available to the contractor, it is quite often the practice to make one set constantly available for inspection by subcontractors or suppliers. Many trade contractors, particularly those whose trades are major ones in a specific project and therefore demand a considerable amount of take-off, will often request the loan of the drawings and the specifications—for an evening, a weekend, or a longer period. This results in an unavoidable amount of "juggling" of the documents, trying to satisfy everyone's needs at the same time; and it is because of this constant movement of the bid documents in and out of the contractor's office, plus the factor of the inevitable issuance of addenda and revised drawings, that it is essential to keep an accurate record of all these events.

Apart from the obvious need to maintain an efficient and organized system, it should be recognized that these documents are the basis of a (possible) future contract; they are, in fact, *potential contract documents*. If the bid is successful, these documents assume a distinct status. They are the documents upon which the *bid was based*. It is not unusual for postbid revisions to be made to both the drawings and the specifications *prior* to the signing of the contract, and there will almost certainly be a number of such revised documents issued after that event. These documents are therefore the best and true record of the *information available to the contractor at the time of bidding*.

On the less positive side, if the bid is unsuccessful, the documents will have to be collected and returned to the architect's office.

Either situation demands that the process of locating and putting together all the bid documents be as smooth and painless as possible. Few activities in a general contractor's office present such a dismal picture of frustration as that of young estimators poking fruitlessly into dark corners of the office when looking for missing drawings and specifications. ("Jack says he gave the structural drawings to *someone* but can't remember *who*!" "Volt Electric Co. say they returned the 'specs.', but no one's seen them!")

Figure 1.3 illustrates an example of a recommended type of record for a specific project. It is divided into two divisions: Receipt and Distribution. To record the receipt of the documents requires such basic information as the date, the *number of sets* received, and the drawing identification numbers, and also information regarding the specifications accompanying the drawings. If, for example, the divisions for Architectural, Structural, Mechanical, and Electrical work are issued in separate volumes, this should be noted.

This record will also be used if and when addenda and revised drawings are issued. (*Note:* It is a good idea to insert a revised drawing into the set immediately *before* the drawing being replaced and note on the original the word "Superseded." This facilitates any necessary checking to ascertain the changes made to the original drawing.)

Under Distribution of the record, the pertinent information is again the date, the details of the documents that are being loaned out, the name of the company borrowing them, and the date they were returned to the contractor's office. The initials of the person picking up the plans is also recommended.

The final column in the sample record is used to write the date on which the documents were returned to the architect's office. This is, of course, the sad announcement that the bid was unsuccessful; those words "plans and specifications returned to the architect's office on such-and-such a date" form the epitaph to many bids prepared in a general contractor's office.

The discipline of maintaining this type of record during the bid-preparation period must be aggressively pursued if it is to be effective and useful. It should never be allowed to become sloppy, especially when the bid closing date is near and a certain "oh well, it doesn't matter now" attitude may develop. Estimators are exposed to considerable work pressures at this time, and the temptation to rely on memory or on hastily written notes on scraps of paper (all done with every good intention of writing up the record at a later time) is very natural; but nobody's memory is foolproof, and those little notes have a habit of disappearing into jacket pockets and do not re-emerge until the jacket goes to the cleaners.

1.3 Checking the Bid Documents

Apart from recording the receipt of the documents, it is also important (*imperative* in fact) to ensure that *all* the documents have been received. The drawing numbers should be checked against those written on a transmittal sheet or an index provided either in the specifications or on one of the drawings. Failing the provision of such an index or transmittal sheet, the drawing numbers will need to be checked for sequence and a query put to the archi-

Bid Documents: Receipt
Estimate No: 27/82
Project: *New Research Wing, Jackson University*

Bid Documents: Distribution

Date	Dwg.	No.	Description	No. of Sets	Date: Out	Date: In	Dwg. No.	Description	Firm's Name	Initials	Date ret'd. to Arch.
4/24/82	A1-A9 S1-S6	)))	Architectural Structural	2 2	4/26/82	4/30/82	S1-S6	Structural (1 set of specs.)	Bar-Rod Reinf. Co.	B.W.	
	M1-M8 E1-E5	)))	Mechanical Electrical	2 2	5/2/82	5/7/82	A1-A9	Architectural (1 set of specs.)	Centreville Drywall Co.	A.J.B.	
			Specifications: Architectural & Structural	2	5/5/82	5/26/82	M1-M8	Mechanical (1 set of mech. specs.)	B.T.U. Plumbing & Heating Co.	D.H.	
			Mechanical Electrical	2 2	5/7/82	5/14/82	A1-A9	Architectural (1 set of specs.)	Monarch Precast Co. Ltd.	S.F.	
5/19/82			Addenda Nos. 1 & 2	2	5/7/82	5/26/82	E1-E5	Electrical (1 set of elec. specs.)	Volt Electric Co.	P.N.	
5/23/82	A3, A6	)))	Revised Architectural)))	2	5/23/82	5/25/82	-	A3, A6 (Revised) Addenda Nos. 1 & 2	Centreville Drywall Co.	A.J.B.	
		))	Revised Mechanical)								

All Documents ⟶ 5/30/82

Figure 1.3.

tect's office regarding the number of drawings included in a set. It is not sufficient to know that architectural drawings numbered A1 to A9 have been received unless it has been ascertained that the set is limited to *nine* drawings.

Checking that *all* the pages have been included in the set (or *sets*) of specifications is, admittedly, a somewhat awesome chore calculated to provoke teeth-gnashing and eye-rolling on the part of a junior estimator to whom this task will almost certainly be delegated. Frequently, the meticulous page-by-page check will be evaded, and some shortcuts devised. Reliance will be placed on the improbability of the *same* page (or pages) being accidentally excluded from *two* sets of specifications. Confidence will be expressed in the certainty of missing pages surely becoming obvious to *someone* reading the specifications during the bid period! With so many demands on an estimator's time during the preparation of the bid, the decision to avoid a proper, but time-consuming, check can be appreciated. Nevertheless, estimators should always be aware of the harsh truth of a building owner's unsympathetic response to a plea that a contingency sum of $300,000 was omitted from the bid amount because "that page was missing from our set of documents." That is a very extreme and exaggerated event and quite unlikely to happen, but it is always possible!

1.4 Checklist of Trades

Construction company estimators become conditioned to the reality of the clock ticking away the minutes to the bid-closing hour while the drawings are still being unrolled in the office. It is imperative that all available time be used as constructively as possible. Idly thumbing through these documents, getting absorbed in some challenging detail on the drawings, attempting to decipher an obscure specification clause picked at random, muttering phrases like "how the hell do you build *that*?" or "I can't figure out what's holding that beam up!"—all such diversions are natural to construction personnel, but indulging in them will not assist in the effective organization of an estimate or provide an early all-round comprehension of the project.

One way to start is to compile a checklist of all the trade divisions noted in the specifications. This list can then be used to establish those trades where quantity take-offs will be necessary (usually for that work to be performed by the contractor's work force), the trades for which quotations from subcontractors will need to be solicited, and the trades falling into both these categories, that is, those trades upon which subcontractors will quote on a "supply only" basis.

Figure 1.4 shows a suggested format for such a checklist. It will be noted in this example that some trades have been further subdivided into additional sections than might have appeared in the actual specification. For example,

Estimate No. 27/82

New Research Wing, Jackson University

	Division	Take-Off	Subtrade Quote.	Take-Off: Start	Complete	Estimator
02200	Earthwork	√	√	4/28/82	5/5/82	B.E.W.
02480	Landscaping		√			
02500	Paving and Surfacing		√			
03100	Formwork	√		4/28/82	5/12/82	J.D.
03200	Reinf. Steel: Supply/detail		√			J.D.
	Placing		√			
	Wire Mesh	√		4/28/82	5/12/82	
03300	Cast-in-Place Concrete	√		4/28/82	5/12/82	J.D.
	Concrete Floor Finishing	√	√	4/28/82	5/12/82	J.D.
03400	Precast Concrete: Wall Panels		√			
	Paving	√	√	5/14/82	5/16/82	J.D.
04200	Unit Masonry	√	√	5/7/82	5/15/82	B.E.W.
05300	Metal Decking		√			
05500	Metal Fabrications	√	√	5/19/82	5/22/82	J.D.
06100	Rough Carpentry	√		5/16/82	5/20/82	B.E.W.
06200	Finish Carpentry	√	√	5/21/82	5/23/82	B.E.W.
07100	Waterproofing		√			
07500	Membrane Roofing		√			
07900	Sealants		√			
08100	Metal Doors and Frames	√	√	5/22/82	5/23/82	J.D.
08200	Wood and Plastic Doors	√	√	5/22/82	5/23/82	J.D.
08500	Metal Windows		√			
08800	Glazing		√			
09250	Gypsum Wallboard		√			
09300	Tile		√			
09500	Acoustical Treatment		√			
09650	Resilient Flooring		√			
09680	Carpeting		√			
09900	Painting		√			
10000	Specialties	√	√	5/23/82	5/26/82	B.E.W.
14200	Elevators		√			
15000	Mechanical		√			
16000	Electrical		√			

Figure 1.4.

Item 03200 "Reinforcing Steel" has been subdivided into three categories:

Supply, fabricate, and detail
Placing
Wire mesh reinforcement

The reason for these subdivisions is the estimator's anticipation (from experience) of the various options open to subcontractors quoting on this trade. Some may quote on the basis of both supplying and placing the reinforcing bars, and others on the basis of "supplying only." Another subcontractor who specializes in the placing of reinforcing bars will quote on that part of the work, or the estimator may decide to prepare an estimate for this work to be performed directly by the contractor. The wire mesh reinforcement will usually be purchased and installed by the general contractor.

Note also a similar situation with "Precast Concrete" being split into two sections: (a) precast concrete wall panels, and (b) precast concrete paving slabs. Here again the estimator is prepared for the likelihood that one or other of the precast concrete companies bidding will either not include for subdivision (b) or will quote for the "supply only" of material. A requirement for quantities is therefore noted in order to estimate the cost of installation.

This checklist of trade divisions can also be used to establish some sort of bid-organization schedule by the use of columns showing "target" dates for the start and finish of the various quantity surveys required. In a large contracting company employing a considerable number of estimators, this would be supplemented with the initials of the personnel to whom the various sections of the work have been delegated. All this will be subject to revisions during the course of the bid period. Some take-offs will prove to be more demanding than initially considered; other trades that appeared to contain complexities will turn out to be quite straightforward and will not require the scheduled time. Also, some estimators will have to double-up on trades because of the work-load urgencies of other bids in the office.

1.5 Bid-Info Reports

Following the preparation of the list of trade sections (or *preceding* it, according to an estimator's preference) a further perusal of the documents should now be made for the purpose of identifying and recording those items and details that will quickly produce a clear outline of the project. The information provided on these capsule reports will be in the nature of answers to the many questions that estimators and other personnel in a construction office ask when new drawings are being reviewed: How big is it? What is the gross floor area? What kind of a structure is it? Any feature immediately identifiable as being unusual or unique should be noted down.

Most specifications include a section usually entitled "Instructions to Bidders." This section usually includes certain data pertinent to the bidding procedures that should be included in these Information Bulletins.

Figure 1.5 presents a suggested format for this type of brief report. The title and the location of the project along with the names of the owner and

Bid-Info Report

Re: Estimate No: 27/82

Project Title and Location:	New Research Wing, Jackson University, Centreville, Ontario
Architect:	Dodgson and Carroll
Building Owner(s):	Board of Governors, Jackson University
Bid Closing Time and Date:	3:00 p.m., May 27th, 1982
Gross Floor Area:	31,485 ft^2 (2925 m^2)
Estimated Value:	$1,754,000
Description:	Three-story building. Partial basement area approx. 13 ft (3.3 m) below grade. Reinf. concrete foundation and superstructure, metal roof deck at small single-story portion. S. and E. elevations—face brick. N. W. elevations—precast concrete panels, concrete block backup, aluminum strip windows. Concrete block partitions. Interior finishes: drywall to walls (painted), acoustic ceilings, resilient flooring, ceramic tile to washrooms. Carpet in offices.
Bid Security:	Bid Bond: 10% of bid amount.
Bonds:	50% performance bond 50% material and labor payment bond
Misc. Information:	30 days to award contract Completion date: October 31, 1983 Liquidated damages: $200.00/calendar day. Include all sales taxes

Figure 1.5.

the architects are obvious requirements, as are the closing time and date of the bid.

The general description of the project should be concise and emphasize the major elements: the structure (reinforced concrete, structural steel, precast concrete, etc.); any noted requirements for perimeter shoring and/or underpinning; the materials of the exterior cladding ("skin"); a brief catalog of the most prominent interior finishes; plus any special equipment requirements, such as laboratory furniture, hospital or kitchen equipment, exotic wood finishes, or extensive landscaping. Information regarding mechanical and electrical systems is also useful.

The information concerning bid deposits (bid bonds or certified checks), performance and other bonds, and sales tax exemption (usual in bids for public or institutional works) should also be stated.

The gross floor area (GFA) not only indicates the magnitude of the project; it is also necessary in establishing a preliminary valuation of the total cost. This area given in square feet (square meters) should be computed in accordance with the recommendations made in *Measurement of Buildings by Area and Volume*, as prepared and published by the Canadian Institute of Quantity Surveyors.

This gross floor area will be multiplied by a unit cost applicable to the building's function (school, hospital, office complex, etc.) and based on the costs of similar buildings within the estimator's experience. A good source for this information will be a company bid analysis format, which is discussed in the last chapter. In the example shown, a new research wing to a local university has a gross floor area of 31,485 ft^2 (2925 m^2). The estimator will have checked through previous estimates and identified one for a building comparable in size and design and with a similar function or use. The cost per square foot for that building was \$50.63/ft^2 (\$544.98/m^2) and this unit has been adjusted to \$55.70/ft^2 (\$599.55/m^2) to allow for labor and material increases that have occurred since that other bid was prepared. This unit multiplied by the GFA produces an amount of \$1,754,000.00 which is noted as being the estimated value of the project.

In some cases the owner may have had a preliminary budget prepared and this amount stated to the contractor at the time of the bid invitation; but an experienced estimator would still check this amount by making a gross floor area cost comparison with previous estimates for similar projects. If, for example, the owner's budget amount for the research wing *divided* by the gross floor area had produced a unit of say \$48/ft^2 (\$516.67/m^2) then the estimator would be justified in reporting an anticipated higher estimate of (probable) cost based on the data noted in an earlier estimate.

When a mandatory completion date for the project is stated in the specifications, it should be noted in this report, and also any clause regarding "liquidated damages" for noncompletion on that date.

It must be emphasized again that these bid-info reports should be restricted to those pertinent details that can be readily observed in the bid documents. At this time, only the broad outline and shape of the tree is necessary; the minute details about the leaves and branches can follow later. The intent is to present brief but relevant information on a single sheet of paper.

In large contracting organizations, these reports could be routed out to other personnel or departments, senior management, accountants, contract departments, and so on. They would be of assistance to managerial decision making when debating the pros and cons of bidding a particular project. (A list of other known bidders would also be useful on this info report; the question "Who else is bidding the job?" will invariably be asked by someone.)

1.6 Soliciting Bids from Subcontractors

Potential subcontractors and material suppliers should be contacted for quotations as soon as possible after the checklist of pertinent trades has been prepared. Several years ago it was not uncommon for many contractors to have something akin to an entourage of faithful subcontractors for the various trades, and these would probably be the only companies those contractors would approach for quotations. "We only use Smith and Co. or Jones and Sons for plumbing and heating work," a contractor would proclaim. "We know them and they know us and we've always used one or the other on our jobs, never anyone else!"

In present times, and particularly in those areas where competition is fierce, every contractor bidding a project wants to receive the lowest price available for any given trade. In every city or region there exists a large body of subcontractors with established reputations for good workmanship and reliable performance who are known to most of the general contractors in that area; and these will be the companies from whom probably all the contractors will solicit quotations. This statement must not be construed to imply that contractors might not experience smoother or more comfortable working relationships with some subcontractors than with others; nor let it be hastily added, that the reverse situation of subcontractors' preferences for certain contractors no longer exists. However, the deciding factor in selecting a subcontractor is usually the lowest bid received for a particular trade.

Although it is recommended that general contractors do make direct requests for quotations from the trade contractors, it should be observed that when a certain bid call has been advertised or announced in trade journals, or because the documents have been registered at a local construction association office, it will most often be the subcontractors themselves who will decide to prepare and submit their quotations to all the general contractors listed as bidding the project, irrespective of whether or not they receive any formal requests for quotations from anyone.

Most estimating offices compile a directory of local or regional subcontractors. Some directories may contain the names of *all* known subcontractors in a particular area with the names arranged in alphabetical order and the appropriate trade noted against the name:

Gibson and Son (address) - plaster, drywall, acoustics.
Goldwater Construction - excavation contractor.
And so on.

The problem here is that only someone with an excellent memory and familiarity with the local construction scene can speedily run through this directory picking out the drywall and excavation contractors. As specifications are prepared in the format of trade sections, it makes sense for the contractor's directory of subcontractors to follow the same pattern:

<u>Plaster and Drywall</u>
Acorn and Beech Drywall Ltd.
Supreme Plaster Enterprises
And so on.

This type of directory should preferably be patterned on a standard specification format (Masterformat).

The most common method used by general contractors to request quotations is to mail standard printed cards (or letters) to the selected subcontractors. Figure 1.6 shows an example of such a card. The details to be added to the printed wording will be the project title, the architect's name, and the bid closing time and date. On the reverse side of this card (not shown) will be printed or typed the name and address of the subcontractor.

This information can, of course, be *typed* onto the cards; but as the quantity of cards to be mailed out will often be considerable, this could become a very time-consuming and uneconomical operation. Most contractors use some patented system to speed up the processing of these cards or letters. There are a number of systems available: metal plates, with corresponding equipment (automatically or manually operated) for the actual printing, special "stick-on" labels, and so on. Most of these systems will be coordinated with the subtrade directory previously discussed, and estimators will adopt the method and system most suitable to their own organizations. One factor to be considered when setting up and organizing any system is the inevitable implementation of address changes, company name revisions (Brown and Son Ltd. to Brown Construction Innovations Ltd.), deletions (out of business), and additions (new companies). The system that permits these changes to be made quickly, cheaply, and easily, should be given full consideration. Allowing backlogs of such revisions to accumulate will result not only in a lot of communication problems with subcontractors, but time-consuming administrative work in updating a lapsed system could aggravate the normal bid-preparation operations of the Estimating Department.

REQUEST FOR QUOTATION

We would be pleased to receive a quotation for the following:

PROJECT: New Research Wing, Jackson University, Centreville, Ontario

ARCHITECT: Dodgson and Carroll

BID CLOSES: 3:00 p.m., May 27th, 1982

Bid documents are available for inspection at the address below, or at the architects' office, or at the offices of the local construction association.

GELLEM CONSTRUCTION COMPANY,
23, North Street West,
Centreville, Ontario.

Figure 1.6.

Contractors usually supplement their direct solicitations for quotations by placing advertisements in trade journals for two or three days prior to the bid-closing deadline. Figure 1.7 shows an example of such an advertisement.

Neither the direct approach to subcontractors by mail nor the indirect approach of advertising guarantees that *any* quotations will be received by the contractor. The only known *facts* are the actual mailing of the cards or the physical appearance of the ad in the paper. The inclusion of a polite R.S.V.P. on the printed cards would provoke a very limited response. Apart from the knowledge of certain subcontractors who visited the office to examine or borrow the drawings and would therefore be classed as "definitely quoting," the estimator has no real assurance of the intention of other subcontractors. Therefore, at some time during the bidding period, the method of telephone communication will need to be exercised, at least to the subcontractors for the most contentious or specialized trades in the project.

Probably the combination of all three methods of bid solicitation will be the most effective in yielding the maximum response from subcontractors and suppliers:

1. Printed cards to those particular companies with whom the contractor has a past history of cordial relations. (This is a business courtesy gesture, indicating that the contractor is preparing a bid, that the subcontractor's particular trade is included in the project, and that a quotation would be welcome.)
2. A trade journal advertisement (to appear in one or more issues) to catch the attention of those other subcontractors who will also be bidding, who are

NORTH YORK ONT.

TENDERS FOR SUB TRADES

TENDERS will be received by the undersigned until 2:00 p.m.

FRIDAY, MARCH 23, 1973

for all sub-trade and material prices required in the construction of additions and alterations to St. John's Convalescent Hospital.

Architects, Mathers & Haldenby, 10 St. Mary Street, Toronto, Ont.

Lowest or any tender not necessarily accepted.

V. K. MASON
CONSTRUCTION, LTD.,
181 Eglinton Avenue East,
Toronto, Ont. M4P 1J9
Phone: 485-8621. KM23

Figure 1.7.

equally competent to do the work, and with whom the contractor is prepared to do business.

3. "Zeroing-in" by telephone to the subcontractors for the most pertinent trades.

1.7 Recap

Although a tremendous amount of work lies ahead for the estimators, the following groundwork for the bid preparation has been accomplished:

1. A system has been set up to record the receipt and distribution of the documents.
2. The trades applicable to the project have been identified and listed.
3. A schedule for the preparation of the quantity surveys is established.
4. The main details about the project are made known on capsule information reports.
5. The subcontractors have been alerted and their quotations requested.

The activities most essential to the bid preparation—quantity surveys, scheduling, and pricing—can now be started. The next chapter will deal with an aspect of bid preparation that is not always recognized as being a significant factor to the production of a realistic estimate—*communication*. It exists in the form of a "background" series of activities continuing right through the bidding period and merits some discussion.

2
Prebid Communication

2.1 Initial Communication

The last chapter discussed some recommended procedures for recording the receipt of the bid documents when they are received at the outset of the bidding period. The rolls of drawings with accompanying volumes of specifications received in an estimating office are the instruments of communication used by the building owner's appointed design team—architects, engineers, and other consultants—to convey all the pertinent information necessary for general contractors to:

1. Establish within a defined period of time an estimate of the cost of the building.
2. Properly construct the building.

The first event is naturally the one of primary concern to the estimator. The second event is the obvious objective of the first event and will only be carried out by the general contractor who submits the most competitive and successful bid. (*Note:* "Successful" in the context of *winning a contract,* not necessarily a guarantee of a profit-yielding project.)

There are many factors contributing to the preparation of an accurate estimate of cost, not the least of which is the ability to assimilate and correctly interpret everything contained in this package of communication from the building designers. The duration of time between the receipt of the bid documents and the deadline date for the completion and submission of the bid is all too often very short. Even the most experienced estimator will flinch at the prospect of studying, reading, absorbing, and thoroughly understanding, within this short time period, everything shown in a roll of drawings about 12 inches in diameter and described in an 8-inch thick volume (or volumes!) of specifications that will probably contain more words than the *Bible* and *War and Peace* combined (and be probably just as controversial)!

This book is mainly concerned with the preparation of a bid or tender for a stipulated price (*lump-sum*) contract, and general contractors should be conditioned to accept *two* hard, inescapable facts common to all bids for this type of contract.

Fact 1. The date and time set for the bid submission, the ominous deadline which warns of the hour when the sands will run out and everything, rightly or wrongly, must be finished.

Fact 2. This is expressed in statements contained (with varying phraseology) in almost all Forms of Agreement, General Conditions, or other similar documents. The Canadian Standard Construction Document for a stipulated sum contract, CCDC 12-1979, words it this way:

> 1.2 The Contract Documents are complementary, and what is required by any one shall be as binding as if required by all.
> 1.3 The intent of the Contract Documents is to include the labour, products and services necessary for the performance of the Work in accordance with these documents. It is not intended, however, that the Contractor shall supply products or perform work not consistent with, covered by or properly inferrable from the Contract Documents.

The American Institute of Architects Document A201 hammers the same message home with similar wording:

> 1.2.3 The intent of the Contract Documents is to include all items necessary for the proper execution and completion of the Work. The Contract Documents are complementary, and what is required by any one shall be as if required by all . . . [etc.].*

Fact 1 stresses the time limitations for the preparation of the estimate; fact 2 is a solemn reminder that the completed bid must include the estimated costs of *everything* required by the drawings, the specifications, and any other documents pertinent to the bid.

Estimators in a general contractor's office must not only be satisfied that they themselves understand the intent of the bid documents; they must also be satisfied that potential subcontractors and suppliers have equal compre-

*AIA copyrighted material has been reproduced with the permission of The American Institute of Architects under permissison number 82048. Further reproduction is prohibited.

hension as it applies to their specific trades. A quotation from a subcontractor that *demonstrates* a misinterpretation of something in the documents and is accepted by the contractor *without challenge* for inclusion in the bid, becomes in effect an error for which the *general contractor* will ultimately bear the responsibility. This leads to all kinds of subsequent conflicts and disputes. The estimator must be continually alert to the possibility of these situations happening and take all precautions to avoid them. For example, a specification for section 07200 Insulation might state that: "Rigid insulation to be 2 in. (50 mm) thick, *or as noted on the drawings*." The drawings might include special details for certain areas in the building to require 2½-in. (62-mm) or 3-in. (75-mm) thick insulation. If an insulation subcontractor provided a low quotation that included the statement "All rigid insulation to be *2 in. as specified,*" the contractor would find it difficult at a later date to make this subcontractor provide material of any greater thickness than was qualified in the quotation. It is true the subcontractor misinterpreted the specification clause, but the contractor was made aware of the misunderstanding at the time of the bid.

Apart from the obvious requirement that information be presented clearly and concisely, effective communication also requires that this information be properly understood by the people to whom it is addressed. Certainly, the chances of misunderstanding will always be greater when the given communication is vague or confusing, but even the most carefully considered phraseology or the most excellent draftsmanship can still be, and probably will be, misinterpreted by someone. Worse still, this misinterpretation might be passed along to a third person and accepted as a valid statement. A clear directive like "All interior wood doors are to be painted with black paint" will pop out of some branch of the communication pipeline network as a negative statement that they must not be painted *white!*

2.2 Drawings

The drawings, being a graphic or visual mode of communication, are often less subject to misinterpretation than the specifications or other written documents. "Draw me a picture" is a common enough expression often heard where there is difficulty in understanding an oral or written description of something.

However, bad or sloppy draftsmanship can impede the process of understanding a drawing. A lack of explanatory wall sections, a bewildering cluster of notations and dimensions, or absence of any dimensions, indistinct lettering—all these things can be frustrating to someone stoically endeavoring to decipher a somewhat complex detail. Nevertheless, it is difficult to imagine how an elevation of a wall noted on the drawings as being constructed of "brick" could be misinterpreted as being something other than a brick wall!

The length and height of this wall can also be ascertained on the drawing; the thickness of the wall might also be noted. The drawing can communicate this information quite clearly; however, to properly estimate the cost of this wall, the estimator seeks more information. This information would include:

Brick sizes, types, special brand names, color, and so on
Mortar materials and mixes
Type of bond
Type and thickness of mortar joints
Masonry anchorage and reinforcement materials
Laying the brick, the workmanship expected
Cleaning and pointing
Winter heat and protection requirements
Other similar items

This information will, or should, be provided in the specification.

2.3 Reading the Specification

The specification could be defined as the document that expresses in *words* those things that cannot be properly demonstrated graphically. It is also often described as the document that *supplements* the drawings. Document CCDC (Article GC 2.5) states that *"specifications shall govern over drawings,"* and many other similar documents confirm the status of the specification in relation to the drawings, particularly with reference to conflict between these documents.

Specification writing is a profession with its own standards of methodology and performance; *effective reading* of specifications also requires an expertise that estimators should learn to develop.

If the specification is well arranged in appropriate trade sections (as Masterformat or similar) and uses clear language, with sentences short and concise, then the intended meaning should not be difficult to understand. But if a path to the exact meaning and intent has to be beaten and hacked through an undergrowth of ambiguities and lengthy and involved paragraphs, some of which trail into further obscurities, then the estimator must determinedly strip this verbiage down to a more concise and comprehensive format. The specification has to be streamlined into something that is brief but still explicit, reducing lengthy technical data to a few short statements that highlight the most pertinent items.

It is recommended that the specification be considered in terms of the following three groups, when reading and making notes, each group differing as to the amount of in-depth study required on the part of the contractor's estimator:

1. *General conditions:* This colloquialism encompasses a number of specification sections with titles such as General Instructions, Temporary Facilities, General Work, and so on, according to the differing practices in the design offices. (Masterformat Division 0, Bidding and Contract Requirements, and Division 1, General Requirements, provide a comprehensive list of applicable items.)
2. *General contractor's work:* The sections devoted to the trades that the general contractor would consider carrying out with his own labor force, and for which detailed quantities and cost estimates will be prepared. These sections would probably include Excavation, Shoring, Underpinning, Concrete and Formwork, Masonry, and Carpentry Work.
3. *Subtrade sections:* These apply to the trades that the general contractor intends or is prepared to subcontract in whole or *in part*. These trades could include those already mentioned in group 2.

The specification sections falling under the categories of groups 1 and 2 must be read thoroughly and in their entirety, with the most important items effectively noted and recorded. This can be done by utilizing one of the following methods:

1. Underlining the items with a colored pencil.
2. Using a special marking pen to highlight the items.
3. Making brief notes on a separate sheet of paper.

It is recommended that method 3 be followed because this makes it possible to reproduce all the necessary information on one or two sheets of paper, expressed briefly in simple and comprehensive terms, thus simplifying the task of checking that all items are covered. The other two methods will necessitate thumbing through several pages of a large, probably unwieldy, volume of specification to locate and recheck the noted items, with the accompanying irritant of the book's refusal to remain flat and open at the appropriate place.

Figure 2.1 shows a page from a specification, in this instance an extract from a section for Concrete Work. Note that the pertinent items have been ringed, as required in methods 1 and 2.

Figure 2.2 shows an example of method 3 with the same information repeated in the format of a few notes on a separate sheet of paper.

The following is how a complete section for Concrete Work, which might run anywhere from 20 to 30 pages in the original specification format, could be reduced to a series of brief notes representing nearly all the information

Division 03300 - Concrete Page 5 of 10

4. *Slabs on Fill*
   a) Place one layer of polyethylene vapor barrier over granular fill. Place in continuous length, lap joints a minimum of 6″. Keep joints to a minimum.
   b) Slab on fill to be 4″ thick of 3000 p.s.i. concrete. Maximum slump to be 2½″. Mix design to be subject to the Architect's approval.
   c) Slab to be reinforced with 6 × 6 - 6/6 wire mesh reinforcement, placed in flat sheets, lapped 6″. Reinforcement to be extended within 2″ of construction joints and slab edges, and placed 1½″ from top of slab.
   d) Provide screeds for leveling of concrete slab. Engineer's level to be used for setting.
   e) Concrete to slab to be placed in continuous strips, with construction joints provided between the strips. Width of strips to be kept at a minimum to achieve fast placing without creating cold joints. Construction joints to be located on column lines.
   f) Provide control joints as soon as possible during concrete curing. Saw cut slab to panels of approximately 20′ x 20′. Saw cuts to be 1½″ deep and should be made on column lines wherever possible. Saw cut joints to be filled with an epoxy resin material.

5. *Column Base Plates*
   a) Base plates to be provided by Structural Steel.
   b) Contractor to grout base after steel frame has been plumbed and levelled. Grout to be a premixed nonshrink material.

Figure 2.1.

needed by the estimator (supplemented, of course, by the drawings) to prepare an estimate for this trade:

Estimate No. 3-81
Concrete Mixes:
- Skim slabs, 2,000 p.s.i.

Estimate No. 3-81

Notes Re: 03300 Concrete

Polyethylene vapor barrier under slab, 6″ laps (Query: gauge?).
4″ thick slab on earth; 3,000 p.s.i. concrete.
6″ x 6″ - 6/6 wire mesh reinforcement (6″ laps).
Provide screeds set to engineer's level.
Place in continuous strips, const. joints between strips (refer Typ. Detail Drgs.).
1½″ dp. sawcuts, rectangular 20′0″ x 20′0″ panels, filled with epoxy resin, column lines.
Premixed nonshrink grout to col. baseplates.

Figure 2.2.

- Footings, pile caps, slabs on earth, 3,000 p.s.i.
- Suspended slabs, shear walls, beams, columns 4,000 p.s.i.
- Fill to metal deck, lightweight concrete.
- Toppings. 3/8″ Aggregate.

Grout base plates, nonshrink grout. (Base plates supplied by structural steel subcontractor.)
Water reducing admixture to concrete in slabs.
Clean and slurry coat slabs for toppings.
Sawcuts in slabs, panels 20′0″ x 20′0″
Slab on grade to be placed checkerboard fashion.
6″ x 6″ - 6/6 wire mesh to slab on grade.
Chamfers to beams and columns.
Rub exposed concrete as per CSA A.23 1-1973.
Inspection and testing *by owner*.
Construction joints.

- Vertical, keyed to walls.
- Horizontal, keyed to wall slabs (run re-steel through joint).
- 6″ polyvinyl waterstop in all construction joints below grade (welded at joints).
- Install waterstop between walls and slab on grade.

Curing

- Keep exposed surfaces continuously wet 7 days.
- Membrane curing to finished surfaces of slabs.
- Protect cured floors (tarps or plywood).

Forms

- Reshore floor and roof slabs after stripping (maximum spacing 8′0″ each way).
- Vapor barrier ("No-Moist") under floor slabs.
- Dovetail anchor slots for masonry.
- Asphalt-impregnated expansion joints.

The estimator should supplement these notes with further information shown on the structural and architectural drawings, and will then have, in effect, a complete checklist of items and work to be measured and included in the estimate:

Footings, pile caps, foundation walls, grade beams.
Slabs on grade.
Skim slab (under footings).
Suspended slabs, beams, drop slabs.
Columns: rectangular and circular.
Fill to roof deck.
Miscellaneous curbs and bases (interior and exterior).
Floor toppings.

and so on. With all this gathered and listed information, the estimator can proceed to measure quantities, summarize the items, solicit material quotations and equipment rental rates, and price the labor, all with a minimum of checking and rechecking back through the pages in the specification. It is also much easier to run through these notes and check off all the items to ensure their inclusion in the estimate.

2.4 Specification Sections Relating to Subtrades

As these sections in an average specification will probably aggregate to approximately 75 to 80 percent of the total, the task of reading and absorbing all the information contained therein would appear ominous and almost impossible to do in the time allowed. Therefore, before starting any laborious

Section 08200 - Plastic Laminate Doors

A) Guarantee doors for three years from date of acceptance against manufacturing defects, including delamination of plastic laminate and warp exceeding 1/4″.
B) Guarantee shall include hanging and refinishing of any replacements that may be necessary.
C) Doors shall be wood solid core slab with plastic laminate faces, manufactured by the following approved companies:
Best-Dor Co. Ltd.
Smith Lumber Co.
J. H. Jackson Ltd.
D) *Size and Thickness* - Fabricate doors to size and thickness noted. If thickness not noted, provide 1-3/4″ doors.
E) *Openings in Doors* - Prepare doors for installation of grilles as indicated. Grilles to be supplied and installed by Division 10, Manufactured Specialities.
F) Undercut or rebate bottom rails as required.
G) Provide hardwood strip 3/6″ thick in all four edges of doors and plastic laminate on both faces. Plastic laminate to be 1/16″ thick, color to be selected by Architect.
H) Thoroughly sand back of plastic laminate to provide a homogeneous bonding surface; bond laminate to door under pressure to provide a perfectly smooth surface free from distortion, waves, ridges or core ghost lines.
I) Plane or sand edges smooth to make laminate and wood edges flush; clearly indicate top and hinge side of each door. (Exposed edges of stiles shall be beveled by carpenter on site as required.)
J) Deliver doors to site in protective scuff resistant wrapping; do not remove wrapping until doors are ready for installation; print door identification on wrapping.
K) *Core* - No. 1 Shop or Cutgrade Ontario white pine kiln dried to 5% moisture content.
L) *Edge Strip* - Hardwood at least 3/4″.
M) *Plastic Laminate* - To be 1/16″ thick, solid color to later selection by Architect. Adhesive as recommended by plastic laminate manufacturer.

Figure 2.3.

reading one should first consider which part of the information is most pertinent (1) to the general contractor, (2) to the subcontractor (or supplier), and, (3) to both the general contractor and subcontractor.

Figure 2.3 illustrates a page from a specification for Plastic Laminated Wood Doors. The items of most importance to the general contractor are circled, and the following is an example of how this would be transcribed in a few notes:

Notes re: Section 08200 Plastic Doors

1. Three-year guarantee, including hanging and finishing.
2. Wood solid core slab doors with plastic laminated faces.
3. Approved manufacturers: Best-Dor Co. Ltd., Smith Lumber Co.; J. H. Jackson Ltd.
4. *Excludes* grilles (see Section 10); cutouts to be included.

The door manufacturer would be concerned with *all* the information in this specification, including the technical data concerning the fabrication, quality, door construction, materials, packaging requirements, and so on. The contractor is mainly concerned with establishing the cost of receiving, handling, and installing these doors.

The estimator will make a count of the required number of doors from the drawings and/or door schedule, grouping them according to their type and dimensions. Some suppliers also might calculate these quantities and present the contractor with a total *package* quotation; the majority, however, will provide a quotation that only states a *unit price* for each door type and will leave it to the contractor to establish the total supply cost.

The following explains the significance and importance of these notes to the estimator:

1. *Guarantee:* it is essential to remember to check the quotations from manufacturers or suppliers to ensure that this guarantee is confirmed. Also, the estimator may consider the probability of one or more of these doors subsequently becoming defective and include a contingency amount in the tender to cover the cost of removing these doors and hanging and finishing the replacement doors. The "small print" at the back of the quotation will usually state that this work is not covered by the manufacturer's guarantee.
2. This note is merely a brief outline description of the items involved.
3. The names of the approved manufacturers remind the estimator that quotations from *other manufacturers cannot be accepted for inclusion in the "base" bid amount,* but could be offered separately as possible savings to the building owner if the prices are cheaper than those quoted by the approved manufacturer. (*Note:* This process of offering potential savings is discussed further in Chapter 11.)
4. The item regarding grilles is important. It reminds the estimator to check that the door manufacturer has allowed for making the necessary cutout in

> the doors to receive these grilles. Also, a check should be made that the Specification Section 10A does include these items; if omitted, a query should be directed to the architect. An experienced estimator knows that those very brief words "door grilles to be included in the work of Section 10A of these specifications" throws onto the contractor's shoulders the responsibility for providing these items if they are not covered in any other section of the specifications.

This method of identifying and noting the items that most affect the general contractor can be applied in varying degrees to all other specialist or subtrades. The trainee or junior estimator will tend to read almost every word in a trade specification before writing down the pertinent information, and will probably make more notes than necessary; the ability and the *confidence* to recognize those items of vital importance while scanning rapidly through the specification can only be acquired through experience and repetition.

2.5 "Work by Others" Clauses

The problem of an item (or items) of work being noted in one trade division to be provided by another trade was touched on in the example of the notes for the section Plastic Laminated Doors. These type of clauses are negative and can result in some problems if not challenged during the bid-preparation period. (It is useless to raise the issue at a later time!)

For example, a clause in the trade specification for Section 07800 - Sealants might say something like this:

> Excluded from this division is the caulking and sealant work to be provided by the following trades:
> 03400 - Precast Concrete
> 08500 - Aluminum Windows

The estimator will note this statement and then check those other trade divisions. Section 03400 might clearly specify the caulking requirements for the precast concrete work, thereby confirming that the cost of this work is intended to be included in the precast concrete contractor's quotation. However, Section 08500 stays "silent" on the subject and *makes no reference to this caulking whatsoever*. Experience cautions the estimator into expecting that the trade contractors normally will only read those sections devoted to their own specific trades, and will usually refer to any other sections *only if and when directed to do so* in their own trade specification.

Prior notice of these discrepancies should warn the estimator that the following things could (and might) happen:

1. The caulking contractors will exclude the cost of this work in their quotations, in accordance with the specified instructions.
2. The aluminum window contractors *will also exclude this work from their quotations,* not having read any directive to do otherwise in the specification section applicable to their own trade.

If the contractor is negligent in pursuing this matter, and assuming that all the subcontractors base their quotations in strict accordance with the requirements of their own trade specifications, the contractor is left exposed to the unhappy situation of being contractually responsible for an item of work the *cost of which is excluded in the bid*.

Remember, the architects did not stipulate this item as being excluded from the prime contract, only from *one trade division*.

This kind of situation warrants the following recommended procedures:

1. Inform the aluminum window contractors that a clause relating to *their trade* is noted in the division for *another trade*. (In practice, of course, experience will prompt many of these contractors to query the omission of this work.)
2. Notify the architects regarding this omission and request the issuance of an addenda to rectify this discrepancy.
3. Suggest to the caulking subcontractors that they prepare a separate quotation for this work. This is in the event that the architect does *not* formally clarify the matter, with the result that some window contractors will include the work and others will exclude it. This separate quotation will ensure that the general contractor will have a cost estimate for the item to include in the bid. (Alternatively, and with time permitting, this work could be "taken-off" and the materials and labor priced by the contractor's estimator.)

Estimators should watch very closely for these and similar discrepancies that can occur in the various trade divisions of a specification. Most specifications and/or forms of contract have clauses that hold the *general contractor* responsible for the allocation of the work to the various trades, *irrespective of where a specific item of work is located in the specification*.

2.6 Items Relative to Normal Trade Practice

The contractor's estimator should also take note of the items of work that are customarily carried out by one particular trade but are sometimes included in the specification for another trade. The specification writer may be strictly correct in the allocation of certain items according to some standard specification system (Masterformat, for example), but local or regional trade practice may decree that another trade usually performs this work.

A good example would be roof insulation. This work is generally included in the Roofing Division (Masterformat 07500) of the specification, but sometimes it shows up (not illogically) in the trade division for Insulation Work (Masterformat 07200). The estimator should make prebid contact with the various subcontractors for both these trade divisions to ascertain their intentions. In most cases it will be established that the roofing subcontractors intend to include this item because it is normal practice for them to do so; and for the same reason most of the insulation subcontractors will exclude it. However, some subcontractors in either trade may decide for one reason or another to ignore normal trade practice and quote in strict accordance with the specifications. The contractor's estimator should check with all the potential subcontractors in these circumstances in order to avoid the same set of circumstances that were considered in Section 2.5 concerning the problems relating to the caulking trade. These circumstances would be that (1) two contractors representing different trades will include the same item of work, or (2) *neither* trade will include it.

Again the estimator is faced with the problem of either a duplication of items in the bid, which could make it less *competitive*, or the alternative situation of the omission of both items of cost. (It is fair comment to say that if the bid is successful and the first condition, that is, duplication, is found to exist, it will probably be considered as a piece of shrewd strategy on the part of the estimator! Not so the opposite situation, of course!)

2.7 Approved Trade Contractors or Manufacturers

Some mention was made of this in the example of note making on a specification for Plastic Laminated Doors. The estimator should note carefully the names of all *approved* subcontractors or manufacturers. He or she should also examine the specifications (usually the General Conditions) for the exact meaning of the clause that often follows the specified names of trade contractors or products: ". . . or approved equal." The usual definition of this clause is that approval of the work or products of companies other than those named in the specifications must be formulated by written instructions from the architect (usually in the form of an addenda) *prior to the closing of the bid*. Only when this procedure is followed may the general contractor accept for inclusion in the bid any quotations from these companies; to do this without this prior written approval renders the bid liable to rejection on the grounds of informality.

Remember: Only the architect can grant this seal of approval. The general contractor does not have the authority to do so; nor can this approval be *self-imposed by the companies themselves*. ("Our product is as good as so-and-so's, in fact it's better and cheaper. . . .")

If the specifications do not include a clause that clarifies the intent of this term, "approved equal," then the estimator should query this matter with the architect. Also to be queried is the exact meaning of statements such as "The overhead doors shall be as manufactured by Wilco-Pritchard Ltd."

The operative word here is "*as*." The architect could mean two different things. He or she could be implying that:

1. Only doors actually manufactured by Wilco-Pritchard will be considered for the project; or
2. The name is merely stated for the purpose of establishing the standards of workmanship and quality required.

In the latter case, the general contractor is permitted to accept quotations from other companies without requiring the written prior approval of the architect. The only risk the general contractor is exposed to here is the possibility of the architect subsequently rejecting the proposed doors as being inferior in quality to those manufactured by Wilco-Pritchard and requesting a substitution without *any additional costs being allowed to the contractor*.

2.8 Making and Recording Queries

After the receipt and study of the bid documents, the communication process will now be reversed, and queries, suggestions, and comments will now flow from contractors, subcontractors, and manufacturers back to the designers.

Subcontractors and suppliers may submit their queries to the general contractor for transmission to the designers, or they may make them directly to those authorities. Most of this communication will be made orally by telephone, because time will limit the possibility of a large amount of written correspondence.

Although general contractors and subcontractors may communicate their questions *orally* to the designers, the reverse flow of information should be in writing, usually in the form of addenda or bulletins. Estimators should always be aware of the following statement, which appears in most bid documents:

> The architect will not be responsible for any *oral instructions or revisions*.

This implies that any clarification or directive given orally will have no contractual value. However, a designer will often give an oral answer to a query at the time, and confirm it formally and in writing before the tender closing date. This is quite satisfactory, but it is important for the general contractor's estimator to keep a detailed record of all oral queries and answers. This record is useful for checking that all replies are subsequently confirmed by addenda.

Such a record should show the date the query is made, the name (or initials) of the estimator, the name of the designer's representative receiving the call, a description of the query, and the nature of the reply. Figure 2.4 is an example of such a record.

The following are some comments on this example:

1. The first query regarding the thickness of a cavity wall insulation would probably have been originated by a subcontractor specializing in insulation work. It could be questioned if, on the basis of the "specifications shall

PROJECT: MILL STREET HIGH SCHOOL ESTIMATE NO. 3-79

ARCHITECTS: FLOTSAM AND JETSAM

Date	*Estimator (Initials)*	*Architect's Rep.*	*Question*	*Reply*
Aug. 21/79	J.K.	Bill Jones	Spec. Div. 7D states cavity wall insulation to be 2″ thick. Wall Sections on Drg. A-6 show 3″. Which is correct?	2″ thick as per spec. Dimension on Drg. A-6 will be revised by Addenda.
Aug. 23/79	B.Y.	Bill Jones	Section 5/6 Drg. A-10 shows damp-proofing at basement walls. No specification for this item.	Addenda will include spec. for this damp-proofing.
Aug. 24/79	J.K.	Bill Jones	Drgs. and specs. indicate fill is required under concrete slab on grade: What is the material? Thickness of the bed?	6″ bed of 3/4″ dia. crushed stone, to be confirmed by Addenda.
Aug. 24/79	J.K.	Bill Jones	Re. Spec. Item 9D, Para 1-A "Warranty." Please clarify this clause. Does it apply to materials only, or does it include workmanship?	Will look into matter, and if further clarification necessary will be covered by Addenda.

Figure 2.4.

govern" clause, this query is really necessary. This contention is not unreasonable. However, most specifications require that all such discrepancies be drawn to the attention of the designers *before* the tender closes and querying is always the best course to follow. It should also be noted in this example that, although the answer has been stated (and accepted) *verbally*, the architect has expressed the intention to confirm his reply formally in an addenda.

2. In the answer to the second query the architects are (rightly) not attempting to indulge in a brief trade specification over the telephone to one contractor; they merely state that a specification for this work will be prepared and issued immediately.
3. This is similar to the first query and has been answered quite straightforwardly by the architect, with the promise of a confirmation by addenda. When this addenda is received, this particular item should be checked to ensure that it conforms to what was stated orally.
4. This query is of a slightly different nature. Let us assume it was raised in the first instance by a subcontractor. The question relates to an item in the specification that is ambiguously worded and its intent is not clear. It could mean one or two different things. The subcontractor has raised the question with the contractor's estimator and has requested an interpretation. In this example the estimator is following the *recommended procedure* by passing the query immediately to the architect. It is inadvisable for the contractor's estimator to attempt an interpretation of a hazy clause in a specification, particularly to a third party. If the subcontractor presses for some kind of an interpretation from the contractor, then any statement made by the contractor should be qualified as being merely an *opinion*.

A common statement in most contract documents recognizes the status of the architect as being "in the first instance the *interpreter of the contract*." This applies to problems that may arise out of the documents during the actual construction phase, but it is also valid during the bidding period. Therefore, where there is doubt, *query the matter*.

Estimators must be aggressive in this area of communication; every doubtful wrinkle ironed out during this phase could eliminate many future disputes and conflicts. When the bid is in the owner's hands, it is too late to ask questions about the bid documents. Keeping an organized record of queries to designers is important for checking addenda to ensure that everything queried has been answered, and that the written clarification confirms the oral statement with the same or similar wording and meaning. Also, although these query sheets do not have any contractual status, they could carry some weight in the event of an answer being given verbally but never confirmed in writing, and then later challenged by the designer.

To expostulate at a later date that "one of our people called someone at your office about four months ago . . ." is not as impressive as, "According to our records, on May 16th, 1981 our Mr. Knight telephoned your Mr. Jones with this question, and he stated that . . . ."

Of course, if Mr. Jones no longer works at the designer's office, then the impact of this statement is somewhat deflated! He might also (in all honesty or otherwise!) deny any knowledge of the incident. It does indicate, however, that such a query was made.

2.9 Addenda

Addenda (or bulletins) could be considered as *refinements* of the original communication. They are issued by the designers to accomplish:

Corrections of errors in the original documents
Approval of material substitutions
Authorization of design changes agreed to, or required by, the owner
Response to queries from contractors and subcontractors

Addenda often include a large amount of fussy "house-cleaning" in terms of correcting minor mistakes in spelling or grammar, irrespective of whether such errors were glaringly obvious. Estimators gradually become conditioned to wading through myriads of items such as "for 'rump' read 'ramp'" or "delete the sentence beginning 'provide decorative *slots* to the architect's approval' and insert 'provide decorative *slats* . . . etc.'"!

Addenda become part of the contract documents and *take precedence over the original documents*. Most bid forms require that contractors acknowledge the receipt of such addenda, confirming numbers and date of issue. The importance of ensuring that all potential subcontractors or suppliers are made aware of this additional communication is obvious. It is unwise for a general contractor to acknowledge on his bid form the receipt of Addenda Nos. 1 to 4 without ensuring that all subcontractors' quotations also confirm examination of all these addenda. The issue of addenda is another reversal of the flow of communication, which is once again coming from the designers to the contractors, for onward transmission, where applicable, to subcontractors and suppliers.

Sometimes revised drawings may supplement the addenda. The more common procedure, however, is for the written addenda to contain a number of items pertaining to drawing revisions, stating the applicable drawing and/or section numbers. The task of reading, checking, and noting all these revisions can be very demanding on an estimator's time, requiring great concentration and considerable patience. This applies particularly to a whole page or two of very minor revisions to dimensions that might have little or no influence on the actual cost (although they will become very essential during construction).

Figure 2.5 shows an example of a typical page from an addenda revising the specifications. Attention is drawn to the first item in this addenda. This

Port Cragfield High School (Project No. PC8-81)

Addendum No. 4

Section 02220 Earthwork
Page 6: Para. 4. Fill - Add: Provide 3/4″ crushed stone fill under the concrete slabs on grade.

Section 05500 Miscellaneous Metals
Page 3: Corner Guards - Add: Thickness of corner guards shall be 1/4″.

Section 06200 Carpentry
Page 3: Wood Railing - Delete: Wood railing at north side of Corridor No. 4.
Page 5: Valances - Change: "solid red oak" to "oak-veneered particle board".

Section 09250 Gypsum Wallboard
Page 1: Para. 2 - Add: Item 2.6, Install metal door frames in gypsum wallboard partitions (frames supplied by Section 08100 Metal Doors and Frames).

Figure 2.5.

refers to one of the queries noted in the example (Figure 2.4) of a Query Record Sheet. In that example a query was raised regarding the thickness and type of material to be used for underfloor fill. This answer in the addenda *only refers to the material*, but has still not confirmed the required thickness of the bed. A further query to the architects will now be necessary!

2.10 Review

As was demonstrated in the preceding pages, a great amount of communication flows back and forth during the bid-preparation period between all the concerned parties—contractors, design consultants, owners, trade contractors, and suppliers. This communication starts with the issuance of the bid documents and finishes with the final delivery of the bid into the owner's hands. One effect of this prebid communication is that it has probably improved the clarity of the bid documents, enabling contractors to prepare their bids with more confidence and probably eliminating a number of disputes during the construction period.

In summing up, it must be stressed once again that:

1. Only persistent querying and checking will dissipate haziness and discrepancies in the bid documents and make the information more definitive and decisive. In other words, when in doubt, *shout!*

2. Estimators should never permit sensitivity to somebody's feelings or "toe-treading" to restrict their aggressiveness in seeking necessary clarification. Certainly, it will often be obviously irritating to the designers to be subjected to a barrage of questions, but most architects would endorse the value of having things clarified in January rather than have them disputed in December! However, queries should never be made irresponsibly without a careful check to see if the matter has been clarified somewhere in the documents or a previously issued addendum.
3. Those doubtful items that are not clarified before the bid submission will come back to haunt the contractor at a later time and could result in a reduction of anticipated profit for a project.
4. Equally, it is essential that subcontractors fully understand all information relating to their trades, so that when a contractor is expecting a quotation for "oranges" he is not presented with one for "apples"! If a subcontractor has raised a query to the architect, the contractor's estimator should make sure that when an answer is received the subcontractor is satisfied with the answer. "Does that answer your question?" should be asked repeatedly.

3

Take-off: General Comments

3.1 Basic Principles of Quantity Surveying

Basic rules and recommendations for taking off quantities from drawings have been affirmed and stressed in every text or reference book written on the subject; they justify some reviewing, endorsement, and repetition. The following are some of these established precepts:

1. Items should be measured as "net fixed in place" and in accordance with accepted guidelines as discussed in Section 3.2 and the examples of take-off in the ensuing chapters.
2. Dimensions should be rounded off to:
   (a) Nearest inch for Imperial measurements. Examples: 1′ 5½″ would become 1′ 6″ and 1′ 5¼″ would be written 1′ 5″. (Note: All dimensions to be stated in duo-decimals, e.g. 1′ 6″ to be written 1.6, not 1.5.)
   (b) Two decimal places for metric measurements. Examples: 456.764 would be recorded as 456.76; 456.768 as 456.77.
3. Figured dimensions should be used in preference to scaled dimensions.
4. Dimensions relating to "deductions" or "voids" should be either written in red (pen or pencil), or enclosed in brackets—e.g. "(4.6) × (5.0) = (20 SF)".
5. Adjustments for waste and similar factors will be added to the *total net quantities* of each item; they should never be considered during the actual measuring. (Refer to Section 3.3.)
6. Adherence to a systematic order of measuring and recording dimensions is essential. The dimensions should be written consistently in the sequence of length, breadth (width), and depth (height). Where there is more than a single item with the same dimensions in a specific category, a group of

spread footings, for example, the dimensions should be written once and prefixed with the applicable digit. (This is commonly known as "Timesing.") For example, if a structure contained six column footings with the same dimensions, 4′6″ × 4′0″, these would be recorded as "6/4.6 × 4.0".

7. Identify and record on the take-off sheets information regarding the locations of the various items as they are identified on the drawings, such as column lines, floor elevations, room numbers, building elevations, anything in fact that will simplify the process of checking back on items to verify they have been taken off. The small amount of extra time necessary to do this is worthwhile and eliminates the futile and nonproductive time spent by estimators who return from lunch with complacent stomachs but their heads full of confusion as to what had been taken off before dashing off to the cafeteria!
8. Study the drawings carefully and meticulously before actually starting any take-off, making as many notes as possible. This time will not be wasted if used constructively. Careful examination of the drawings will alert the estimator to items that are repetitious, where things start and finish, what member is supporting or is tied in with what other member, and so on. The items should be measured in a methodical order and preferably, wherever possible, the same sequence in which they will be constructed on the site. In other words, don't start at the roof and work down; or, worse, don't meander from foundation walls to suspended floor slabs, then switch to footings followed by the toppings and floor finishes, and so forth!
9. Adopt a system of marking items on the drawings as they are taken off; use colored pencils if necessary, and do this as neatly as possible. A sinister statement in the specifications may warn estimators about possible adjustment or cancellation of the refund of the monetary deposit on the documents if the drawings and specifications are "unduly marked or mutilated." What is meant by "unduly marked" is sometimes obscure.
10. Where the company estimating system requires the transferring of the (reduced) quantities to separate summary sheets for pricing *(the system recommended in this book)*, a distinctive check mark should be placed against the item with a colored pencil indicating that the item has been "posted." Estimators should always be on the alert against the ironic situation of having an item meticulously taken off, with all the arithmetical computations correctly made and rechecked, and then completely overlooking the item when posting to the summary! Distinctively marking each item as it is transferred will afford some protection against such omissions.
11. Formulate a take-off method that permits a number of items to be calculated from *one* set of dimensions. Refer to Figure 3.1. This illustrates the recording of measurements for a group of isolated concrete footings. Figure 3.2 is a second example, this one for continuous wall footings. In the first example the single set of dimensions could be developed to provide the quantities of both concrete and formwork; and in the second example the quantities for the additional item of the footing "key" were also established. This is a time-saving method that avoids "double-measuring" and provides a consistent relationship between the quantities for each item. *Note:* the formulas involving *A*, *B*, and *C* are necessary if someone (calculator operator, clerk, etc.) other than the estimator is going to do the arithmetical extensions.

Description of work	No. pieces	Dimensions A	Dimensions B	Dimensions C	Concrete A × B × C	Forms 2 × (A + B) × C	
Concrete to column footings (3000 lbs)							
(Refer footing schedule Drg. 5.4)							
Type A	7	4.0	4.0	1.3			
Type B	3	4.0	3.6	1.0			
Type C	10	4.6	4.6	1.6			
							S.F.
					÷ 27		
					=	C.Y.	

Figure 3.1.

Description of work	No. pieces	Dimensions A	Dimensions B	Dimensions C	Concrete A × B × C	Forms 2 × (A × C)	Key (2″ × 4″) A	
Concrete to perimeter wall footings (2500 lbs)								
Col. lines 1+4	2	150.0	2.0	1.0				
Col. lines A		60.0	2.6	1.0				
Col. lines D		60.0	2.0	0.8				
							S.F.	L.F.
					÷ 27			
					=	C.Y.		

Figure 3.2.

3.2 Methods of Measurement

Construction estimators are advised to formulate and agree upon a standard schedule of units and methods of measurement to be used within their own organization for taking off quantities. These schedules would be prepared for all those trades normally taken off in the individual contractor's offices and should be adhered to as closely as possible in all estimates. Familiarity with these agreed rules and methods will usually speed up the process of quantity take-off (less time wasted due to an estimator agonizing about "Should this be in cubic yards? or should it be in square yards and state the thickness?"); it can also simplify the task of making comparisons with similar items in previous estimates or cost reports when pricing a particular trade.

A construction company's schedule of measurements and items is also useful to site personnel—engineers, superintendents, project managers, site accountants, and others—in ensuring that "field quantities" taken off for the purpose of cost records are prepared in compliance with the methods employed by the estimators. This ensures a true comparison between actual and estimated quantities.

The Canadian Institute of Quantity Surveyors (CIQS) publish a document called a *Method of Measurement for Construction Work,* which is self-described as "a definition of principle rather than an inflexible document," and this excellent publication could usefully be employed as a model for a company schedule of items and measurements, or be adopted and used without any modifications to suit company methods or procedures.

Some general contractors would prefer to identify and price separately certain items of work that in the CIQS document are suggested for inclusion in the estimated unit price, items such as scaffolding, formwork hardware and oil, and falsework. Integration of a number of activities into single items can lead to possible misinterpretations by site supervisory personnel and be a hindrance to effective cost control and accurate cost reporting. Therefore, some contractors will prepare their own schedules of measurement methods and rules, which might still follow closely the basic principles set forth in the CIQS document.

Schedules of items and measurements are included in the chapters relating to quantity take-off for specific trade divisions. They are similar to the CIQS document and, like that document, follow as closely as possible well-established standard trade practices; also like the CIQS document, these schedules should be considered to be flexible.

This consideration should be given to any set of estimating procedures or methods formulated in a contractor's office. Estimators must be allowed, and also allow themselves, the latitude to modify or revise any rules when good judgment indicates the justification of such revisions or modifications. The mere existence of a written rule or procedure should never become an overriding factor! Estimators should always seek to know the reason *for* and the logic *behind* each procedure rule; just knowing and being able to quote them parrot-fashion is not satisfactory.

3.3 Net and Gross Quantities

The difference between *net-in-place* quantities (which are basically what are measured on the drawings) and the *gross* (or "gross-on-site" might be a suitable title!) quantities is something of a perennial controversy between a construction company's personnel on the site and the estimators in the office. Superintendents and foremen are conditioned by experience (not unnaturally) to consider construction materials in terms of the methods by which they are purchased, delivered, and installed. They will tend to consider these items not so much in quantity surveying terms (volumes or areas or lengths), but in the more realistic context of truck or carloads, cartons, barrels, drums, rolls, sheets, and so on.

Trained and experienced estimators and quantity surveyors are equally aware of these realities, but their training and experience discipline them to be consistent in the initial establishment of the net-in-place quantities *before* proceeding to add adjustments as compensation for wastage and other factors. An estimator confronted with an accusation that the quantities for a specific item were "very short" will often confound a superintendent with the statement that "there was nothing wrong with the *actual quantities,* it was the *waste factor* that was wrong." This statement is small comfort to a foreman who has only been allowed 8000 bricks in the estimate for a structure that will require 10,000 to build. This image bears overtones of comedy, but there is some logic lurking in the wings; the estimator by establishing the accuracy of the quantity take-off has also established that the waste factor was inadequate and should be adjusted for future estimates. (The alternative, of course, is for the estimator, if foolhardy enough, to accuse the foreman of undue and excessive breakage and waste.)

To attempt the establishment of an accurate and foolproof adjustment for every variable condition and material would be a time-consuming and hazardous operation. It is more sensible to determine a range of *high* and *low* percentage limitations for the different materials (based on previous experience or calculations that have proved satisfactory). These will usually satisfy most conditions.

The terms "cutting and waste" have been employed in previous statements regarding adjustments to net quantities, but there are many other conditions that require the use of adjustment factors to develop the net quantities into the area of actual conditions. Not all these conditions will demand consideration in the average bid, but it is important that estimators appreciate their existence and also the impact they exercise on estimates and quantities. The following are those normally encountered in building projects and should receive consideration in the estimates:

1. *Laps:* The overlapping of one piece of material over another piece of the same material. One example would be welded wire mesh reinforcement. This material is usually sold in 6-ft (1830-mm) wide rolls, and most specifications require that this material be lapped a minimum of 6 in. (300 mm.). This means that except for the first roll in a given area the actual surface covered will be 5 ft. 6 in. (1530 mm); therefore, the net quantity would require an adjustment of at least 8.5 percent to provide sufficient material for the job. As this material would still be subject to further cutting and waste, it is very apparent that a minimum percentage to be added would be 10 percent.
2. *Seepage:* The best example for this condition would be the concrete lost due to seepage through a stone or gravel underbed. The drawings might call for a concrete slab placed on stone fill to be 6 in. (150 mm) thick net, but the actual quantity of concrete placed to achieve this thickness might be equal to 7 to 8 in. (175 to 200 mm). This condition can be compensated for in the estimate by either adjusting the net quantity with a percentage factor or by actually adding an additional 1 in. or 2 in. to the specificed thickness. If this is done, it must be recorded clearly on the take-off sheets in the "waste" columns; this will enable anyone checking the take-off sheets to see how the adjustment was made.
3. *Overbreak:* When rock is excavated by either blasting or drilling, there will be spalls of breakage, and where concrete is to be placed on the rock surfaces (for footings, grade beams, slabs, etc.), additional concrete will be required to make up for the concrete filling up the broken areas. It is a similar condition to the problem of seepage, but a much greater extra thickness of concrete will be necessary to achieve the actual specified thickness.
4. *Compaction:* the change in a quantity of any loose material due to consolidation by compression. This usually applies to the backfilling of excavations with earth, gravel, stone, sand, or other materials, and adjustment to the net quantities is necessary to compensate for shrinkage. This condition, and also the inverse condition of the *swell* of excavated soil, are discussed in more detail in Chapter 4.

Table 3.1 shows a schedule of suggested adjustment factors to be applied to certain materials. Excluded from this table are the factors for soil compaction and swell, which as already stated are included separately in Chapter 4. Also the adjustment for bonding in masonry work is dealt with separately in Chapter 6.

There are other factors to be considered for quantity adjustments not shown on the schedule in Table 3.1. For example, there is often a small wastage of ready-mix concrete materials due to spillage; also, often excess concrete in

TABLE 3.1 Schedule of Adjustment Factors

Material	*Condition*	*Adjustment Factor, %*
Wallboards: plywood, gypsum board, fiberboard, hardboard, etc.	Cutting and waste	10–30
Wire mesh reinforcement	Laps plus cutting and waste	10–20
Lumber (this is premised on lumber being sold in lengths of 2-ft multiples)	Cutting and waste	20–30
Face brick (excludes bonding adjustment)	Cutting and waste	5–15
Concrete block	Cutting and waste	5–10
Glazed concrete block	Cutting and waste	10–20
Clay tile units	Cutting and waste	5–10
Glazed structural tile	Cutting and waste	10–20
Building paper, polyethylene, etc.	Laps and waste	5–10
Wood sheathing, T & G	Cutting and waste	10–15
Wood sheathing (diagonal)	Cutting and waste	15–25
Rigid insulation board	Cutting and waste	10–15

the truck has to be paid for even though it is not used. Many estimators consider these conditions are compensated for by things like the volume of concrete displaced by the reinforcing steel bar or other items embedded in the concrete, and that adjustments are not usually made for small openings, voids, or recesses. Other estimators lean toward the prudence of adding 1 to 2 percent to allow for these small discrepancies.

Although best considered at the "pricing" stage, estimators should bear in mind that many materials are sold on a "minimum purchasable quantity" basis, and when there is a considerable gap between the net requirement of a material and this minimum quantity, a compensating adjustment should be made. Sometimes the excess material could be used on another project, in which case probably no adjustment would be made; however, if it is an expensive material not often encountered in most projects, the minimum purchasable quantity should be included in the bid.

Because of all the variables applicable to the procurement and installation of materials, it should be obvious how essential is the accuracy of the net-in-place quantity take-off. Agonizing over the most realistic adjustment factor for a given material is an exercise in futility if the net quantities are incorrect due to sloppy take-off methods. Any investigation into the reason for a discrepancy between *actual* and *estimated* quantities should start with the examination of the original take-off. If that stands up to inspection, the answer will either be the estimator's lack of practical knowledge about construction materials (a superintendent's opinion!) or bad organization at the site resulting in excessive and unjustifiable waste (an estimator's viewpoint!).

3.4 Take-Off Sheets

The examples given in the ensuing chapters for specific trade divisions will be based on the use of sheets designed for take-off purposes only; that is, no pricing will be done on these sheets. Each item will be taken off, the arithmetical extensions made and totaled, and then the items with the totals will be transferred to another summary sheet.

The alternate method, and one favored by many estimators, is to have the sheets designed for take-off on one side, with columns for pricing at the opposite side.

There are advantages and disadvantages in both methods. When the pricing is done on the same sheet a certain amount of time is saved from having to rewrite the quantities on the second sheet. That is certainly an advantage.

The disadvantage is that certain items applicable to a specific trade might require writing up one, two, or more sheets of dimensions; this means that an item can only be priced on the *last sheet* for this item (where the total quantity will be stated). An estimate for a major project will result in a huge number of sheets with the *totaled and priced items* occurring spasmodically throughout. With the separate summary method, all the items for a specific trade are gathered together on one or two summary sheets; this not only facilitates pricing the items, it also facilitates the checking over of the priced items by a contract or project manager or senior supervising estimator. It could be protested, with some justification, that an item could also be omitted in the process of posting to the separate summary. That is true; but equally it is also possible to overlook an item for pricing on the "combined sheet" method.

3.5 General Contractor's Trades

The schedules of methods and measurements and the quantity surveying examples in this book will be limited to those trades considered as traditional for general contractors to perform with their own work forces. This no longer holds completely true, as many of these trades are now subcontracted in part or in whole; but most general contractors are prepared to do this work if subcontractors are not available or the contractors consider they could do the work more economically than the subcontractor and so ensure a more competitive bid. Also, the number of traditional trades that are subcontracted or worked by the general contractor varies in different regions of the country. In Western Canada, for example, nearly all masonry work is subcontracted, while concrete and formwork operations (particularly in the Prairie provinces) are still very often carried out by the general contractors' work forces.

The trades considered in this book include:

1. Sitework (e.g., excavation, grading, backfilling)
2. Concrete, formwork, and concrete floor finishing
3. Masonry (e.g., brick, concrete block, clay tile)
4. Carpentry and millwork (*Note:* It is becoming common for millwork contractors to include the installation of the millwork items in their quotations)
5. Miscellaneous items. These would include:

- Hollow metal doors and frames
- Hollow metal partitions
- Wood doors and frames (often included in the quotation from millwork subcontractors)
- Miscellaneous metals (*Note:* for those items to be *embedded* in concrete, masonry, or other work)
- Specialties (washroom accessories, mat sinkage frames, roof hatches, toilet partitions, etc.)

3.6 Drawings

The examples of quantity take-off demonstrated in Chapters 4, 5, 6, and 7 are based on Figures 3.3 through 3.10 for a 3-story university research building.

To supplement the information shown on these drawings brief specification notes are provided in Chapters 4, 5, 6, and 7 for the pertinent trade to be taken off. All take-off examples are in accordance with the appropriate "Schedule of Items and Measurements" included in each chapter.

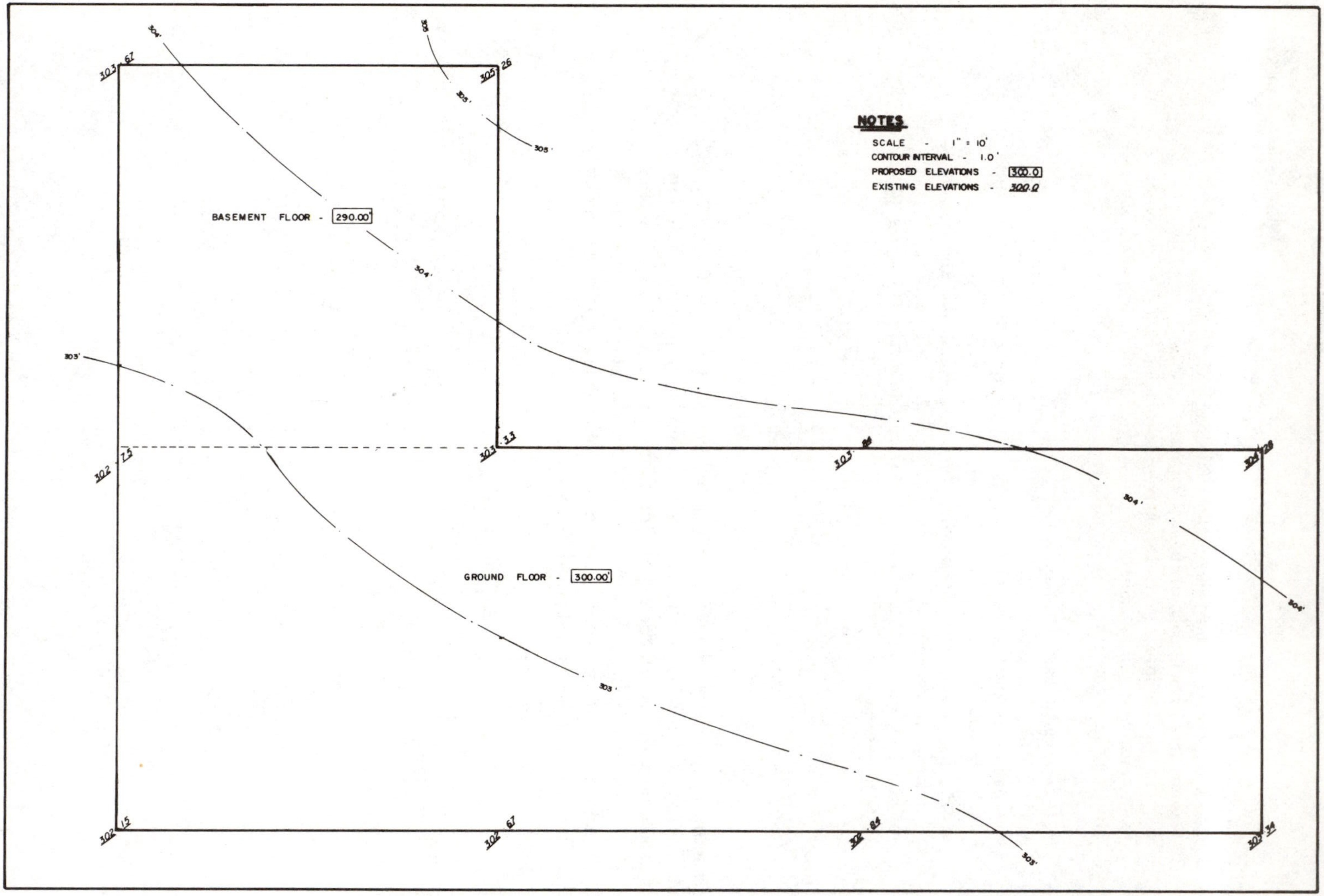

Figure 3.3. Plot plan.

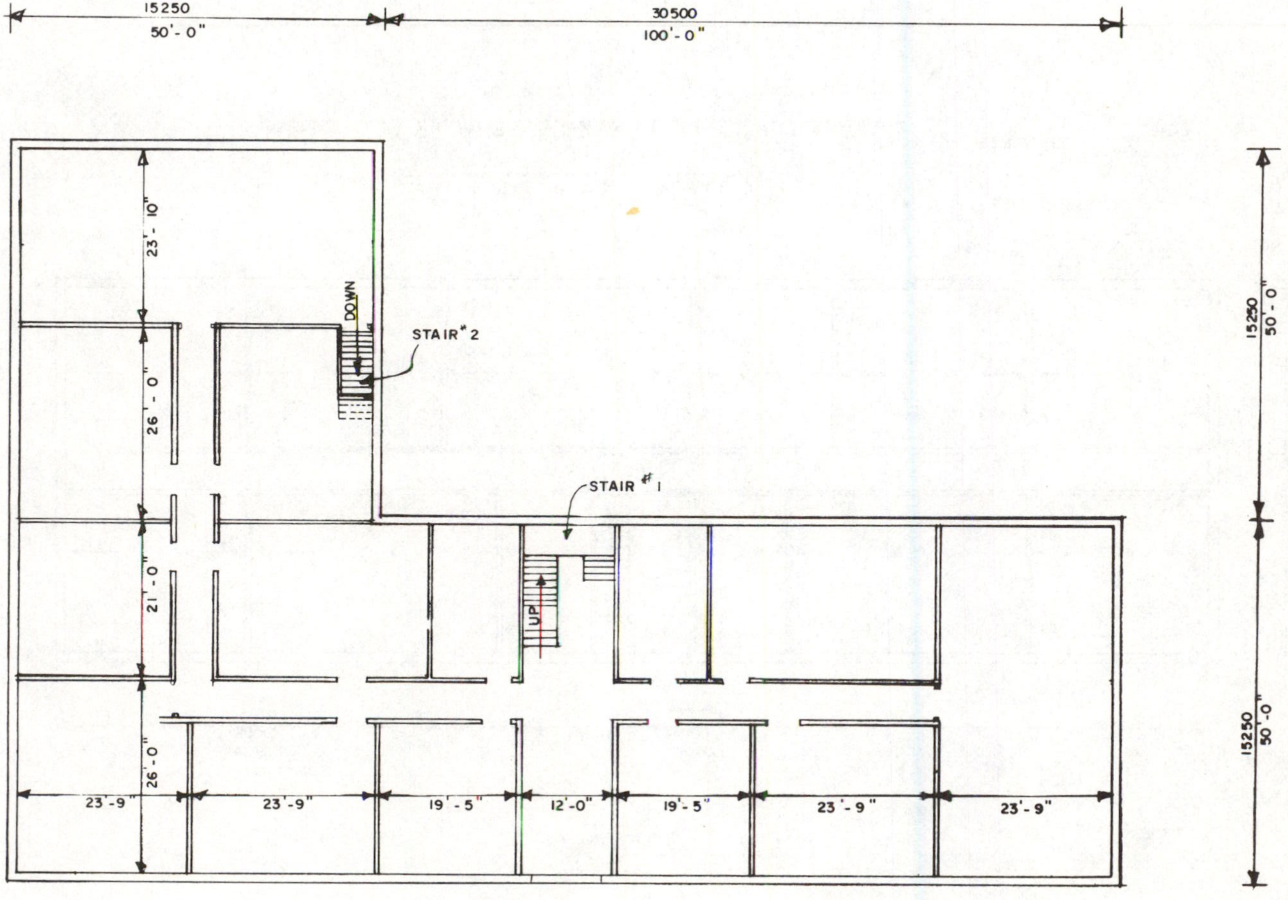

GROUND FLOOR PLAN

Figure 3.4. A.1 ground floor plan.

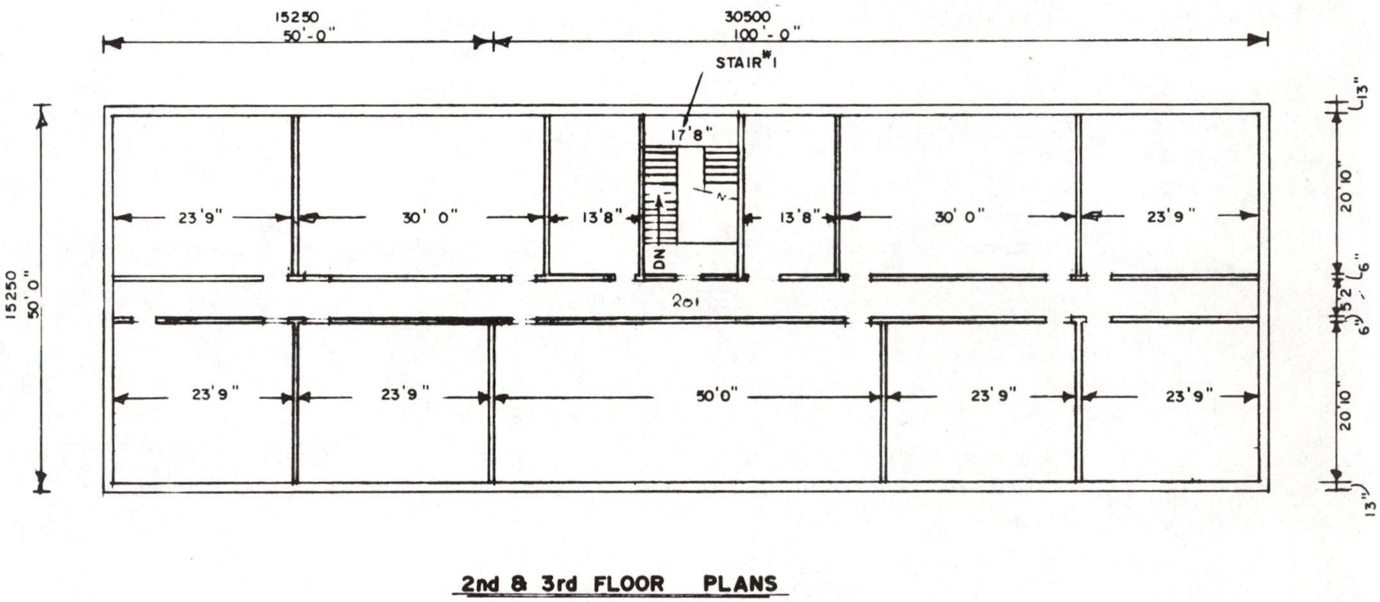

Figure 3.5. A.2 second and third floor plans.

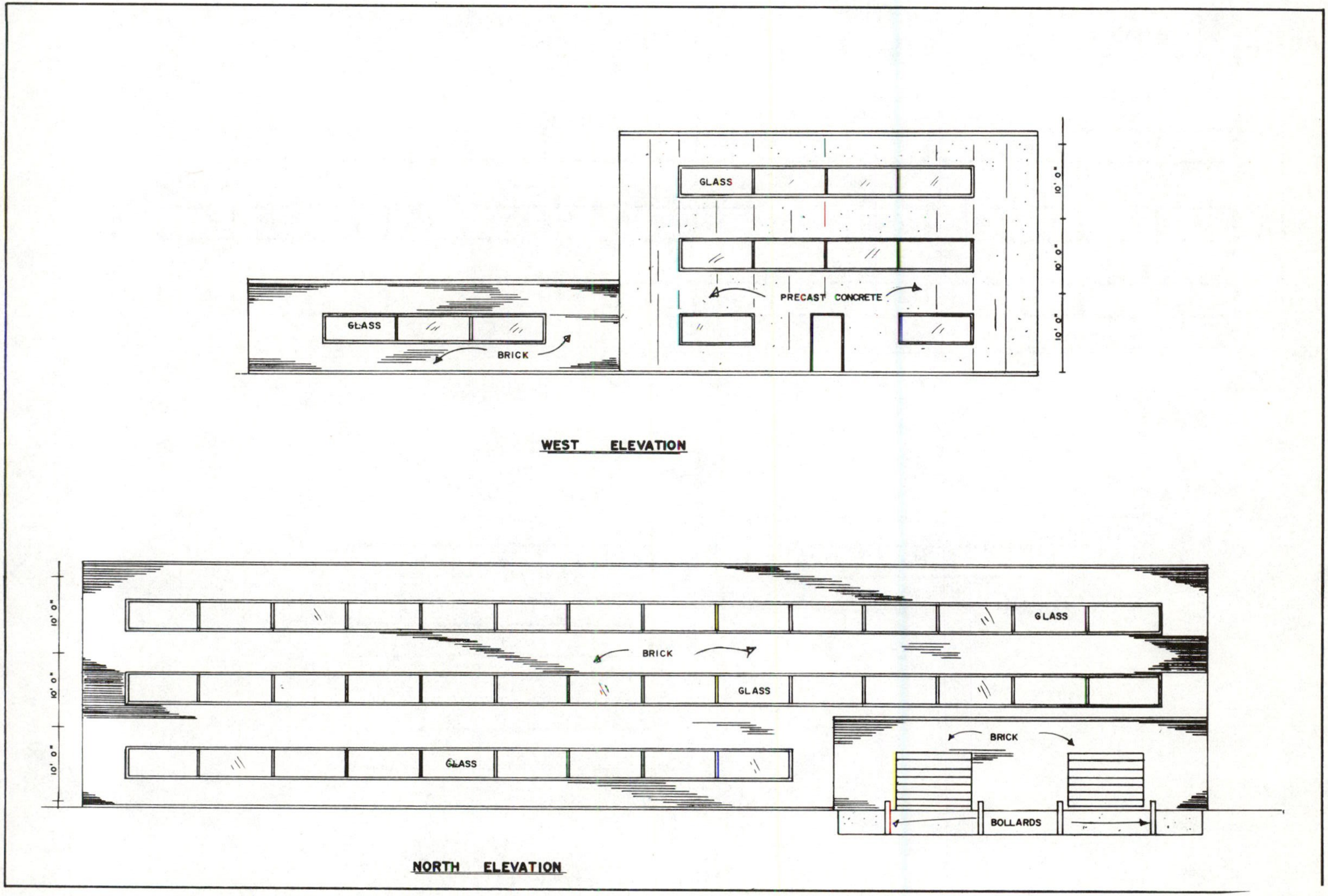

Figure 3.6. A.3 west and north elevations.

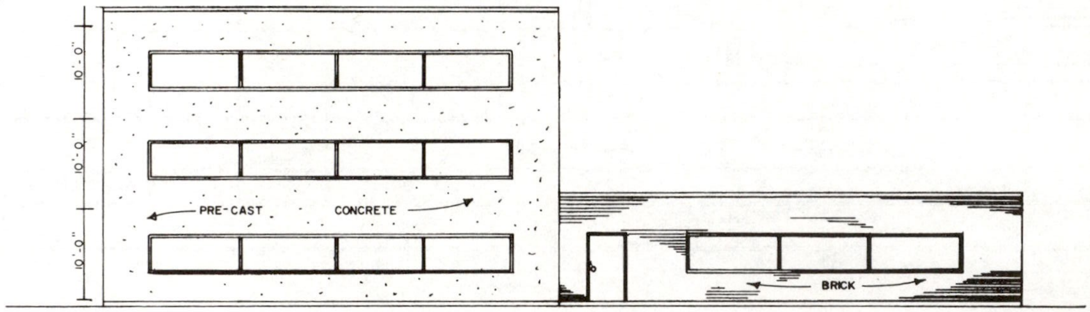

EAST ELEVATION

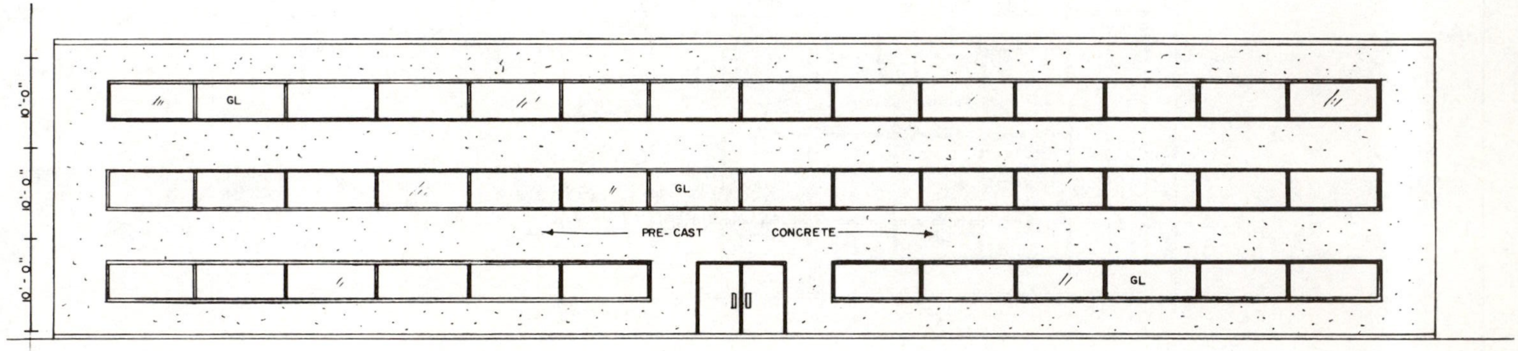

SOUTH ELEVATION

Figure 3.7. A.4 east and south elevations.

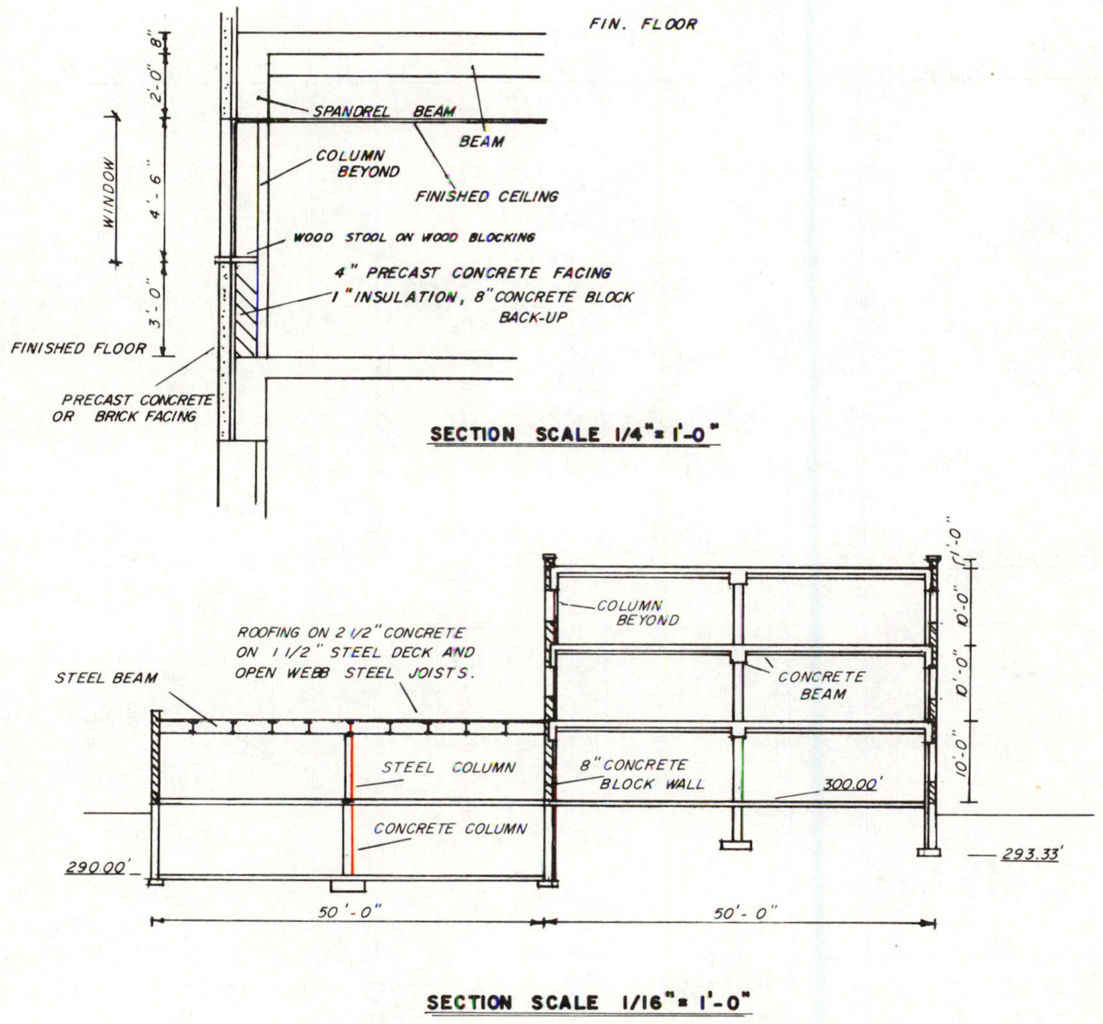
FIN. FLOOR
SPANDREL BEAM
BEAM
COLUMN BEYOND
FINISHED CEILING
WINDOW
2'-0"
8"
4'-6"
3'-0"
WOOD STOOL ON WOOD BLOCKING
4" PRECAST CONCRETE FACING
1" INSULATION, 8" CONCRETE BLOCK BACK-UP
FINISHED FLOOR
PRECAST CONCRETE OR BRICK FACING
SECTION SCALE 1/4" = 1'-0"
ROOFING ON 2 1/2" CONCRETE ON 1 1/2" STEEL DECK AND OPEN WEBB STEEL JOISTS.
STEEL BEAM
COLUMN BEYOND
CONCRETE BEAM
STEEL COLUMN
8" CONCRETE BLOCK WALL
CONCRETE COLUMN
300.00'
290.00'
293.33'
1'-0"
10'-0"
10'-0"
10'-0"
50'-0"
50'-0"
SECTION SCALE 1/16" = 1'-0"

Figure 3.8. A.5 building section.

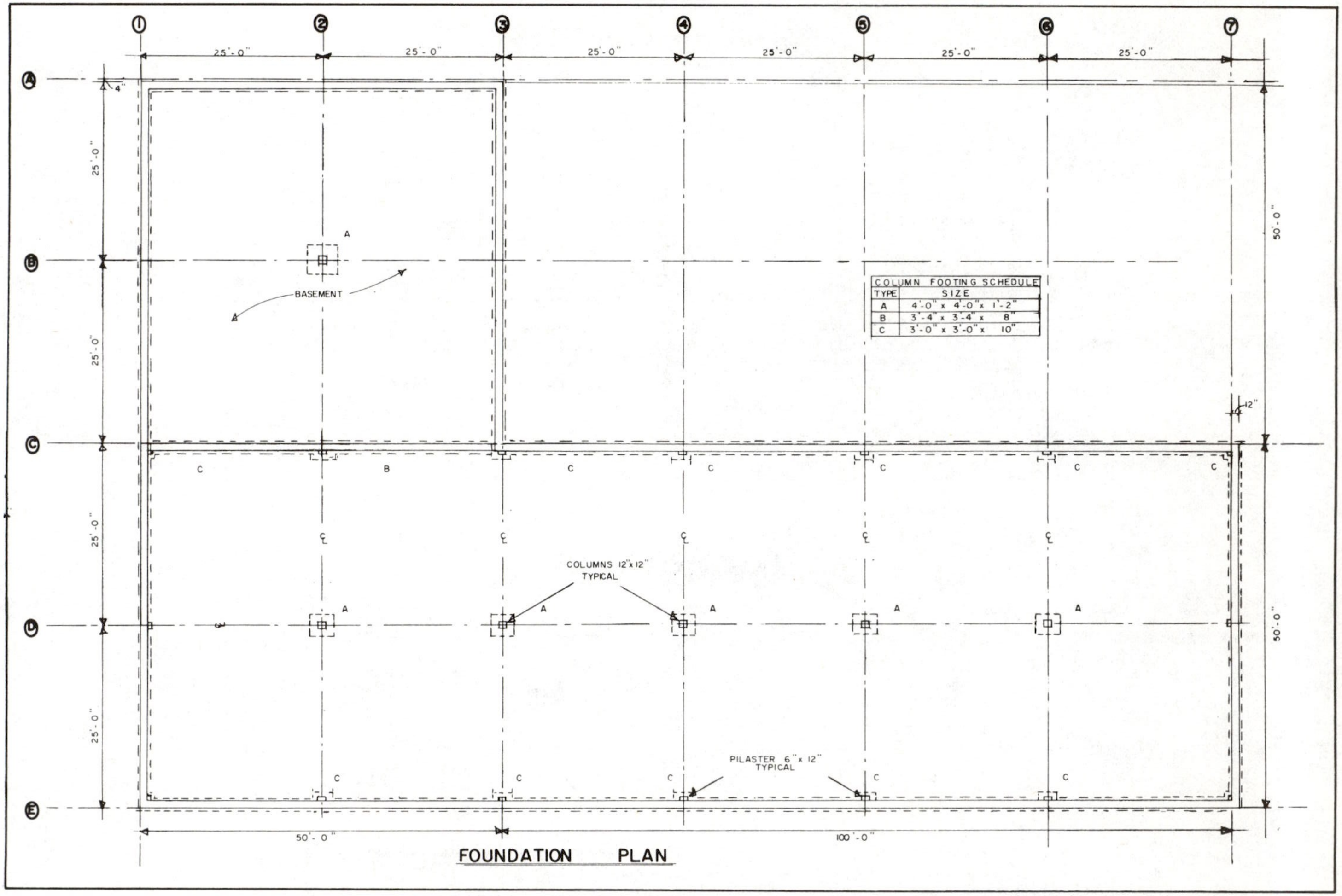

Figure 3.9. S.1 foundation plan.

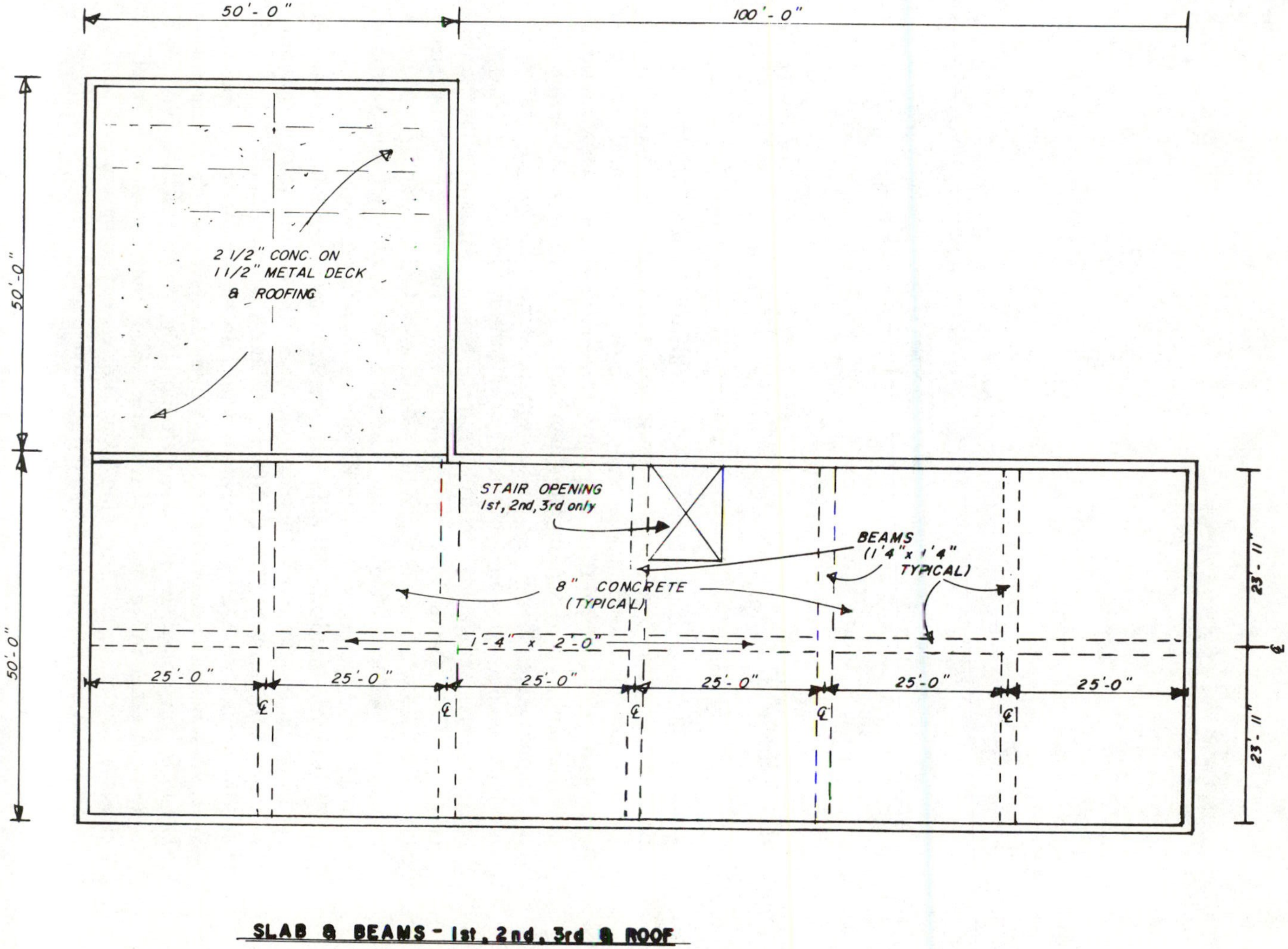

Figure 3.10. S.2 structural floor plans—1st, 2nd and 3rd floors

4

Take-off: Sitework

4.1 General

Sitework (site clearing and general excavation work) is one of the first operations performed on a construction project, but this does not mean that it is logically the initial trade taken off in the estimate. Experienced estimators often leave this trade until at least after the concrete substructure work has been taken off, and very often later than that. An early site visit is also essential before taking off sitework, and in some instances the use of a surveyor's level may be necessary for spot checks of existing grades.

Another recommendation is to have the estimator responsible for the concrete quantities also take off the excavation work. The measurement of structural work below grade will mean the recording of the locations, enumerations and size of footings, pile caps, pits, and such like, all of which data will facilitate taking off the excavation and backfill for these same items.

Probably the fundamental difference between measuring the quantities of earthwork in comparison with taking off the work of other trades (concrete, masonry, carpentry, etc.) is that, with the possible exception of civil engineering projects, the actual *excavation details* do not appear on the drawings. What are usually shown are the details of those items for which the *excavation has to be performed,* be it a complete building, or foundations, pits, manholes, and other miscellaneous structures. Also, only the *neat lines* of the excavation are reflected in the dimensions. For excavation measurements, these basic dimensions have to be projected to provide for:

1. Additional working space.

2. Side slopes to prevent the caving in of the banks, usually legislated by jurisdictional authorities (unless a system of perimeter shoring or sheet piling is to be used to support the banks).

Figure 4.1 shows how these neat-line dimensions would be expanded for take-off purposes.

Another factor that affects the quantities for earthwork estimates is the swelling of the soil after it has been loosened and excavated. This factor is usually expressed as a percentage factor applied to the net-in-place (*bank measure*) quantities. As an example, if the appropriate adjustment factor was 15 percent, then 100 cubic yards of earth would become 115 cubic yards after excavation (*loose measure* volume).

Although this book primarily addresses itself to stipulated-sum bids, it is recommended that this *bulking* factor be dealt with by incorporating it into the estimated unit rate, rather than applying it to the net quantities. This would appear to be a reversal of all previous recommendations that adjustment factors for wastage, cutting, compaction, and so on, should be applied against the quantities. The principal reason for this inconsistency is that in building construction work (as opposed to heavy engineering works), it is usual for a general contractor to subcontract the excavation work, and excavation contractors will often only quote unit rates to the general contractors, leaving it to the contractor to compute the quantities and establish a total cost. This bulking factor will usually be included in these unit rates, and a possible duplication could occur if it was also reflected in the quantities.

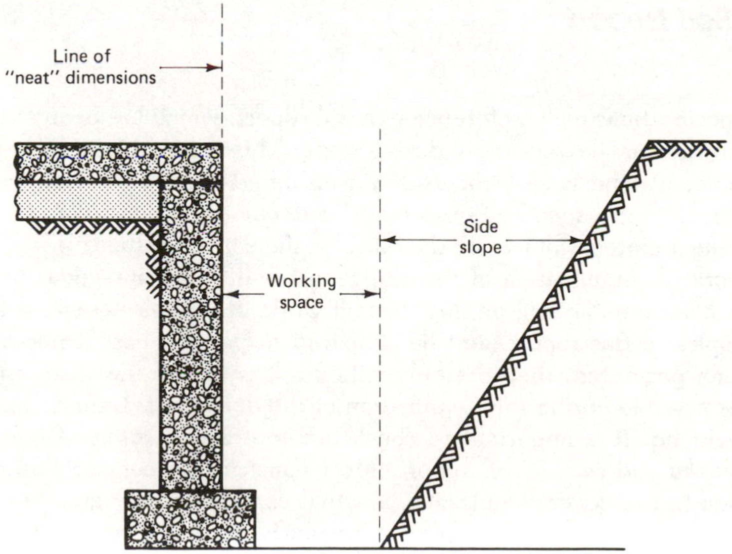

Figure 4.1.

The measurement of excavation work is influenced by methods and equipment. This applies more particularly to heavy engineering construction than to building projects; in heavy work, very often the quantity take-off will not be started until equipment and methods have been predetermined. This book is mainly concerned with *building construction,* and the methods of measuring and estimating earthwork will follow the principles adopted by most general contractors. The various items will be categorized according to the type of operation (e.g., mass, trenching) or the function of the item for which excavation is required (e.g., basement, footing, pit, manhole, underfloor drainage).

These classifications naturally have some influence on the methods and equipment to be used; certain items will preclude the use of one particular type of equipment, others will lend themselves to a choice. For example, a scraper would hardly be considered practical to dig out a number of isolated column footings, whereas a major item of "cut and fill" would be suitable for that piece of equipment. The matter of final equipment selection is best left until the pricing stage of the estimate, rather than complicating the estimator's work at the take-off stage. Discussions with superintendents and other supervisory personnel will yield sound advice, based on practical experience on earthwork operations. If necessary, the quantities could be regrouped into separate categories of selected equipment; for example,

Backhoe operation = 9,000 cubic yards
Scraper work = 14,000 cubic yards
And so on

4.2 Soil Report

Most specifications make reference to a soil report, which has been authorized by the owner in the very early design stage. This is not always included as a *bid* document (and is also not usually considered a *contract* document); the usual directive in a specification is that this document is "*available for inspection* at the architect's office, or the office of the soil consultant."

A thorough examination of this soil report will be advantageous to the estimator before embarking on any take-off work. It will be beneficial to make photocopies of this report (and be prepared to pay the cost if necessary); if this is not permitted, then the only option left is to make as many pertinent notes as possible during the examination of the document, time consuming as this might be. It is important to check the contractual status of information provided *by* and *in* this soil report. Most construction contracts allow compensation to the general contractor if actual conditions vary greatly from the information given in the soil report, particularly if the discrepancies could not be observed on a site visit. However, some specifications sound the ominous warning that "the soil report is provided for information only and the owner accepts no responsibility for the accuracy of the information contained therein."

Even if the soil borings and information are shown on the drawings or in the specifications, estimators should take note that these are often only a *portion of or extracts from the official report*. The complete document should be studied. One item experienced estimators look for is the groundwater table. The consultant's report will probably also make recommendations regarding methods to dispose of groundwater: drainage sumps, perimeter ditching, well-point systems, and the like.

4.3 Compaction

Just as an adjustment factor has to be allowed for the swell of excavated materials, another factor has to be considered for the compression or *compaction* of materials after being placed as fill in the structure. The recommendation for this item is that it should be measured as the *compacted volume*, with the neat quantities projected to include all allowances for compaction. In the unit-price type of contract, this compaction would obviously be included in the unit rate, but for other contracts, where payments to the contractor are *not* to be based on measurements and prices, it would seem desirable to consider such material items in the context of the actual quantities to be purchased. Unless a site superintendent had been properly enlightened, there could be misunderstandings about both the *quantities* of material required and the estimated *unit cost* of the material. Therefore, if 1000 cubic yards bank measure of a granular material is required, and the compaction percentage is considered to be 20 percent, the estimate should show a quantity of 1200 cubic yards *priced at the unit rate quoted by the supplier*. These materials are usually quoted by the ton (tonne), and need to be adjusted by an applicable conversion factor to cubic yards or meters.

Table 4.1 shows some recommended compaction factors for various material classifications. Estimators, engineers, superintendents, and soil consultants could debate interminably as to the right percentage to use for a specific condition; the only solution is to exercise the best possible judgment and to make use of whatever past experience is available.

TABLE 4.1 Backfill Compaction Factors

Soil Classification	*Factor, %*
Soil	25–30
Sand and gravel	20–25
Crushed stone	15–20

4.4 Measurements: General Principles

Earthwork should be measured (with certain exceptions) in cubic yards (cubic meters) and to *bank measure*. Excavation should be stated separately for the following soil classifications:

1. Earth (this might be further divided into categories for hard, soft, or medium soil; clay; hardpan, etc.).
2. Rock or shale (again could be categorized as hard rock, soft shale, broken shale, etc.).

Excavation by machine should be measured to the full depth required by the drawings, and any final hand trimming or breaking should be measured separately and recorded as an "extra over."

Items that can only be excavated *by hand* (a different category from the *trimming* just described) should be measured and stated as separate items, and it is recommended that explanatory descriptions be included with the item (e.g., "hand excavation to shallow trenches"). Also included in this category are items that could not be excavated at the time of the major earthwork operations but do not carry a cubic volume sufficient to justify the *float charges* of bringing the equipment back to the site.

A working space allowance should be added to the basic dimensions. Recommended *minimums* are 12 in. (300 mm) plus the distance of the footing projection from the wall face or 2 ft. 6 in. (750 mm) from the wall face, whichever is the greater. (Remember, these are recommended *minimums!*)

Side Slopes. These are expressed as a ratio based on the number of feet *horizontal* to the number of *feet in depth*.

Example: A 1 : 1 slope requirement for a trench 10 ft deep means that the width of the excavation at the top will be 10 ft at *each side* of the trench.

These side slopes will vary according to the different soil classifications, but estimators will find that in most regions there will be permissible slope ratios required by the authorities having jurisdiction (local, provincial, state, or federal). In Ontario, for example, the Construction Safety Act (1973) requires that the excavation sides have a 1 : 1 slope *from four feet above the bottom of the excavation*. Table 4.2 shows some recommended slopes according to soil classifications.

Excavation to confined and/or restricted areas should be stated separately. (Machine excavation might still be possible in such locations, but productivity would be greatly impeded.)

TABLE 4.2 Side Slope Ratios

Soil Classification	*Slope Ratio*
Sand or gravel	1:1
Earth	1:1 to 1:2
Clay	1:3 to 1:4
Rock or shale	Nil.

State whether excavated material is to be side-cast, stockpiled, or removed from the site. Some estimators measure everything as side-cast, and state the other two categories as extra over. The site plan should also be checked to ensure that stockpiling is practicable: there may not be sufficient space, and other vital operations might be impeded.

Small items requiring excavation of less than 10 cubic feet (300 mm^3) each should be stated in cubic feet and the number of such items given. For example,

Excavate for small isolated piers (20 in number) = 55 cubic feet.

All work in rock should be measured separately and stated if to be drilled and blasted, ripped, or broken up with hand tools. The cleaning off of rock or shale surfaces must also be stated separately; this can be a very expensive item.

4.5 Schedule of Items and Measurements: Excavation

Item	*Comment*	*Unit of Measurement*
Clearing site	Includes the clearing and "grubbing" of all shrubs, small trees, brush, vegetable matter, etc.	Square yard or acre (Square meter or hectare)
Tree removal	This will include the grubbing and removal of the roots. On most projects this item will require a physical count at the site. The drawings do not usually give this information, unless there are only a few selected for removal. Keep separate as follows: • 12–24 in. dia. (300–600 mm) • 24–36 in. dia. (600–900 mm) • over 36 in. dia. (over 900 mm)	Numerical
Protection of existing trees	Specifications and drawings may identify some trees that must be protected against damage	Numerical

Item	*Comment*	*Unit of Measurement*
	during construction, and will describe the protective materials (wood boards, snow fence, etc.).	
Breaking up of existing foundations	State material (concrete, masonry, stone, etc.) if known. Small items (isolated piers for example) should be enumerated. Existing foundations known to be heavily reinforced should be stated separately. If possible state in separate categories for: • breaking up by tools and compressor • breaking up with hand tools • breaking up with excavation machinery	Cubic yard (m^3)
Removal of rubble or debris	This item will include the removal from the site by trucks or garbage containers of the items previously measured for breaking up. An adjustment factor will be made to the net quantities to allow for "bulking." *Note:* Some estimators will prefer to amalgamate this item with the breaking up item rather than price it separately.	Cubic yard (m^3)
Removal of miscellaneous obstructions	These would include but not be limited to: • fences and gates • manholes, catchbasins, sumps • hydro poles, light standards and bases • small structures (sheds, garages, kiosks, etc.) • other existing obstructions	 Linear foot (m) Enumerate Enumerate Enumerate Enumerate
Strip topsoil	This will be classified as either (a) stockpiled or (b) removed from the site. State average depth.	Cubic yard (m^3)
Machine excavation	General classifications should be: • main building (basement) • excavate over site to reduced levels • spread footings, pile or caisson caps • trenches for foundations • trenches for mechanical and electrical trades • tunnels • manholes, catchbasins, pits • other items *Note:* The main reason for keeping the excavation work for mechanical and electrical trades as separate items is that, although the architect's specifications may stipulate this work to be performed by these particular trades, some (or all) of these subcontractors may elect to exclude it in their bids, qualifying it as work to be done "by the general contractor." Estimators	Cubic yard (m^3)

Item	*Comment*	*Unit of Measurement*
	should always be prepared for such eventualities. They should also remember that such work usually demands pricing at a higher unit cost to allow for a slower rate of productivity due to the speed at which such services can be installed, and also for special excavation equipment if required.	
Hand excavation	This falls into two categories: (a) Trimming, cleaning and grading of surfaces after machine excavation. Trimming the sides and/or bottom surfaces of excavation for spread footings (or similar items) not exceeding 10 ft^2 (1 m^2) could be *enumerated*.	Square foot (m^2)
	(b) Excavating for items that are too small, or shallow, or inaccessible for excavation by machine. These would include items such as small bases, thickening of concrete slabs under masonry walls, weeping tile, shallow trenches, curbs, etc. *Note:* Handwork requiring double handling to be stated separately.	Cubic foot (m^3)
Line drilling to rock surfaces	This is required to control the amount of work loosened or shattered by blasting. State depth and centers.	Linear foot (m)
Removal of caissons (or piling) spoil	This item is quite often identified as an "exclusion" in quotations from piling subcontractors.	Cubic yard (m^3)
Stripping overburden	This is an operation within the category of machine excavation, but should be shown as a separate item. State if less than 18 in. deep (450 mm).	Cubic yard (m^3)

4.6 Fill and Backfill: General

As already stated, all fill and backfill operations should be measured to provide the total *compacted* quantities. This means that a percentage will be added to the net quantities to allow for the necessary additional volume of material.

The specifications should be checked carefully regarding the possible use of excavated materials for fill and backfill. A common phrase in a specification is that this material can be used "*if* approved by the architect or engineer," a statement that rarely gives any comfort or feeling of confidence to an estimator!

Where the degree of compaction is specified as a percentage (e.g., 95% Proctor) and a specific grade of material is also specified, the estimator is advised to check with the material supplier (possible gravel pits) to ascertain that the required compaction can be obtained with that material. If the suppliers express any doubts, the architect or engineer should be consulted. The contention here might be that the contractor could allow for another grade of material in his bid, which would give the specified compaction, but this material might be more costly and would affect the competitive nature of the contractor's bid.

Fills and backfills should be measured and stated separately according to the (1) material classification, and (2) the compaction requirements.

Items such as small holes, pockets, bases, in fact anything with a volume of less than 3 cubic feet, should be measured separately in cubic feet and the total number stated.

Where underfloor fill or bedding is placed on rock surfaces, an additional thickness of material should be allowed for overbreak. This additional thickness could range from 3 in. (75 mm) to 6 in. (150 mm) (or greater) according to the estimator's judgment of site conditions.

4.7 Schedule of Items and Measurements: Fill and Miscellaneous Earthwork Items

Item	*Comment*	*Unit of Measurement*
Backfill	Recommended separate items for: • fill to grade or under slabs • perimeter foundations (this could be further divided into *outside* and *inside* faces if different labor and equipment methods were pertinent) • spread footings, pile or caisson caps • miscellaneous pits, manholes, catchbasins • mechanical and electrical trenches Estimators should make some judgment (where possible) between backfill items that require placing solely "by hand," as opposed to those locations where the fill can be machine deposited into place, with handwork only necessary for trimming and compacting. All backfill at underpinning or perimeter shoring work must be stated as separate items. The placing of backfill to fill the small space left after the removal of	Cubic yard (m^3)

Item	*Comment*	*Unit of Measurement*
	timber lagging (mandatory in some municipalities) is a costly item.	
Underfloor fill to concrete slabs	State if stone, gravel, or sand. It may be necessary to keep separate underfloor bedding to small platforms, pits, steps, and similar. Also bedding to walkways and sidewalks should be treated as separate items.	Cubic yard (m^3)
Bed and surround to drainage tile	Should be kept separate for interior and exterior locations.	Cubic yard (m^3)
Spread topsoil	Stated as separate items for: • excavated and hauled from stockpile • imported topsoil It is also necessary to separate the placing of topsoil to planting beds, or plants, all of which would have to be hand placed.	Cubic yard (m^3)
Sand blinding over stone or gravel	This is often required to receive a polyethylene vapor barrier. Because of the loss in stone or gravel voids, a waste percentage should be allowed, or it might be more practical to increase the specified thickness by an additional 1 in. (or more if the estimator considered it necessary).	Cubic yard (m^3)
Drainage tile	State diameter of pipe and material classification. The total length of pipe measured should include all "specials" (i.e., tapers, wye pieces, bends, etc.), but these items should be enumerated as separate items for extra over to *material costs only.* (This is really up to the estimator's discretion; preference might be to measure and state every item in detail.)	Linear foot (m)
Vapor barrier under floor slabs	Describe the material and allow 5% to 10% for laps.	Square foot (m^2)
Timber sheeting	This would be required in locations where sloping was not practical, and would particularly apply to trench for pipes or conduits. Keep separate categories for light, medium, or heavy. Keep separate if to be machine driven.	Square foot (m^2)

4.8 Perimeter Piling and Shoring

This is usually a mandatory requirement in large projects in the downtown areas of towns and cities where side sloping is restricted. This is an operation that is becoming increasingly common for a general contractor to subcontract to a specialist company. However, there are certain items of work that are not always included by these subcontractors, or the quotations might only reflect unit rates for the applicable items, requiring the general contractor to compute the quantities.

The following is a checklist of some items to be considered for an estimate of this work, with some recommendations regarding measurements:

1. Preboring for H-piles (state diameter and total length).
2. Driving H-piles (linear foot or meter). (*Note:* Items 1 and 2 would probably be quoted by a specialist contractor either on a lump-sum or unit-rate basis.)
3. Weak concrete fill to piles, including subsequent removal. State in cubic yards (cubic meters).
4. Concrete fill to base of piles. State in cubic feet (cubic meters).
5. Timber lagging. State the type of wood and the thickness, and also if creosoting is required. Measure this item in square feet (square meters) and state if removal is also necessary (or state as two separate items).
6. Rakers, walers, struts, and the like. If not included by the subcontractor, these items should be measured and stated in tons (tonnes).
7. Sand fill behind lagging should be measured in cubic yards (cubic meters).
8. Mobile crane, welding and burning equipment, cables, slings, and the like.

Other items to be considered in their applicable trade divisions would be the excavation of the berm; concrete footings ("deadmen") for the rakers, provision of holes through the concrete wall and slabs (i.e., the formwork) for the rakers, raker and tie-back pockets (including subsequent filling in and making good); and setting and grouting of miscellaneous base plates and anchor bolts. Other items that might be exluded from a subcontractor's quotation would include:

1. Removal of lagging and upper portion of H-pile where required by a municipality.
2. Demolition and removal of sidewalks and any excavation and backfill to facilitate the removal of lagging and piles, and in some circumstances, the removal of the rakers.

In some instances the subcontractors might quote for the complete work on the basis of a unit rate per square foot, in which case only the net face area of the earth to be supported would be measured.

4.9 Underpinning

Excavation work to locations where underpinning is required will be measured separately as already stated; the same will apply to applicable concrete and formwork. Other items to be taken into account with underpinning operations would include:

1. Timber sheathing against the earth at each section or "pit" of underpinning. (The sequence in which these sections will be worked is usually noted on the drawings.) This sheathing can be measured in either square feet (square meters) or per board foot measure (cubic meters) of lumber.
2. Grouting at the point where the new wall comes into contact with the bottom of the existing wall or footing. This should be measured in cubic feet (cubic meters) to both the sides and the rear portion of the pit. The sheathing at the rear of the pit will need to be noted as "left in place."

4.10 Dewatering

The rental and operation of pumping equipment for removal of water from the excavation is usually included in the estimate of site overhead or *indirect* costs. For sites where the specification or soil reports indicate excessively high groundwater content, it will be necessary to consider other methods of removing the water, such as well-point installations or the provision of *relief wells*.

Well-point systems are provided by specialist companies, usually on a monthly rental basis. On major projects where the equipment will be required for a lengthy time period, the specialist company will often quote higher rental rates for the first, second, and third months, and a lower rate for the ensuing months. Jet-eductor equipment (if applicable) will usually be quoted separately. Other items to be considered when analyzing a proposal from a dewatering specialist would include:

1. Installation and removal of the equipment, sometimes quoted on a per diem basis.
2. Operation of the system, also on a per diem basis. If not provided by the specialist company, the estimator will have to allow for the total hours and rates of operating engineers.
3. Freight and loading charges (at the specialist company's yard).
4. Unloading and loading costs at the site. This will usually have to be done by the contractor's work force.
5. Charges for electric service.

If it is considered that the dewatering can be handled by the installation of *relief* or *deep* wells, the following items should be considered:

1. Drilling for the casings, per linear foot (meter), stating the diameter.
2. Supply and placing of the casings, per linear foot (meter),
3. Granular filter surround to casings, per cubic yard (cubic meter).

4. Pump equipment, rental or purchase.
5. Additional hose, per linear foot (meter).
6. Electrical wiring, item.
7. Removal of surplus soil cuttings, cubic yard (cubic meter).
8. Screen sections, per linear foot (meter) stating the width.
9. Attendance on pumping equipment, total man-hours.

Other dewatering systems, or variations on the systems described, are available for consideration. Soil engineering consultants and dewatering specialists should be contacted for advice and proposals.

4.11 Demolition

This is also a division of sitework (Masterformat 02050), although the demolition work usually measured and priced by general contractors is for the breaking out and removal of *parts* of an existing structure; the complete demolition of existing buildings is usually subcontracted to demolition or wrecking contractors. Very often a new building will connect into or be adjacent to an existing building, a new hospital or university wing, for example, and the contract will require the contractor to perform renovations and alterations in that building. This work would include the breaking out and removal of partitions, ceilings, flooring, miscellaneous concrete or masonry, and similar items.

There are three separate cost factors involved in most of these items:

1. The actual breaking out, with hand tools or pneumatic or similar equipment.
2. Removing the rubble or debris to a location where it can be loaded into a truck or special garbage container. This could involve wheeling barrows along corridors, down freight or other elevators, through exits to the exterior ground level. If this was in an existing hospital, for example, where the normal activities of such an institute were to be unimpaired by construction work, the productivity factor would be exceedingly low.
3. The loading up of a truck or container, either by hand or with a front-end loader.

It is recommended that factors 1 and 2 be considered as one operation for measuring and pricing purposes. It would be difficult to allocate separate costs with any real accuracy; factor 3, on the other hand, would often be a separate operation done periodically, and could be more easily identified for cost allocation. An exception to this ruling would be when the debris could be wheeled to a rubbish chute for instant deposit into a truck or container.

Although a considerable amount of quantities of demolition items can be taken off from the drawings, a site visit is essential to fully appreciate all the items and work to be considered. Also, certain items may not be spelled out in the written documents but could only be inferred from the description of other work to be done. For example, the drawings and specification might contain a schedule of locations where existing ceilings were to be removed and new ceilings installed, but make no reference to other areas where the removal of ceilings would be essential for mechanical and electrical renovations.

Dustproof partitions will sometimes be shown and specified for certain locations and at defined stages of construction; more often than not, the specification will stress the obligatory provision of these partitions, describing the construction details, but leaving the scheduling and location details to the contractor's judgment.

Items that are to be removed and later reinstalled or relocated should preferably be split into separate items, one for the removal and another for the reinstallation or relocation. Where new materials are to be installed in lieu of replacing the existing materials, they will often be specified in their appropriate trade divisions (gypsum wallboard, tile, acoustic ceilings, etc.), and the estimate should allow for this work being included in the trade contractors' quotations for those sections.

The following schedule refers to some of the items of demolition work usually performed by general contractors in projects where renovations and alterations are necessary. Large items of mechanical and electrical work or other specialized trade items (sections of aluminum curtain, for example) should be stated as lump-sum items and the appropriate trade contractors consulted if necessary.

4.12 Schedule of Items and Measurements: Demolition

Item	*Comment*	*Unit of Measurement*
Break-up and remove:	(*Note: removal* is to a place for loading into trucks, to a rubbish chute, or to storage)	
Exterior masonry	State type of material (e.g., brick, block, etc., or a combination). Keep separate walls greater than 10 ft in height.	Cubic foot (m^3)
Interior masonry partition	State type of material.	Cubic foot (m^3)
Existing concrete	State separately and describe according to location and function (e.g. slab, footing, wall).	Cubic foot (m^3)
Strip roofing and flashings		Square foot (m^2)

Item	*Comment*	*Unit of Measurement*
Ceilings	State separately for plaster, gypsum wallboard, acoustic tile, or other materials. State if suspension system included.	Square foot (m^2)
Nonresilient finishes	State if tile, terrazzo, marble, quarry tile, etc.	Square foot (m^2)
Glazed wood partitions		Square foot (m^2)
Metal roof or floor decks		Square foot (m^2)
Resilient tile and base	Allow for cleaning off of adhesive.	Square foot (m^2)
Existing doors and frames	State average size and if wood or metal.	Enumerate
Existing windows and frames	State material, also average size if enumerated.	Square foot (m^2) or enumerate
Load and remove debris	State if into trucks or containers.	Cubic foot (m^3)
Dust screens	Keep separate: • fabrication and erection • relocation • dismantle and removal	Square foot (m^2)

4.13 Take-Off Example

Figure 4.2 provides an example of quantity take-off for earthwork. The plot plan (Figure 3.3) and foundation plan (Figure 3.9) provide most of the information applicable to this trade section. The following brief specification notes supplement the data provided on the drawings:

Strip topsoil average 6 inches, stockpile on site.
Excavated material for backfill at exterior side of perimeter foundations.
Backfill at other locations: imported granular fill.
Stone underfill to concrete slabs on ground.
6 inches diameter perforated drainage pipe and fittings.
Pea gravel surround to drainage pipe.
Remove surplus excavated material from site (dump—2-mile haul).

QUANTITIES

SHEET No. 1 OF 5

PROJECT Research Centre — ESTIMATE No. 27/82
LOCATION — BY B.E.W. — CHK'D
SUBDIVISION 02200 – Earthwork — DATE

DESCRIPTION OF WORK	NO. PIECES	DIMENSIONS	AREA 1	AREA 2	AREA 3
Refer Site Plan					
			304·28	303·33	302·75
Gr. Floor : 300·00			303·34	303·84	303·33
6" Slab : ·50			302·84	302·84	302·67
299·50			303·84	302·67	302·15
8" Stone ·67			1214·30	1212·68	1210·90
298·83					
		Average =	303·58	303·17	302·73
		Less 6" Topsoil	·50	·50	·50
			303·08	302·67	302·23

Areas 1. 2. 3 — Av Grade

303·08
302·67
302·23
907·98

÷ 3

= 302·66

Less U/side of Fill 298·83
3·853 = Av Depth of Cut = 3'·10"

Basement Floor 290·00
Slab + Fill 1·17
288·83

Area 4

303·67
305·26
303·33
302·75
1215·01

Average = 303·75
Less 6" Topsoil ·50
303·25
Less U/side of Fill 288·83
14·42 = Av Depth of Cut = 14'·5"

Figure 4.2.

QUANTITIES

SHEET No. 2 OF 5

PROJECT ____________ ESTIMATE No. 27/82

LOCATION ____________ BY B.E.W. CHK'D ____________

SUBDIVISION 02200 EARTHWORK DATE ____________

DESCRIPTION OF WORK	NO. PIECES	DIMENSIONS A	B	C	EXCAVATION A×B×C	HAND TRIM SURFACE A×B
MASS EXCAVATION TO BUILDING						
AREAS 1 & 2.						
100'-0"						
+WORKING SPACE · 2'-6"						
102'-6"						
50'-0"						
WK SPACE · 2' × 2'6" 5'-0"						
55'-0"						
AREA 3						
50'·0"						
W/S · 2'6"						
52'6"						
50'·0"						
DEDUCT WALL · (1'0")						
49'·0"						
		102·6	55·0			5638
		52·6	49·0	3.10	31472	2573
AREA 4						
50'·0"						
WALL 1'·0"						
W/S · 2' × 2'·6" 5'·0"						
56'·0"						
SLOPE 14'5" × 2 / 2 = 14'5"						
70'5"						
50'·0"						
W/S (2) 5'·0"						
SLOPE 14'·5"						
69'·5"		70·5	69·5	14·5	70470	4888
ADJUST LINE "C"		(69·5)	(8·11)	(3·10)	(2373)	(619)
" SIDE SLOPES FOR TRENCH EXCAV. (REFER SKETCH)		55·0				
AREA 1: 5'·6"; 4'3"/2 2'·2"; 7'·8" — AREA 2: 5'·6"; 4'·0"/2 2'·0"; 7'·6"	2/	50·0				
	2/	7·8	7·8	4·3	5550	
	2/	50·0	7·6	4·0	3000	
		52·6				
AREA 3		49·0				
5'·6"; 3'·5"/2 1'·9"; 7·3"		7·3	7·3	3·5	2694	
					110813 CF	12480 SF
					= 4104 CY.	

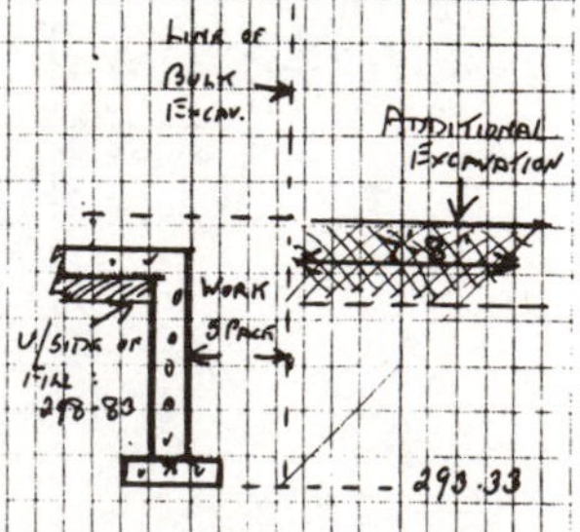

Figure 4.2. *(continued)*.

QUANTITIES

SHEET No. 3 OF 5

PROJECT ____________________ ESTIMATE No. 27/82

LOCATION ____________________ BY B.E.W. CHK'D ________

SUBDIVISION 02200 EARTHWORK DATE ________

DESCRIPTION OF WORK	NO. PIECES	DIMENSIONS A	B	C	TRENCH EXCAV A×B×C	TRIM BOTTOM A×6'0"
TRENCH EXCAV FOR FOOTINGS						
MEASURED FROM ELEV: 298.83						
U/SIDE FOOTING: 293.33						
5.50						
WIDTH OF WALL: 1'0"						
W/SPACE: 2×2'6": 5'0"						
SLOPE 2×5'6"/2: 5'6"						
11'6"						
50'0"						
2'6" 2×5.9 (11'6")						
2'9" 38'6"						
5'3"						
50'0"						
(6'9")						
43'3"						
LINE C	2/	100.0				
	2/	5.3				
		38.6				
		50.0				
		5.3				
		43.3	11.6	5.6	21979	2085
STEPPED FOOTINGS	2/½	12.0	6.0	4.6	324	72
293.33 1'0"	2/2/½	12.0	4.6	7.9	837	144
−288.83 2×2'6"=5'0						
4.50 6'0"						
5'6"						
½×4'6"=2'3"						
7'9"						
ADJUST B/MENT EXCAV	2/	(11.0)	(16.0)	(10.0)	(3520)	
1'0" 1'0"						
2'6" 5'0"						
½×14'11"=7'6" 6'0"						
11'0" 10'0"						
16'0"						
5'6"						
4'6"						
10'0"						
PERIM. COL. FTGS.	13/	5.6	2.0	5.6	787	A×B 143
	2/	5.6	2.0	10.0	220	22
					20627 CF	2466 SF
					= 764 CY	

Figure 4.2. *(continued)*.

SHEET No. 4 OF 5

QUANTITIES

PROJECT ________________ ESTIMATE No. 27/82

LOCATION ________________ BY B.E.W. CHK'D ________

SUBDIVISION 02200 - EARTHWORK DATE ________

DESCRIPTION OF WORK	NO. PIECES	DIMENSIONS A	B	C	EXCAVATE A×B×C	HAND TRIM No. × 16'.0
EXCAV INT. COL FOOTINGS						
4'.0"						
2×1'.0" 2'.0"	5/	12.0	12.0	6.0	4320 CF	80 SF
SLOPE 2×3'.0" 6'.0"						
12'.0"						
					= 160 CY	
					EXT B/FILL (EXCAV SOIL) A×B×C	INT B/FILL (IMPORTED GRANULAR) A×B×C
BACKFILL - PERIMETER FOUNDATIONS						
BACKFILL to (ASSUMED) NEW EXTERIOR GRADE						
SLAB = 300.00						
LESS 1.50						
298.50						
U/SIDE FTG. 293.33						
5.17						
½×5'2" = 2'.7"						
W/SPACE 2'6" LINE "E"		150.0				
5'.1" " 7		50.0				
" "C"		100.0	5.1	5.2	7879	
DEDUCT B/MENT	2/	(10.0)	(5.1)	(5.2)	(525)	
½×14'11" = 7'6" LINE 1		50.0	5.1	5.2	1313	
W/S 2'6" STEPS	2/½/	12.0	2.6	4.6	135	
10'.0"	2/½/	12.0	4.6	7.9	419	
CORNERS	3/	5.2	5.2	5.2	414	
BASEMENT	2/	60.9				
" 50'.0" 50'.0"		59.9	7.3	9.8	12703	
4'9" 5'0" 9'9" 4'9" 1'0" 5'0" 10'9"						
59'9" 60'9"						
4'9" 298.50						
2'6" 288.83 INTERIOR		149.0				
7'3" 9.67	2/	48.0				
		100.0	5.2	5.6		9804
CORNERS	3/	(5.2)	(5.2)	(5.6)		(440)
COL LINE "C"		49.0	7.6	10.0		3675
					22338	13039
298.83		COMPACTION =		20%	4468	3260 ←25%
288.83					26806	16299
10.0						
					993 CY	604 CY

Figure 4.2. *(continued).*

QUANTITIES

SHEET No. 5 OF 5

PROJECT ______
LOCATION ______
SUBDIVISION 02200 - EARTHWORK

ESTIMATE No. 27/82
BY B.E.W. CHK'D ______
DATE ______

DESCRIPTION OF WORK	NO. PIECES	DIMENSIONS A	B	C	A×B×C		
B/FILL TO INT. COL. FOOTINGS							
TOTAL EXCAV VOLUME (SHEET 4) =					4320		
DEDUCT CONCRETE	5/	(4.0)	(4.0)	(1.2)	(93)		
	2/	(3.4)	(3.4)	(.8)	(15)		
PIERS	5/	(1.0)	(1.0)	(4.10)	(24)		
					4188		
COMPACTION 20%					838		
					5026 CF		
					186 CY		
STONE FILL TO U/SIDE CONC FLOOR SLAB					A×B×C		
		48.0 48.0	48.0 49.0	.8	6304		
ADD 20% COMPACTION					1261		
					7565 CF		
					280 CY		
WEEPING TILE AT PERIMETER B/MENT WALLS					PIPE A	SURROUND A×B×C	
	2/ 2/ 4/2/	50.0 51.0 .10	3.6	4.9	209 LF	3469 +20% 694 4163	
						÷27 =	154 CY
EXCAV INT TRENCHES FOR MECHANICAL SERVICES					EXCAV A×B×C	B/FILL A×B×C	
	4/	150.0 100.0 50.0	7.0	4.9	14963	14963 2993 ← 20% 17956	
				=	554 CY		÷27 = 665 CY

Figure 4.2. *(continued).*

COMMENTARY ON TAKE-OFF: EARTHWORK

1. Refer to Sheet 1. In this example the building area has been subdivided into four separate areas (or rectangles) as defined by the existing elevations noted on the perimeter wall lines. The average existing grade is determined for each of these areas.

The first operation will be stripping of topsoil over the entire site (these measurements are not shown). The average depth of the topsoil is 6 in. (150 mm), and the average existing grade elevations are adjusted to allow for this preliminary operation. The thicknesses of the concrete floor slab and the underfloor fill are deducted from the average grade elevation (302.66) to establish the grade to which the cut will be made (298.83).

Areas 1, 2 and 3 could have been computed as a total area, and the average grade levels and depth of cut calculated as follows (refer to sketch):

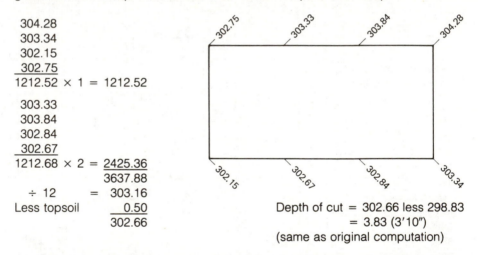

304.28			
303.34			
302.15			
302.75			
1212.52	× 1	=	1212.52
303.33			
303.84			
302.84			
302.67			
1212.68	× 2	=	2425.36
			3637.88
	÷ 12	=	303.16
Less topsoil			0.50
			302.66

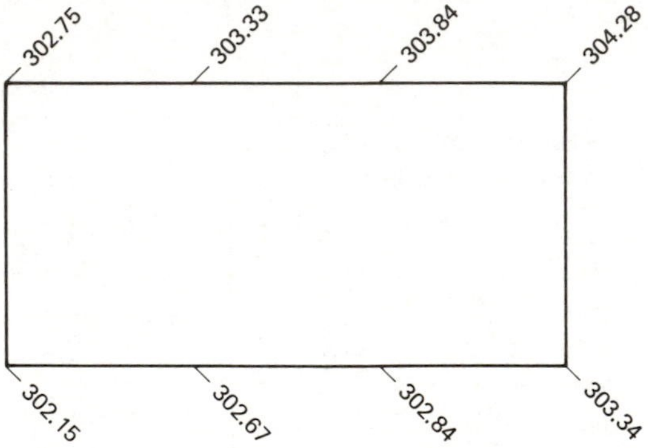

Depth of cut = 302.66 less 298.83
= 3.83 (3′10″)
(same as original computation)

A more accurate computation of excavation depth would be achieved by 'shooting' a series of additional levels at regular intervals at the site, and plotting the results on a grid on the drawing. Each grid would then be computed separately and the results aggregated to a total. This method is most useful for determining 'cut and fill' quantities.

In this example the excavation for the basement (area 4) has been computed from the original ground level (average 303.75). In practice the excavator would probably excavate over all the areas to the reduced level at 298.83 and the basement excavated from this level; and many estimates would show the quantitites computed on this basis. The "end result" in the computed quantities would be the same whichever method of measurement was followed.

2. Refer to Sheet 2. The side calculations demonstrate how the given dimensions are extended (or reduced) to provide for (a) working space, and (b) side slopes (in this instance 1:1 slopes). The calculations for line 1 at area 3 make no mention of working space. This is because the addition of this dimension at E

is offset by the required deduction at C to allow for the basement excavation in area 4.

The adjustment for line C is necessary to compensate for that portion of the excavation to the basement already included in the measurements for excavation to elevation 298.83 (see sketch).

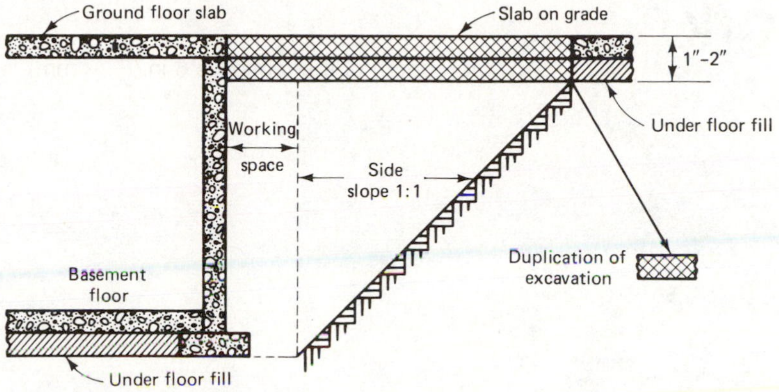

The adjustments to allow for the future side slopes to the trench excavation have been added to this mass excavation item on the assumption the excavator would be alerted to this necessity and perform the work at this time; also mass excavation can usually be performed at a cheaper rate than trench excavation. It has also been assumed that the exterior grading to reduce the existing levels to this new finished grade of 298.50 would be done at a later date. The sketch on the "Take-Off" sheets illustrates the intent of these adjustments.

3. The last item on this sheet shows measurements for the additional *width* of the perimeter column footings. In practice an excavator would most likely dig the continuous perimeter trench to the width to accommodate these footings, and many estimators would measure the quantities on this basis. In this instance the additional volume is not very significant, but on large complex projects this could amount to a fairly substantial quantity. It must always be remembered that doing this also increases the backfill quantities; this could become quite costly if a special grade of imported fill material was specified!

4. Refer to Sheets 4 and 5. The backfill measurements are from the trench bottom to elevation 298.50 which is 1 ft 6 in. below the finished ground floor level.

The material to the interior side of the trenches is an imported granular fill.

5. The weeping tile and the pea gravel surrounding are not shown on the drawings. No deductions are made in the backfill and surround quantities to compensate for displacement by the piping.

6. The interior trenches for mechanical piping are not detailed on the drawings, and the examples are given for a demonstration of measuring and pricing. In practice these details would probably only appear on the Mechanical drawings supplemented by a statement in the specifications that "excavation and backfill is the responsibility of the general contractor."

5

Take-off: Concrete and Formwork

5.1 Concrete: General

The various items applicable to the supply and placing of concrete should be taken off and described according to:

1. Material classification regarding strength mix, aggregate, and so on.
2. Specific function in the structure (i.e., footing, slab, beam, etc.).

A typical estimate item might be "3,000 p.s.i. concrete in perimeter wall footings." The "3,000 p.s.i. concrete" refers to the material classification and the "perimeter wall footings" describes the structural function. If an addenda to the specifications changed this item so that it now became "4,000 p.s.i. concrete in perimeter wall footings," the only difference in the estimated cost would be in the price from the ready-mix concrete supplier; the labor cost of *placing* the concrete would remain unchanged, as it is not affected by the change in strength mix. Equally, a second item of "3,000 p.s.i. concrete in foundation walls" would show the same price for material, but a different unit for placing the concrete than was stated for the perimeter footings.

The material cost is dependent on the specified classification for strength mix and other factors; the labor cost is influenced by the structural function, size, and location of the item. To avoid a lot of repetitious pricing of identical material items, it is recommended that when all the items have been taken off they be regrouped into separate categories for pricing purposes as follows:

1. *Concrete materials:* aggregate all the items pertinent to a particular mix (say, 3,000 p.s.i. concrete) and transfer the total quantity for this material

category to the estimate summary for pricing. Adoption of this method eliminates the repetition of the same material price against a large number of items and also reduces the number of arithmetical extensions to be made and checked. Also the supplier's prices for ready-mix concrete are usually related to the quantities applicable to the particular strength mixes, and this method enables estimators to quickly identify and estimate quantities of each mix when asked by the ready-mix supplier.

2. *Concrete placing:* collection of the items into separate categories according to their structural functions.

Example: The quantity take-off sheets record the following items and quantities:

3000 p.s.i. concrete to perimeter footings	30 cubic yards
3000 p.s.i. concrete to foundation walls	70 cubic yards
3000 p.s.i. concrete to slab-on-grade	100 cubic yards
4000 p.s.i. concrete in suspended slab and beams	200 cubic yards
4000 p.s.i. concrete in columns	80 cubic yards

To facilitate pricing, these would be regrouped into the following categories:

Concrete Materials

3000 p.s.i. concrete	200 cubic yards	
4000 p.s.i. concrete	280 cubic yards	

Concrete Placing

Perimeter footings	30 cubic yards	
Foundation walls	70 cubic yards	
Slab-on-grade	100 cubic yards	and so on accordingly.

This method of collection into categories will be further demonstrated in the examples of take-off and pricing for concrete work.

The general unit of measurement for concrete is the cubic yard (cubic meter). Concrete items with small quantities (less than 5 cubic yards) should, under the Imperial System of Measuring, be given in cubic feet for the cost of placing; in the metric system no such convenient unit as a cubic foot exists. There is, of course, nothing to prevent estimators from using the cubic foot formulas in a metric designed project if they so wish. All that is necessary is a "soft conversion" to cubic yards and then dividing by 27. Where a total quantity represents the aggregate of a number of small items spread throughout the structure (e.g., small equipment bases or pedestals), then both the concrete volume and the number of the items should be stated.

Example: Place concrete to equipment pedestals (15 each) = 30 cubic feet.

It will be easier to take a more realistic approach when pricing these items. The displacement of concrete by reinforcing steel or other items embedded in the concrete will not be taken into account, and no adjustment will be made to the quantities.

All work applicable to architectural concrete must be kept separate. The usual criteria for concrete work under this heading is that little or nothing will be done to the concrete after the forms have been stripped—no patching or rubbing and, sometimes, no cleaning. However, estimators should take note that, where walls in architectural concrete are of a considerable height and require to be poured in lifts,there could be a seepage of concrete at the upper lifts, which would run down to the lower part already *placed and stripped;* to avoid staining, this should be cleaned off immediately. Therefore, an item of cleaning should be measured in square feet (square meters); also an item for protection with polyethylene might be necessary, as additional to the cleaning.

Most ready-mix concrete suppliers quote special charges for underloads usually grouped into the categories of:

Less than 6 cu. yards
Less than 5 cu. yards
Less than 4 cu. yards
Less than 3 cu. yards

with a charge per load for each category, ranging from $10 to $30.

Also, these quotations are subject to a maximum discharge time, usually 30 minutes per load or 10 minutes per cubic meter (whichever is the greater), and a demurrage charge is made for additional time at a rate per 15-minute interval.

Where concrete is to be placed with a concrete pump, there is an invariable additional charge per cubic yard (say $2) for "pump mix" for all mixes of less than 4,000 p.s.i.

Estimators have to exercise judgment regarding the inclusion in their estimates for these special *premium* charges on ready-mix concrete. The decision might be made to assess them as accurately as possible and price them accordingly, or a contingency item might be included for "ready-mix premiums" providing a quantity and rate per cubic yard established, which (hopefully) would be close now to the average amount actually expended. The most important thing is to be realistic and aware that such charges exist and some money will have to be expended on them during the course of the job.

5.2 Schedule of Items and Measurements—Concrete

Item	*Comment*	*Unit of Measurement*
1. Concrete materials	State in separate categories of strength, mix, and aggregate. This item may	Cubic yard (m^3)

Item	Comment	Unit of Measurement
	require a small percentage factor to allow for waste or surplus quantity not placed.	
2a. Admixtures integral with ready-mix concrete: air entrainment retarding admixture	Should be stated separately from the item with which it is to be integrated, and described as "Extra for . . ." (type of admixture).	Cubic yard (m^3)
2b. Admixtures non-integral with ready-mix	According to manufacturer's unit of sale (e.g., a waterproofing compound might be sold in liquid form, and would therefore be stated in gallons or quarts). The applicable quantity would be calculated according to the manufacturer's recommendations.	Gallon, pound, etc. (liter, kilogram)
3. Winter delivery	This is a charge made by ready-mix companies for the heating of the concrete during certain winter months (this varies according to the region of the country, usually within the November to May limits). The estimator must assess all the concrete quantities to be purchased and placed during this period, and state the item as being "extra over" the basic cost of the concrete.	Cubic yard (m^3)
4. Calcium chloride	Keep separate as 1% or 2%.	Cubic yard (m^3)
5. *Placing concrete:* a. wall footings b. spread footings c. pile or caisson caps d. grade beams	Where concrete is to be placed on rock or shale, an allowance should be made for additional quantity necessary to compensate for rock "overbreak." This could vary from an additional 3 to 6 in. or more, according to the estimator's judgment.	Cubic yard (m^3)
6. *Walls:* a. foundation walls and pilasters superstructure: b. shear walls, c. elevator core walls d. stair walls	The various categories are given as a recommended "checklist" and estimators may expand into additional items, or amalgamate where it is not considered the cost will differ considerably or the quantities are not significantly large. Interior foundation walls should be stated separately from perimeter walls if different placing	Cubic yard (m^3)

Item	*Comment*	*Unit of Measurement*
e. misc. walls to: f. pits g. loading docks h. ramps	methods are to be considered (e.g., poured with slab for example).	
7. Retaining walls		Cubic yard (m^3)
8. Dwarf walls	Applies to walls with heights less than 3 ft (1 m) and includes but is not limited to such items as parapets, balconies, balustrades, and similar.	Cubic yard (m^3)
9. Columns and piers	Measured to the underside of suspended slab or soffit of beam or drop slab. Where capitals occur they should be included with this item.	Cubic yard (m^3)
10. Skim slab on grade	This is usually not greater than 3″ thick, and additional depth should be allowed for concrete loss (1″ to 2″). (*Note:* Skim slabs under wall footings, small pits, etc, should be measured and stated separately.)	Cubic yard (m^3)
11. Slabs on grade or fill including but not limited to: a. floors b. ramps c. pits d. loading docks	Apply an adjustment factor to compensate for concrete loss in ground or fill, either a percentage or additional depth 1″ to 3″. Where placed on rock, allow additional 3″ to 6″ or more, according to the estimator's judgment of the conditions.	Cubic yard (m^3)
12. Slab on waterproofing membrane	This slab is placed over the membrane material, which is itself installed on the skim slab. There is no adjustment necessary for concrete seepage or uneven grade surfaces.	Cubic yard (m^3)
13. *Suspended slabs:* a. flat slabs		
b. beam and slab	*Note:* Although the beams will be measured separately, the quantities will be added to and included with the slab quantities for pricing, as the concrete for both slabs and beams is placed at the same time, and cost separation is very difficult.	
c. slabs on structural steel		

Item	*Comment*	*Unit of Measurement*
d. slabs on: metal pans, waffle pans	The normal method is to measure the slab to the gross depth and then deduct the displacement volume of the pans or waffles to arrive at the net quantity.	Cubic yard (m^3)
e. slabs on fiber tubes	Measure as for pans.	
f. slabs with tile fillers	Measure as for pans.	
g. slabs on V-rib forms	Allowance should be made for deflection minimum 30%.	
14. Fireproofing structural steel		Cubic yard (m^3)
a. beams		
b. columns	Measured to underside of slab or beam.	
15. Stairs	Include treads, risers, landings, soffits. Keep interior and exterior stairs separate.	Cubic yard (m^3)
16. Exterior slabs on grade or fill	Allow for concrete loss due to seepage.	Cubic yard (m^3)
17. Exterior steps	Allow for concrete loss due to seepage.	Cubic yard (m^3)
18. Curbs:		
a. exterior		
b. interior	If isolated throughout building in small quantities (e.g., around showers, to lockers, etc.), state in cubic feet for Imperial measurements.	Cubic yard (m^3)
19. Equipment bases a. large b. small	State number if there is a considerable quantity spread throughout the building. This presents a more realistic picture for purposes of pricing.	Cubic yard (m^3)
20. *Floor toppings:* a. separate b. monolithic	Thickness of topping should be stated. Toppings with traprock aggregate should be kept separate.	Cubic yard (m^3)
21. Fill to steel stair pans	State in cubic meters for metric measurements.	Cubic foot
22. Trenches		Cubic yard (m^3)
23. Duct banks		Cubic yard (m^3)
24. Manholes and catchbasins	Include walls and base.	Cubic yard (m^3)
25. Pipe bed and surround		Cubic yard (m^3)

Item	*Comment*	*Unit of Measurement*
26. Light standard bases	Indicate total number of bases.	Cubic foot (m^3)
Miscellaneous items:		
27. Base plates, setting and grouting	State average size. Keep separate if greater than 2 ft. 6 in. × 2 ft, 6 in. Note, this item will include the grout materials. Some estimators may prefer this item for grout to be measured and stated in cubic feet.	Numerical
28. Anchor bolts	State diameter and keep separate as follows: • not exceeding 3 ft. in length (1 meter) • exceeding 3 ft., not exceeding 6 ft. • 6 ft. and over	Numerical
29. Expansion joints:		Linear foot (m)
a. less than 12 in. wide	State thickness, width, and material classification.	
b. 12 in. wide and larger	As above, but excluding the width.	Square foot (m^2)
30. Liquid joint filler	State width and thickness.	Linear foot (m)
31. *Finishing formed concrete surfaces:* a. walls and columns b. soffits and beams c. curbs d. stair risers	This item includes patching of tie holes, cleaning and rubbing of exposed concrete. Keep separate according to specification: sack rub, grinding, etc.	Square foot (m^2)
32. Steel fireproofing • mesh wrapping	State gauge, etc. Add factor for lapping and waste.	Square foot (m^2)
33. Miscellaneous embedded items	This would include such items as plates, lintels, steel angles, lintel anchors, bolts, etc. Estimators should use their own judgment as to the most suitable method for take-off and pricing. Generally, a numerical count will be sufficient for plates, lintel anchors, bolts, etc.; other items may be stated in square or linear feet; and in some cases these items might be stated by weight in pounds or kilograms. It is very important to make a distinction among embedded	Linear foot (m)

Item	Comment	Unit of Measurement
	items that must be attached to the formwork (e.g., inserts for shelf angles). These become a labor on the formwork costs.	
34. *Floor finishing:*		Square foot (m^2)
a. screed finish		
b. wood float		
c. steel trowel • hand		
d. machine trowel		
e. hardeners	State pounds per square foot if powdered hardener. Color hardener to be stated separately. (*Note:* State the color green as an "extra over".)	
f. curing	State whether membrane curing, wet curing, polyethylene curing, etc.	Square foot (m^2)
g. stairs and landings		Square foot (m^2)
h. bases		Linear foot (m)
i. saw cuts	State separately if filled.	Linear foot (m)
j. stair nosings		Linear foot (m)

5.3 Formwork: General Remarks

One of the basic principles that estimators learn regarding the measurement of formwork to concrete structures is that it is not (with some few exceptions) the *formwork* that is measured, but the concrete. To be precise, it is the surface of the concrete that will be *in contact with the* forms, known as the *contact area*. This is another of those items that often confuse the practically minded site personnel, who if requested to take field measurements will often measure the actual area of the forms, which in many cases will project above or beyond the concrete structure that they envelope, resulting in a difference in quantity from that stated in the estimate.

As the drawings only show the "finished product" of a formed concrete structure, the contact area is all that can be accurately measured. Contrary to what was recommended for other materials, the adjustment factors for cutting and waste will *be included in the unit prices and not in the quantities*. The conversion of the contact area to the actual lumber and plywood requirements is usually achieved in the pricing of formwork, as will be demonstrated in Chapter 9.

Experienced estimators appreciate that certain factors that might influence the cost of formwork do not necessarily affect the cost of placing the concrete, and the opposite is also true. For example, it is universally accepted that formwork to a curved or circular surface is more expensive than to a straight surface; but the cost of placing the concrete to a curved wall (as an example) will be the same as for a straight wall; the transfiguration of this particular item has no significant influence on its labor cost.

However, the placing of concrete in a wall less than 6 in. (150 mm) in width might be costlier than in a wall of greater width, but the *formwork cost* would be the same in each case. Also, a slab with a sloping surface (especially if the angle was fairly acute) would provide some premium costs to both the *formwork* and the *concrete placing*, and also may require forming on the upper face.

Estimators must also be correct in the pricing of embedded items, distinguishing those that are fastened to the formwork separately from other items (i.e., inserts attached or items requiring support within the forms, such as pipes and flanges).

The general unit of measurement for formwork is the square foot (square meter), but there will be many items that can be more realistically measured and priced on a linear foot basis, and some that should just be enumerated. As in concrete, where total quantity in square feet represents a considerable number of small items in a particular category, this numerical quantity should be stated with the item.

Formwork to exposed architectural concrete work is very expensive and should be kept separate according to the specification classifications. Structural items requiring formwork to "one side only" should be kept separate in the different classifications according to the nature of the unformed surface (i.e., rock, existing structure, timber lagging, or existing walls).

Formwork in locations where stripping is difficult should be identified and so noted. Items where the formwork is to be "left in place" will also be kept separate.

Formwork to underpinning should be measured and stated separately.

Keep separate formwork to items "curved on plan," sloping surfaces, and other irregular shapes. *Note:* Certain shapes may require a different approach when measuring, often requiring a base item for an imaginary straight and regular profile, and an item is taken off separately for the achievement of the "shape" by a system of *boxing out*. There are different options open to estimators for measuring these specialty formwork items, and they will adopt the method that provides the simplest and fastest method for take-off, but that can still be priced realistically. There are also different methods of actually constructing them, and estimators should discuss these items with carpenter foremen and then measure these items in accordance with the proposed method of construction.

It will be noted from the foregoing that the items discussed could be those "exceptions to the rule" of strict contact area.

The CIQS *Method of Measurement for Concrete* (which includes formwork) states:

> a) Formwork shall be measured in square feet (meters) . . . and shall include for erection, oiling, transporting, falsework, stripping, cleaning and all necessary form hardware.

Contractors' estimators might prefer to treat some of those items separately. This would apply most particularly to:

1. *Oil:* As this could not be considered as a "reuse" item, there might be some confusion when embodying it in the unit price (which usually reflects the reuse factor). Preferably, it should be stated in gallons (calculated on the manufacturer's recommendations regarding area coverage per gallon), or it can be given in square feet of *covered* area (which would be identical to the contact area). However, the cost of applying the oil will be included in the unit cost for labor.
2. *Form hardware:* This is sometimes referred to as "formwork accessories" and often means different things to different estimators. It generally represents such items as rough hardware (i.e., nails, screws, etc.), tie wire, and form ties. Many estimators are satisfied to use some tested and tried formula based on the total cubic volume of formed concrete or the net area of the formwork. Others may consider this satisfactory for the nails and wire, but not a realistic approach to assessing the cost of the ties. Form ties can be calculated very accurately, but it becomes a time-consuming task when faced with innumerable items of different heights and widths, and time is something estimators are always short of! However, as these materials are not subject to reuse (except possibly some portions of interior disconnecting ties), they should be considered separately and excluded from the unit price for formwork materials.
3. *Falsework:* This can be included with the item and in the price, but once again the reuse consideration might persuade an estimator to keep this separate.

5.4 Schedule of Items and Measurements—Formwork

Item	*Comment*	*Unit of Measurement*
1. Wall footings 2. Spread footings 3. Pile or caisson caps 4. Grade beams	State separately where concrete is placed on rock or shale where cutting will be required, unless a leveling bed has been applied.	Square foot (m^2)

Item	Comment	Unit of Measurement
5. *Walls:* a. foundation walls *Superstructure:* b. shear walls c. elevator core walls d. stair walls	Generally, *all walls* should be summarized in the following categories: • not exceeding 12 ft. high • 12 ft. to 18 ft. high • exceeding 18 ft. high	Square foot (m^2)
6. Misc. walls to: a. pits b. loading docks c. ramps		Square foot (m^2)
7. Retaining walls	Battered walls to be stated separately.	Square foot (m^2)
8. Dwarf walls	Applies to any walls less than 3 ft. high.	Square foot (m^2)
9. Pilasters	Item to include sides and face (adjustment will be required to the wall form area for the area equivalent to the pilaster face).	Square foot (m^2)

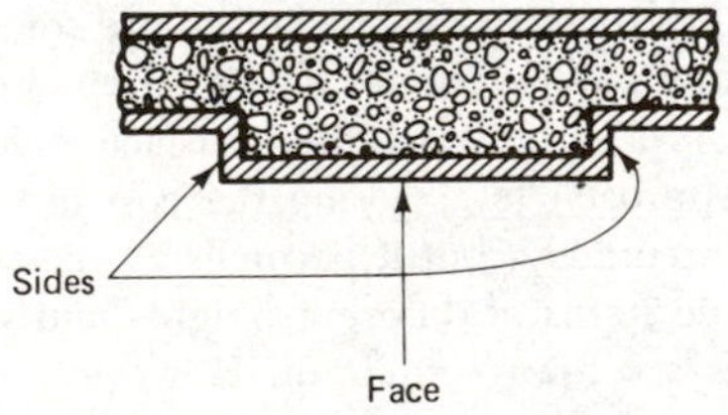

Item	Comment	Unit of Measurement
10. Columns (other than circular)	Measured to the underside of slabs, beams, drops, and capitals. Keep separate where of unusual shape (elongated, triangular, etc.)	Square foot (m^2)
11. Columns (circular)	State diameter and material (metal or fiber material).	Linear foot (m)
12. Suspended beams	To include sides and soffits (adjust slab soffit area). State separately for: • spandrel beams (include slab edge with this item) • isolated beams • beams greater than 3 ft. depth	Square foot (m^2)

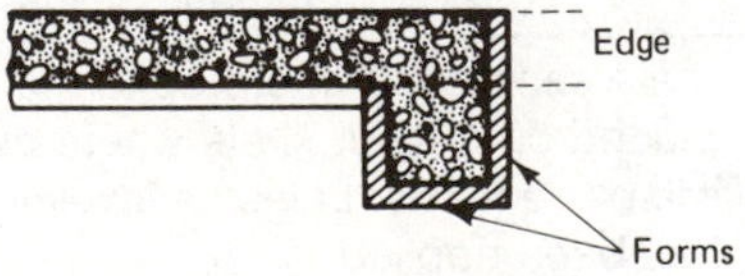

Item	*Comment*	*Unit of Measurement*
13. Up-turned (kick) beams	Sides only.	Square foot (m^2)
14. *Suspended slabs:* a. flat slab b. beam and slab c. slab on structural steel	No deductions to be taken for openings less than 20 square feet. Slabs located at a height greater than 12 ft. to be kept separate and the average height stated; also keep separate slabs located at a height of 30 feet or more above the floor below.	Square foot (m^2)
d. slab on metal pan joists e. slab on plastic dome forms f. others g. canopies h. balconies	Slabs less than 3 ft. high will be kept separate. Miscellaneous small and isolated suspended slabs to be so noted.	Square foot (m^2)
15. *Fireproofing structural steel:*		Square foot (m^2)
a. beams b. columns	Refer to comments regarding concrete beams and columns (page 86).	
16. Drop slabs	To include soffit and edge (adjust slab area).	Square foot (m^2)

17. Column capitals	State average dimensions. Keep separate if in metal and part of assembly with metal column forms (circular).	Square foot (m^2) (or numerical)
18. Suspended stairs and landings	Item to include landing soffits and edges, risers, stringers, sloping soffits, etc.	Square foot (m^2)
19. Steps and stairs on grade	Item to include risers, stringers, edges.	Square foot (m^2)
20. Curbs a. interior		
b. exterior	Combined "curb and gutter" to roadwork to be kept separate.	Square foot (m^2)
21. Equipment bases	State the number where total quantity represents numerous small items.	Square foot (m^2)
22. a. lamp standard bases		Square foot (m^2)
b. pedestals		Square foot (m^2)

Item	Comment	Unit of Measurement
23. Parapet walls		Square foot (m^2)
24. Balustrades		Square foot (m^2)
25. *Edges to slabs:* a. Not exceeding 12 in. high.	"Suspended" edges to be given separately.	Linear foot (m)

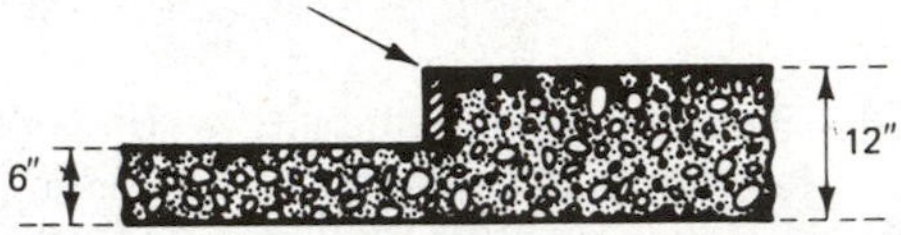

Item	Comment	Unit of Measurement
b. 12 in. high or more.	*Note:* some edges are included with specific items (spandrel beams, "outside" form to a wall, etc.).	Square foot (m^2)

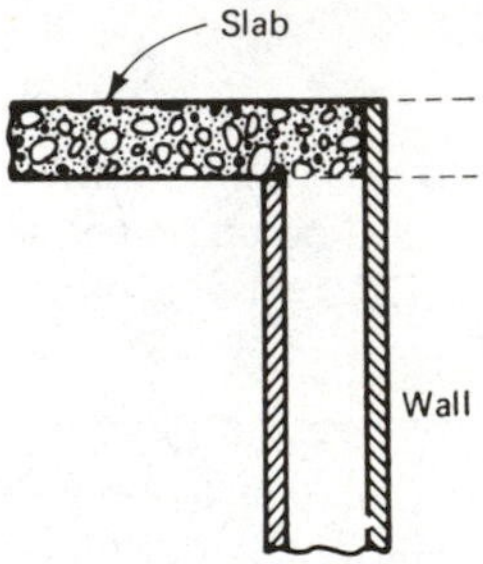

Item	Comment	Unit of Measurement
26. *Construction joints:* a. bulkheads to slabs b. bulkheads to walls		Square foot (m^2)
c. key	State if to be "split" for waterstop.	Linear foot (m)
27. Boxings	Measured to contact area, keep separate to special shapes. (Provide sketch if necessary.)	Square foot (m^2)
28. Chases	State average dimensions.	Linear foot (m)
29. Chamfers, drips, etc.	State average dimensions.	Linear foot (m)
30. Double forms (masonry shelves, etc.)	Measured to contact area.	Square foot (m^2)

Item	*Comment*	*Unit of Measurement*
31. Hanches, nibs, small projections, etc.	State as "extra over" if already *included in the contact area measurements* for a specific item, e.g., a wall.	Square foot (m^2) or linear foot (m) (Estimator's choice)
32. *Metal pan joist forms:* Straight Tapered Closed end	State width and depth (deduct the cubic "void" volume from the concrete).	Linear foot (m)
33. Waffle (dome) pans	State dimensions (the cubic volume of these units can be deducted from the total *gross volume* of the concrete).	Numerical
34. Filler tile Soffit tile End piece	Keep separate and state different tile sizes. (*Note:* this tile–joist construction is not as common as it was several years ago.) The net cubic volume of the tile may be computed as a concrete displacement factor.	Numerical Numerical Numerical
35. Anchor slots	State if filled.	Linear foot (m)
36. Miscellaneous items to be fastened to formwork	Refer to comments regarding "embedded items" in concrete. A numerical count will apply to most of these items, but the estimators must include in this division only those parts of a component *actually attached to the formwork. Example:* With a shelf or spandrel angle bolted into special inserts, only the *inserts* for these items should be taken as an attachment to formwork. The angle itself would be taken with another trade (e.g., Miscellaneous Metals or Structural Steel). Some estimators prefer to "weight" each item and then aggregate all the weights into one single item for pricing, stated in pounds (or kilograms).	

5.5 Take-Off Example

Figure 5.1 provides an example of quantity take-off for concrete and formwork. Building section (Figure 3.8), foundation plan (Figure 3.9), and structural plans for 1st, 2nd, and 3rd floors (Figure 3.10) provide most of the information applicable to this trade section. The following brief specification notes supplement the data shown on the drawings:

3000 p.s.i. concrete to footings, pits and bases.
Lightweight concrete fill to metal roof deck.
4000 p.s.i. concrete to all other items.
Air entrainment to all concrete mixes excluding lightweight concrete.
Rub exposed concrete surfaces (Refer CSA A.23-1).
1/2 inches asphalt impregnated expansion joint junction of slabs and walls.
Concrete slab finishes: plain trowel to floor slabs.
60 lbs nonmetallic hardener to basement floor.
wood float roof surfaces.
membrane curing.
Waterstops at construction joints below grade.
Shelf angle inserts at spandrels.
Anchor slots (provided by Section 04200 Masonry).
Formwork to comply with Publication ACI 347-78.

COMMENTARY: CONCRETE TAKE-OFF

1. The side notes (under "description of work") show the buildup of the figures recorded in the dimension columns. The wall lengths noted on the drawings are extended for the footing projections; where duplication has occurred, deductions are made for doubling up at the corners (see sketch).

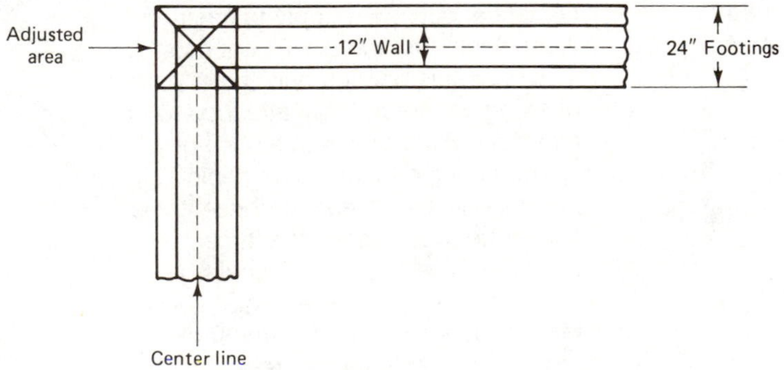

Another method used by many estimators is the center line method for measuring walls and footings which, once the center line is calculated, eliminates the need for further adjustments to the dimensions (as noted on sketch).

2. The column footings type C have been included with the perimeter wall footings. These could have been included with the take-off item for column footings with formwork measured to the four sides, particularly if there was a significant difference between the depth of these footings in comparison with the wall footings. In this instance the difference is small.

3. The dimensions for the stepped footings are a deviation from the normal sequence of length, breadth and height. For simplification reasons the height (4 ft. 6 in.) is taken first, multiplied by the footing width (1 ft. 8 in.), the third dimension

QUANTITIES

SHEET No. 1 OF 9

PROJECT: RESEARCH CENTRE
ESTIMATE No. 27/82
LOCATION:
BY: J.D.
CHK'D:
SUBDIVISION: 03300 – CONCRETE
DATE:

DESCRIPTION OF WORK	NO. PIECES	DIMENSIONS A	DIMENSIONS B	DIMENSIONS C	CONC. A×B×C	FORMS 2×(A+B)×C	
ISOLATED COL. FTGS. – 3000 LBS (25 MPa)							
TYPE A	5/	4.0	4.0	1.2	94	94	
B	2/	3.4	3.4	.8	15	18	
					109	112 SF	
					= 4 CY		
CONTINUOUS WALL FTGS – 3000 LBS (25 MPa)					CONC. A×B×C	FORMS 2×A×C	KEY A
PERIMETER							
100.0							
50.0							
150.0 x 2 = 300.0							
2x2x 50.0 = 200.0							
500.0							
FTG PROJECTION							
2x4x.4 = 2.8							
502.8							
DDT CORNERS							
4x1.8 = (6.8)							
496.0		496.0	1.8	.8	555	665	496
ADD TYPE C FTGS.	11/	3.0	1.4	.8	29	44	33
3.0 − 1.8 = 1.4; .10 − .8 = .2	4/	1.4	1.4	.8	5	7	5
	15/	3.0	3.0	.2	23	15	
INT. WALL FTGS							
2x25.0 = 50.0							
2x.4 = .8							
50.8							
DDT 2x1.8 (3.4)							
47.4		47.4	1.8	.8	53	63	47
STEPPED FTGS	2/	4.6	1.8	1.4	20	24	
					685	818 SF	581 LF
					= 25 CY		
RISER FORMS (STEPPED FTGS)					A×B		
	2/	4.6	1.8		15 SF		

Figure 5.1.

QUANTITIES

SHEET No. 2 OF 9

PROJECT ______________________ ESTIMATE No. 27/82

LOCATION ______________________ BY J.D. CHK'D ________

SUBDIVISION 03300 - CONCRETE DATE ________

DESCRIPTION OF WORK	NO. PIECES	DIMENSIONS A	B	C	CONC. A×B×C	FORMS 2×A×C	PILASTER FORMS SIDES 2×A×C	FACE B×C	
FOUNDATION WALLS									
– 4000 LBS (30 MPa)									
WALL HEIGHTS:									
TOP OF WALL - 300.00									
" " FTG - 294.00									
6.0									
B/MENT WALL - 300.00									
LESS SLAB .67									
299.33									
TOP OF FOOTING 289.50									
9.83									
LINE "C"	4/	25.0							
"E"		150.0							
" 1+7	2/	50.0	1.0	6.0	2100	4200			
DDT CORNERS	2/	(1.0)	(1.0)	(6.0)	(12)	(24)			
BASEMENT	3/	50.0	1.0	9.10	1476	2952			
CORNERS	2/	(1.0)	(1.0)	(9.10)	(20)	(39)			
STEPPED FTGS	2/	4.0	1.0	1.6	12	24			
	2/	4.0	1.0	3.0	24	48			
	2/	4.0	1.0	4.6	36	72			
INT B/MENT WALL	2/	25.0	1.0	9.10	492	984			
	2/	(1.0)	(1.0)	(9.10)	(20)	(39)			
PILASTERS	10/	.6	1.0	6.0	30		60	60	
	2/	.6	1.0	9.10	10		20	20	
	3/	.6	.6	6.0	5		18	9	
		.6	.6	9.10	3		10	5	
					4136 CF	8178	108	94	(DDT FROM WALL FORMS)
						(94)	→	108	
						8084 SF		202 SF	
					= 153 CY				
PIERS BELOW GRADE					CONC A×B×C	FORMS 2×(A+B)×C			
4000 LBS (30 MPa)									
	5/	1.0	1.0	5.6	27	110 SF			
					= 1 CY				

Figure 5.1. *(continued)*.

QUANTITIES

SHEET No. 3 OF 9.

PROJECT
LOCATION
SUBDIVISION D3300 – CONCRETE

ESTIMATE No. 27/82
BY J.D. CHK'D
DATE

DESCRIPTION OF WORK	NO. PIECES	A	B	C	CONC. A×B×C	FORMS 2×(A+B)×C
COLUMNS — 4000 LBS (30 MPa)						
10.0						
SLAB (.8) EXT	3/16/	1.0	1.0	7.4	352	1407
9.4 INT	3/5/	1.0	1.0	8.0	120	480
BM 2.0 ADJ S.O.G.	5/	1.0	1.0	.6	3	10
7.4 B/MENT		1.0	1.0	9.10	10	39
					485 CF	1936 SF
					= 18 CY	

DESCRIPTION OF WORK	NO. PIECES	A	B	C	CONC. A×B×C	FORMS SOFFITS A×B	FORMS SIDES 2×A×C	SLAB EDGES A×8"
SPANDREL BEAMS — 4000 LBS (30 MPa)								
4" FACING	3/2/	150.0						
6" CENTRE LINE OF BEAM	3/2/	50.0	1.0	2.0	2400	1200	4800	804
10" × 2 = 1.8	3/4/	(1.8)	(1.0)	(2.0)	(40)	(20)	(80)	(13)
					2360 CF	1180	4720	791
								4720
								1180
					= 87 CY			6691 SF

DESCRIPTION OF WORK	NO. PIECES	A	B	C	CONC. A×B×C	FORMS SOFFITS A×B	FORMS SIDES 2×A×C
INTERIOR BEAMS — 4000 LBS (30 MPa)							
150.0							
SP. BM. + FACING 2×1.4 (2.8)							
147.4	3/	147.4	1.4	1.4	786	588	1179
BM = 2.0, 50.0	3/5/	46.0	1.4	.8	615	920	920
LESS SLAB (.8), (1.4)					1401	1508	2099
1.4, 48.8							1508
2×1.4 (2.8)					= 52 CY		3607 SF
46.0							

Figure 5.1. *(continued)*.

QUANTITIES

SHEET No. 4 OF 9

PROJECT ____________________

LOCATION ____________________

SUBDIVISION 03300 – CONCRETE

ESTIMATE No. 27/82

BY J.D. CHK'D ________

DATE ________

DESCRIPTION OF WORK	NO. PIECES	DIMENSIONS A	B	C	CONC. A×B×C	FORMS A×B	SET SCREEDS A×B	
SUSP. SLAB (FLAT PLATE) – 4,000 p.s.i (30 MPa)								
50.0 / 1.0 / 51.0; 50.0 / (.8) / 49.4		50.8	49.4	.8	1675	2500 SF	2500 SF	"A"
FACING (.4) / 50.8					= 62 CY			
					CONC A×B×C	SET SCREEDS A×B		SOFFIT FORMS A×B
SUSP SLAB (BM + SLAB) – 4000 p.s.i (30 MPa)								
100.0 / 50.0 / 150.0 / 2×4 (.8) / 149.4	3/	149.4	49.4	.8	14807	22099	"B" DDT SP BM " INT "	22099 (1180) (1508) 19411 SF
	ADD: SP BEAM (P.3)	INT BEAM "			= 548 87 52 687 CY			
					CONC. A×B×C	SET SCREEDS A×B		
L/WT CONC FILL TO METAL DECK								
CONC 2" RIB 1½" / 3½" – 4"		49.4	50.0	.4	822	2467 SF	"C"	
					= 30 CY			

Figure 5.1. *(continued)*.

QUANTITIES

SHEET No. 5 OF 9.

PROJECT ____________ ESTIMATE No. 27/82

LOCATION ____________ BY J.D. CHK'D ________

SUBDIVISION 03300 – CONCRETE DATE ________

DESCRIPTION OF WORK	NO. PIECES	DIMENSIONS A	DIMENSIONS B	DIMENSIONS C	CONC A×B×C	SET SCREEDS A×B
SLAB ON GRADE (30 MPa)						
150·0						
−2×1·0 2·0						
148·0		148·0	48·0			7104
		48·0	49·0	·6	4728	2352
ADD FOR SEEPAGE – 1"		148·0	48·0			
		48·0	49·0	·1	788	
					5516	9456 SF "D"
					= 204 CY	
EXP JOINTS TO SLAB OR GRADE (½" × 6" AIFB)					A	
	2/	148·0			296	
	2/2/	48·0			192	
	2/	49·0			98	
AROUND COLS	6/	4·0			24	
					610	
SLAB EDGE FORMS (NE 12")					A	
B/MENT	2/	48·0			96	
	2/	49·0			98	
STAIR OPENINGS	2/2/	17·0			68	
	2/	11·10			24	
B/MENT STAIR	2/	4·0			8	
	2/	9·0			18	
					312 LF	

Figure 5.1. *(continued)*.

QUANTITIES

SHEET No. 6 OF 9.

PROJECT ____________ ESTIMATE No. 27/82
LOCATION ____________ BY J.D. CHK'D ____________
SUBDIVISION 03300 – CONCRETE DATE ____________

DESCRIPTION OF WORK	NO. PIECES	DIMENSIONS A	B	C	CONC A×B×C	FORMS A×B	FINISH A×1'5"
CONC STAIRS – (30 MPa)							
SOFFITT		21·3	4·0	·4	28	85	30
STEPS	16/½/	4·0	·10	·7	16		
FORMS – RISERS	16/	4·0	·7			37	91
– STRINGER		21·3	·11			20	122 SF
– BOXING		21·3	·11			20	
– BEARING		4·0	·8			3	
					44	165 SF	
					= 2 CY		
					BULKHEAD FORM A	KEY A	WATERSTOP A
CONSTRUCTION JOINTS (VERTICAL)							
ASSUME 40'0" POURS							
TOTAL WALL LENGTH – 298·0 ÷ 40 = 7·5	8/	6·0			48	DO	DO
B/MENT	4/	9·7			38	DO	DO
					86 LF	86 LF	86 LF
					BULKHEAD A	KEY A	
DITTO – (HORIZONTAL)							
S.O.G.	5/	47·6			238	238	
		150·0			150	150	
					388 LF	388 LF	

Figure 5.1. *(continued).*

QUANTITIES

SHEET No. 7 OF 9

PROJECT ______

LOCATION ______

SUBDIVISION 03300 – CONCRETE

ESTIMATE No. 27/82

BY J.D. CHK'D ______

DATE ______

DESCRIPTION OF WORK	NO. PIECES	DIMENSIONS A	DIMENSIONS B	DIMENSIONS C	WALLS/COLS A x B	SOFFITTS A x B			
CLEAN PATCH + RUB EXPOSED CONC. SURFACES									
INT WALLS – B/MENT	2/	48.0	9.4	–	896				
	2/	49.0	9.4	–	914				
COL		4.0	9.4	–	37				
SOFFITT		48.0	49.0			– 2352			
EXTERIOR – ABOVE GRADE		150.0							
	2/2/	50.0							
		150.0	2.0	–	1000				
					2847 SF	2352 SF			
CONCRETE FLOOR FINISHES									
					SUMMARY OF SCREED AREAS				
		AREA "A"	P4		–	2500			
		"	"B"		–	22099			
		"	"C"		–	2467			
		"	"D"	P5	–	9456			
						36522 SF			
					FINISHES				
					MACHINE TROWEL (PLAIN)	DITTO (HARDENER)	ROOF FINISH	CURING	
TOTAL AREA SCREEDS (ABOVE) –					36522			36522 SF	
ROOF AREAS		150.0	50.0				7500		
		50.0	50.0				2500		
							10000 SF		
HARDENER FLOORS		48.0	49.0			2352 SF			
					36522				
DEDUCT – ROOF FINISH					(10000)				
– HARDENED AREAS					(2352)				
					24170 SF				

Figure 5.1. *(continued)*.

QUANTITIES

SHEET No. 8 OF 9.

PROJECT ______________________

LOCATION ______________________

SUBDIVISION 03300 — CONCRETE

ESTIMATE No. 27/82

BY JD CHK'D ______

DATE ______

DESCRIPTION OF WORK	NO. PIECES	DIMENSIONS A	B	C	CONC A×B×C	FORMS 2×(A+B)×C	FINISH A×B
EQUIPMENT PADS — (25 MPa)							
	3/6/	2·6	1·9	·8	52 = 2cy	103 SF	79 SF
MASONRY SHELF — 4"×6"					A		
	3/	50·0			150 LF		
INSERTS FOR SHELF ANGLES AT SPANDRELL BEAMS (2'·0" c/c)							
100/2 =		50+2			52		
2×150/2 =		152+2			154		
					206 PCS		
ANCHORS FOR PRECAST CONC. FACING PANELS (4'·0" c/c)							
N. ELEV	3×150/4 =			113+3	116		
E+W ELEV	2×3×50/4 =			75+6	81		
					197 PCS		
							SAY 200 PCS

Figure 5.1. *(continued).*

QUANTITIES

SHEET No. 9 OF 9

PROJECT
ESTIMATE No. 27/82
LOCATION
BY JD
CHK'D
SUBDIVISION 03300 - CONCRETE
DATE

DESCRIPTION OF WORK	NO. PIECES	DIMENSIONS A	B	C	CONC A×B×C	FINISH A×B			
CONC. FILL TO METAL STAIR PANS — (25 MPa)	2/16/	4·6	·10	·2	21	121			
LANDINGS	2/	12·0	4·6	·2	18	108			
					39 CF	229 SF			
					CONC A×B×C	WALL FORMS 2×A×C	SLAB EDGE (A+B)×2	KEY A	HAND TROWEL A×B
SUMP PITS — (25 MPa)									
BASE		9·10	8·3	·6	41		36 LF		81 SF
WALLS	2/	9·10							
	2/	6·11	·8	4·6	101	306 SF		34 LF	
					142				
					= 5 CY				

Figure 5.1. *(continued)*.

being an *assumed* thickness equal to two times the normal footing thickness (8 in. × 2 = 1 ft. 4 in.). The riser forms are measured separately.

4. The side notes on Sheet 2 (Foundation Walls) show the computations to establish the wall heights.

5. In accordance with the method prescribed in the Schedule of Items and Measurements, the pilaster forms are measured for sides and face, with the face area deducted from the wall face area.

6. The columns are measured from top of slab to the underside of beams.

7. The spandrel beams are measured using the full dimensions for the concrete walls as shown on the drawing, with adjustments made for the thickness of the face brick.

8. Also, no adjustments are made for doubling-up at the corners or for the intersection of interior beams.

9. The suspended slab soffit areas are adjusted for the beam soffits where applicable.

10. The slab on grade has been measured to the net slab thickness of 6 in., and an additional measurement for an assumed 1 in. of loss through seepage. This adjustment could also have been achieved with a percentage factor based on experience and judgment.

11. The construction joints for the foundation walls allow for concrete pours to 40 ft. of wall length. This measurement of this item would usually result from discussion with field superintendents or construction managers, or from the estimator's own judgment of what was reasonable. Also the specifications would probably state some restrictions on length of pours.

12. The item for rub exposed concrete is measured to the interior walls, columns and slab soffits in the basement. The exterior rubbing is measured for that portion which extends from the finished grade (assumed at 300.00) to the top of the wall.

13. The concrete floor finishes are developed from taking the total "screed" area for the predominant finish (i.e., machine trowel) and deducting from this area the separately measured areas for the other types of concrete floor finishes.

14. The equipment pads are not shown on the drawings and the number and dimensions are assumed to provide an example of measuring these items.

15. The inserts set into the concrete (into the *formwork* to be strictly correct) at the spandrel beams to receive the shelf angles are usually supplied and installed by the general contractor. The shelf angle will be supplied by either the structural steel or miscellaneous metals subcontractor (with the contractor's installation measured with the miscellaneous work for those trade divisions).

16. The anchors for the precast concrete wall panels would be supplied by the precast concrete subcontractor to the general contractor for installation in the formwork.

17. The steel stairs extend from the ground floor to the second and third floors. They would be supplied and installed under Section 05500 Metal Fabrications, but the concrete fill to the treads (pans) will be the responsibility of the general contractor. This is one item where the unit of a cubic foot is preferable; a large number of treads are included in one cubic yard (or cubic meter) and the cost of placing the concrete is often as much per cubic foot as per cubic yard. (They could, of course, be measured and priced as a cost per tread.)

18. The sump pits (like the equipment pads) are not indicated on the drawings and are included as an example of measurement and costing.

6

Take-off: Masonry

6.1 General

The general trade practice in Canada and the United States is to express the quantities of the major masonry materials (i.e., brick, block, tile, etc.) in terms of pieces (or thousand piece units). A two-stage procedure is therefore necessary to establish these quantities:

1. Normal measuring to establish wall areas (square feet or m^2).
2. The computation of the masonry units by multiplying the wall areas by a factor applicable to the size of the unit plus thickness of the mortar joint.

This means that the accuracy of the quantities depends not only on the measurements taken off the drawings but also the computation of the factor. An accurate quantity survey of a major masonry project can be spoiled by the careless application of an inaccurate factor.

To take off and price estimates for masonry work on the measured net wall areas for each specific material would appear at first to be the simpler method, but the problems just stated (factors, bonding, waste, etc.) do not then quietly get up and walk away! They now must be reflected in the unit rates, and the possibility of errors is not lessened; in fact, they might be harder to detect! Also, as previously stated in Chapter 3, for purposes of purchasing and cost control the estimate should reflect as closely as possible the actual methods by which these materials are sold and installed.

Superintendents do not normally issue purchase orders or requisitions for so many square feet (square meters) of bricks or blocks; these materials are purchased on the basis of the number of units required. It is advisable, therefore, to prepare and price the estimate accordingly. To provide merely the wall or partition areas of the different materials merely transfers the operation of calculating the required number of units, plus the wastage and bonding factors, to superintendents, purchasing agents, or some other people, when, after all, it is the estimator who is considered to have the best training and expertise to do this work effectively.

Before considering the problems in detail relating to bonding and wastage factors, it is necessary first to review some of the following basic principles to be observed when taking off quantities for masonry work:

1. The quantities will be taken off net in place.
2. Circular work should be stated separately.
3. No deductions should be made for openings less than (10 ft^2) 1 m^2 in area.
4. State the *nominal* dimensions of the materials, and keep separate according to specified classification and type.
5. Keep separate the work in the following categories:
   - Exterior cladding ("skin") to the building
   - Interior partitions and furring
   - Exterior masonry work (retaining walls, landscaping, etc.)
   - Fireproofing to structural steelwork
   - Load-bearing walls
   - Foundation walls below grade
   - Renovation work to existing masonry (including filling in of openings in areas where doors or windows have been removed)
   - Miscellaneous categories

6.2 Schedule of Items and Measurements: Masonry

Item	*Comment*	*Unit of Measurement*
Face brick	Describe material and classification, type of bond, and pointing requirements. State as extra over the numerical quantities of brick units pertaining to: • "snapped headers" • brickwork in decorative patterns • brick on edge • arches • special shape units (bullnose, splayed etc.) • stack bond • other special requirements Glazed brick to be stated as separate category.	Thousand pieces

Item	*Comment*	*Unit of Measurement*
Common brick	Describe material classification, function ("backup", beam filling, etc.)	Thousand pieces
Firebrick	Describe according to manufacturers' literature.	Thousand pieces
Concrete block masonry	Separate categories for: ● low pressure units ● autoclaved units ● lightweight units State as extra over for: ● solid and/or semisolid block ● headers ● specials: bullnose, sash units, piers, bond beams, etc. ● exposed faces (i.e., not covered by plaster, drywall, or other materials). There is an additional labor cost where block is to remain exposed. *Note:* It is the exposed *faces* that have to be measured (enumerated); a block unit in a wall that is exposed on both sides will have *two* exposed faces. The alternative method (preferred by some estimators) is to measure and record the units in categories for: ● block unexposed ● block exposed one side ● block exposed two sides This can, however, slow down the take-off process, and as will be demonstrated in the take-off examples, the method prescribed is faster and no less effective for establishing a reasonably accurate cost factor. Cutting blocks to fit around structural steel columns shall be enumerated and described as an extra over.	Piece
Structural clay tile	State separately for: ● smooth surfaces ● scored surfaces ● rugged surfaces ● other surfaces ● furring tile ● partition	Piece
Structural glazed tile	Keep separate for: ● header units ● stretcher units ● universal units *Note:* Special fittings may be measured	Piece

Item	*Comment*	*Unit of Measurement*
	according to group numbers and described as extra over.	
Glazed concrete block	Refer to the comments regarding concrete block and glazed structural tile.	Piece
Gypsum masonry	State thickness.	Piece
Mortar	To be stated separately according to specified mix proportions. Additives to be stated as extra over. Colored mortar to be described as extra over. Fire temperature and fireclay bonding mortar to be kept separate.	Cubic yard (m^3)
Dampcourses, flashings	Describe specified material classification and (where applicable) weight per square foot (m^2)	Square foot (m^2) or Linear foot (m)
Cleaning down masonry	Keep separate according to the materials to be cleaned (brick, block, tile, etc.). Describe cleansing solution specified. *Note:* These same measurements can be used for enumerating the "exposed faces" of block or tile, by applying a block or tile factor to the measured area.	Square foot (m^2)
Miscellaneous embedded items	Keep separate according to function and/or size. Include (but not limited to): • anchor bolts • bearing plates • sleeves • brackets • other similar items	Piece
Rake out and point mortar joints	This item will be measured when and where the specifications require joints to be raked out and pointed with mortar materials. Mortar specifications to be stated, and the area measured will be the net area of exposed masonry work requiring the raking and pointing.	Square foot (m^2)
Anchor slots	This item may appear in two parts of the estimate: masonry and formwork. It applies to masonry work in direct contact with cast-in-place concrete. It is generally simpler to measure this item with the masonry (the structural drawings rarely show masonry or other materials applied against the concrete) and then transfer the item to the formwork	Linear foot (m)

Item	*Comment*	*Unit of Measurement*
	summary. It can appear in both divisions: the material *supply* in the masonry section, and the *installation* with the formwork section.	
Anchorage material	Classify and describe as per the specification. Various categories will include (but not be limited to): • dovetail anchors (state if dowelled) • ties (state if corrugated) • cavity wall ties • others *Note:* Bronze, brass, or stainless steel anchorage materials to be stated separately.	Piece (or 1000 pieces)
Lintels:		
Steel	State if built up in multiple sections.	Linear foot (m)
Precast concrete	Give width and height.	Linear foot (m)
Reinforced masonry	This applies particularly to concrete block or structural clay tile masonry, and the item should be measured as an extra over, which will provide the additional cost of a bond or lintel beam, reinforcing rods, and concrete fill. Keep separate for different thicknesses.	Linear foot (m)
Control joints	This item usually applies to a rubber control joint, and should be separated into flange widths.	Linear foot (m)
Masonry Reinforcement:		
Reinforcing steel bars	*Note:* This item should exclude reinforcing to masonry lintels, which is included with the item.	Pound (kilogram)
Prefabricated rods or mesh	State overall wall thickness, give all classification details whether standard, heavy duty, extra heavy duty, etc., and other information pertinent to identification in manufacturer's literature and price lists.	Linear foot (m)
Prefabricated corners and tees	Give pertinent information as required for rods or mesh.	Piece
Expansion joints	State thickness and material classification.	Square foot (m^2)
Weep hole plugs		Per hundred pieces
Cavity wall insulation	State thickness and type of material.	Square foot (m^2)

6.3 Masonry Equipment

Apart from the items already covered in the schedule of measurements, there are also items of equipment to be considered. These would include the following:

Mortar mixers: rental cost per month
Scaffold frames: rental per month, plus the cost of erection and dismantling
Masonry saws and blades: rental per month
Masonry hoist: this may be included in the site overhead costs (refer to Chapter 10)
Forklift: rental per month
Hanging scaffolds: this should be divided into:

- rental per month of machine
- erection and dismantling of outriggers and scaffolds
- overhead and winter protection

Winter heat and protection: this would probably be measured and priced in the estimate for site overheads, and would include for:

- space heaters, including fuel and handling
- tarpaulins (including any necessary framework or supports)

Note: The item for erection and dismantling of scaffold frame units may be expressed as square feet (square meters) of wall area, and an appropriate unit rate applied. Some estimators measure the total length of each "lift" of scaffolding; that is, a partition 65 feet long requiring 2 lifts of 5 ft. scaffolding would be expressed as "130 feet of scaffold in lifts of (approximately) 5 ft."

6.4 Conversion Factors: General

The factor by which the square foot (meter) area of a wall constructed of a particular masonry material is multiplied to arrive at the required number of masonry units is not difficult to calculate. To establish a factor, certain basic information about the material must be known.

This basic information includes the obvious ones of length, width, and height; but because the masonry units in a structure are separated by another material, mortar, then the thickness of the mortar joint has also to be taken into account. As the general trade practice is to base the calculations on the number of units per square foot area of wall or partition, then only the *face* dimensions of *length* and *height* are necessary. The thickness of the unit is not necessary for this calculation, unless (as will be explained later) the unit is placed in such a manner that the *thickness* now replaces the *length* for the face area (i.e., *headers*).

The thickness of a unit would, of course, be essential if the factor was to be based on the *cubic volume* of the masonry work, a practice followed in certain regions or by some estimators. However, this book will be restricted to the factors per wall *area*, rather than *volume*.

Taking the example of brick in a wall 4 in. (one brick) thick, with mortar joints specified as ½ in., the factor is derived by dividing 1 ft.² by the *length* of the brick, plus ½ in., multiplied by the *height* of the unit, again plus ½ in.

Example: Face brick, size 8⅜ in. × 2⅜ in. high in a wall, laid in stretcher (running) bond, with ½ in. mortar joints.

$$\frac{1\ \text{ft.}^2}{(8\ 3/8 + {}^1/_2) \times (2\ 3/8 + {}^1/_2)} = 5.63\ \text{bricks/ft.}^2$$

To express a similar example in metric dimensions: face brick size 190 mm × 57 mm high, stretcher bond, with 10 mm mortar joints:

$$\frac{1\ \text{m}^2}{(0.190 + 0.10) \times (0.57 + 0.10)} = 74.6\ \text{bricks/m}^2$$

A *basic factor* can be calculated for each kind of masonry material, utilizing only the dimensions for length, height, and mortar joint thickness. Given an accurate measurement of the wall or partition area (within the parameters outlined in the schedule of measurements) the resultant quantities derived from the multiplication of this area by the appropriate factor will be an equally accurate enumeration of the masonry units actually laid in a specific location. However, once the condition of a single wythe of brick transforms into a condition where greater wall thickness and full *headers* for bonding are necessary, the calculations become a little more complex.

The bonding of solid brick walls affects both the *face brick* factors and the *backup* (common) brick factors. The bonds most commonly used are:

Flemish bond: *alternate* headers and stretchers in *each course*.
English bond: *alternate courses* of headers and stretchers.
Headers every fifth course: (self-explanatory): five courses of stretchers to one course of *full headers*.
Headers every sixth course: same principle as for fifth-course headers.
Full English bond every sixth course: *alternate courses* of stretchers and "snapped" headers, except for each sixth course, where full headers will be used.
Full Flemish bond every sixth course: similar to the variations on English bond for sixth-course headers.

The calculation of quantities of brick per square foot (m²) is made by applying a *correction factor* to the basic factor for a brick laid in stretcher bond.

The following are the correction factors to be applied for the types of bond already mentioned:

Flemish bond: 33⅓ percent
English bond: 50 percent
Full headers, fifth course: 20 percent
Full headers, sixth course: 16.7 percent
Full English bond every sixth course: 16.7 percent (*Note:* The main consideration here is for *wastage factors* because of "snapped" headers, and corresponding increased labor costs.)
Full Flemish bond every sixth course: 5.5 percent

It is important to remember that the correction factors applicable to the specified bonds must be utilized as *additions* to the basic factors for face brick, and as *deductions* from the factors for backup brick, if another (i.e., common) brick is to be used. Table 6.1 provides a table of factors for a limited selection of bonds, brick sizes, wall thicknesses, and mortar joints for Imperial dimensions, and Table 6.2, a corresponding table for metric dimensions. It should be noted that the dimensions shown in Table 6.2 for Ontario size and Quebec size are "soft conversions" from Imperial to metric, and item (a), Table 6.1, gives soft conversions from metric to Imperial. It must also be emphasized that the factors shown in these tables exclude any allowances for waste or breakage. Mathematical purists might contest some of the factors regarding absolute arithmetical accuracy, and, admittedly, in many instances they have been "rounded off" to the nearest decimal; they remain, however, reasonably accurate for estimating purposes.

6.5 Concrete Block Masonry

The factors for establishing the required number of concrete block units per square foot are calculated in the same way as for brick materials. The *length* and *height* dimensions for a standard imperial-sized concrete block are 15⅝ in. × 7⅝ in.

The factor per square foot for block laid with 3/8 in. mortar joints will be

$$\frac{1 \text{ ft.}^2}{(15\ 5/8 + 3/8) \times (7\ 5/8 + 3/8)} = 1.13 \text{ units/ft.}^2$$

Using 5/8 in. joints,

$$\frac{1 \text{ ft.}^2}{(15\ 5/8 + 5/8) \times (7\ 5/8 + 5/8)} = 1.08 \text{ units/ft.}^2$$

TABLE 6.1 Brick Quantities: Imperial

Brick Type and Size	Type of Bond	Mortar Joint	Quantities per Square Foot (ft^2)		
			Facing 4 in.	Backup 4 in.	Backup 8 in.
(a) Modular: 3⅝ × 2¼ × 7⅝ in.	Stretcher	⅜	8.00	—	—
		½	6.44	—	—
	Flemish (full headers)	⅜	10.66	5.34	13.34
		½	8.60	4.31	10.76
	English (full headers)	⅜	12.00	4.00	12.00
		½	9.68	3.23	9.68
	Full headers, fifth course	⅜	9.60	6.40	14.40
		½	7.74	5.16	11.61
	Full headers, sixth course	⅜	9.34	6.67	14.67
		½	7.33	5.38	11.83
(b) Ontario: 4 × 2⅜ × 8⅜ in.	Stretcher	⅜	6.00	—	—
		½	5.63	—	—
	Flemish (full headers)	⅜	8.00	4.00	10.00
		½	7.51	3.76	9.39
	English (full headers)	⅜	9.00	3.00	9.00
		½	8.45	2.82	8.45
	Full headers, fifth course	⅜	7.20	4.80	12.80
		½	6.76	4.51	10.14
	Full headers, sixth course	⅜	7.00	5.00	11.00
		½	6.57	4.69	10.32
(c) Quebec: 3¾ × 2¼ × 8 in.	Stretcher	⅜	6.87	—	—
		½	6.16	—	—
	Flemish (full headers)	⅜	9.16	4.60	11.47
		½	8.21	4.11	10.27
	English (full headers)	⅜	10.31	3.44	10.31
		½	9.24	3.08	9.24
	Full headers, fifth course	⅜	8.25	5.50	12.37
		½	7.39	4.93	11.09
	Full headers, sixth course	⅜	8.02	5.72	12.59
		½	7.19	5.85	12.00

Expressed in metric dimensions:

$$390 \text{ mm} \times 190 \text{ mm}$$

The factor per square meter using 10 mm joints will be

$$\frac{1 \text{ m}^2}{(0.390 + 0.10) \times (0.190 + 0.10)} = 12.5 \text{ units/m}^2$$

TABLE 6.2 Brick Quantities: Metric

Brick Type and Size	Type of Bond	Mortar Joint	Quantities per Square Meter (m^2) Facing, 90 mm	Backup 90 mm	Backup 190 mm
(a) Modular: 90 × 57 × 190 mm	Stretcher (running)	10 mm	74.6	—	—
	Flemish (full headers)	10 mm	99.6	49.8	124.4
	English (full headers)	10 mm	111.9	37.4	111.9
	Full headers, fifth course	10 mm	89.5	59.7	134.3
	Full headers, sixth course	10 mm	87.1	62.1	136.7
(b) Ontario: 101.6 × 60.33 × 212.73 mm	Stretcher (running)	10 mm	63.8	—	—
	Flemish (full headers)	10 mm	85.0	42.6	106.4
	English (full headers)	10 mm	95.7	31.9	95.7
	Full headers, fifth course	10 mm	76.6	51.0	114.8
	Full headers, sixth course	10 mm	74.5	53.2	117.0
(c) Quebec: 95.25 × 57.15 × 203.20 mm	Stretcher (running)	10 mm	69.9	—	—
	Flemish (full headers)	10 mm	93.2	46.7	116.7
	English (full headers)	10 mm	105.0	35.0	105.0
	Full headers, fifth course	10 mm	83.9	56.0	126.0
	Full headers, sixth course	10 mm	81.6	58.3	128.3

6.6 Structural Clay Tile Masonry

The factors required to establish quantities of structural clay tile masonry units will be calculated as were demonstrated for concrete block masonry. There are a greater variety of sizes available in this type of masonry material than for concrete block. The following are some of the normal *length* and *height* dimensions:

Smooth face tile: 5″ × 11 5/8″
Partition tile: 11 5/8″ × 11 5/8″

The factor per square foot for the above units, using 3/8″ joints, will be:

$$\text{Smooth face tile} = \frac{1 \text{ ft.}^2}{(5 + 3/8) \times (11\ 5/8 + 3/8)} = 2.23 \text{ units/ft.}^2$$

$$\text{Partition tile} = \frac{1 \text{ ft.}^2}{(11\ 5/8 + 3/8) \times (11\ 5/8 + 3/8)} = 1 \text{ unit/ft.}^2$$

6.7 *Structural Glazed Tile*

The basic dimensions of length and height for a stretcher unit are 11 3/4 in. long × 5¼ in. high, and the factor per 1 ft.^{2} (¼ in. joints) would be 2.2.

6.8 *Fireproofing Tile for Structural Steel Beams*

This type of steel fireproofing is most uncommon these days, the modern system of spray fireproofing being much more usual. The tile is confined to the sides and flanges of structural steel beams and girders; the conversion factor should be calculated on the basis of the number of pieces per linear foot of beam (or flange).

Example: A steel beam side is fireproofed as follows:

Sides, 1 piece per linear foot of beam side
Flange (shoe tile), 2 pieces per linear foot of flange
Soffit, 1 piece per linear foot of beam soffit

The sides would be calculated using the factor per one side, multiplied by 2. The same would apply to the flanges.

6.9 *Mortar*

There are two types of factors most commonly used for calculating mortar quantity requirements. One factor gives the quantity of cubic yards of mortar per square feet of wall area, stating the mortar joint thickness and the brick dimensions; the other is a factor based on the cubic yards of mortar per so many units of masonry (e.g., 1000 bricks), again taking brick and mortar joint dimensions into consideration.

Basically, all factors are obtained by calculating the total cubic volume of the wall and then *deducting* from this figure the *total net volume of the masonry units;* the amount remaining will be *net volume* of mortar required. Note the two words *"net volume."*

It is not the calculation of this net volume that is difficult. The real challenge is deciding upon the most realistic waste factor! Bricklayers are only happy when the estimate provides enough quantity of mortar to lay all the bricks plus a little bit left over to splatter at the estimators' feet when they

TABLE 6.3 Mortar Quantity Factors

Brick*	Cubic Feet of Mortar per 1000 Brick	
	3/8" Joint	1/2" Joint
4" Standard Modular (3 5/8" × 2 1/4" × 7 5/8")	8.06	10.89
Ontario (4" × 2 3/8" × 8 3/8")	9.67	13.03
Quebec (3 3/4" × 2 1/4" × 8")	8.65	11.66

Concrete Block (15 5/8" × 7 5/8")	Cubic yards of mortar per 1000 Block 3/8" Joint
4" Block	1.1
6" Block	1.6
8" Block	2.2
10" Block	2.6
12" Block	3.3

*These factors based on estimating data prepared by the "Clay Brick Association of Canada"

visit the site! However, it is a difficult material to work with, and the estimated quantities should reflect the realities of actual job conditions. A percentage factor of 25 percent to 40 percent is not unreasonable!

Table 6.3 provides tables of factors for the calculation of mortar. These factors are net and do not include any percentage for waste.

6.10 Masonry Ties and Anchors

These items, like mortar, cannot be measured or calculated directly from the drawings; in most cases they do not even appear on the drawings. They are best calculated on the basis of so many pieces per square foot of wall. Specifications usually give enough information regarding the spacing of these ties to make such calculations. Dovetail anchors, which are attached to anchor slots, can easily be calculated when the total linear length of slot is measured.

6.11 Review

At the beginning of this chapter, it was stressed that preparation of masonry quantities underwent two stages to arrive at the enumeration of the units,

followed by adjustments for waste and bonding. It is worth repeating that, if proper care is not used in all these operations, significant errors can result. A normal masonry take-off is not usually very complicated; measurements of wall areas can be made very accurately. But a good take-off can be useless if the correct factors are not considered and applied, and things go quickly from bad to worse if bonding corrections are inaccurate (or forgotten), and then, finally, lack of judgment may result in an unrealistic factor for waste.

There is nothing wrong with using set printed tables, but estimators must develop their expertise in checking such tables and understanding how they were prepared. They should also prepare their own tables for materials or sizes not included in the printed ones. Research into actual projects should highlight some practical information regarding material waste, based on data regarding the quantities actually purchased and the quantities installed in the structure.

6.12 Take-Off Example

Figure 6.1 provides an example of quantity take-off for masonry. Floor plans (Figures 3.4 and 3.5), elevations (Figures 3.6 and 3.7) and building section (Figure 3.8) show most of the information applicable to this trade section. The following brief specification notes supplement the data shown on the drawings:

Face brick, modular size, red rug, laid in 6th course headers.
⅜ inch joints, Type "N" mortar.
Lightweight concrete block—for backup and interior partitions.
Dampcourses and flashings: 2 oz laminated copper paper.
Cavity wall ties—Z-bars $\frac{3}{16}$ inch wire.
Dovetail anchors, hot-dipped galvanized, 16 gauge—1″ × 3½″ × ⅜″
Anchor slot (supply to formwork trade for installation).
Cavity wall insulation—1 inch polystyrene type 4.
Stone coping at parapet, fixed with ½″ diameter × 1′-6″ anchors.
Concrete fill to block lintels, two No. 4 reinforcing bars.
Clean down exposed masonry (muriatic acid).

COMMENTS ON MASONRY TAKE-OFF

1. The side notes show the computations of the drawing dimensions and levels to arrive at the wall heights. The face brick at the low-rear portion of the building extends below the floor slab and sits on a shelf formed in the concrete wall.

2. Openings in the wall are deducted from the gross area using the *net* door dimensions (i.e., the extra widths for frames is not included).

QUANTITIES

SHEET No. 1 OF 6

PROJECT Research Centre ESTIMATE No. 27/82

LOCATION ______ BY B.E.W. CHK'D ______

SUBDIVISION 04200 – Masonry DATE ______

DESCRIPTION OF WORK	NO. PIECES	DIMENSIONS A	B	C	FACE BRICK A×B	CLEAN DOWN FACE BRICK A×B	
Face Brick - Exterior Walls (6th Course Headers) - Modular 3/8"		Joint					
1 - Storey Area							
Roof 310.0							
Gr. Fl. (300.0)							
10.0							
Parapet 1.0							
Slab + Shelf 1.0							
12.0	3/	50.0	12.0		1800	Do.	
N. Elev.							
3×10.0 = 30.0 2×10.0 = 20.0							
Parapet 1.6 1.6							
31.6 21.6		100.0	31.6		3150	Do.	
		50.0	21.6		1075	Do.	
DDT. Windows	2/	(137.9)					
		(89.7)					
	2/	(29.6)	(4.6)		(1908)	Do.	
Overhead Doors	2/	(10.0)	(8.0)		(160)	Do.	
Ext Door		(3.0)	(7.0)		(21)	Do.	
					3936 SF	3936 SF	
Factor = 6 Course Hdrs = × 9.34 =					36762		
Add 5% Waste					1838		
					38600		
				=	38.6 M pcs.		
Stone Coping at Parapet					Coping ft		Anchors (2'0" c/c)
	2/	150.0			300		300-0 / 2 = 150+2 = 152
	5/	50.0			250		250 / 2 = 125+5 = 130
					550 L.F.		282 Pcs.

Figure 6.1.

QUANTITIES

SHEET No. 2 OF 6

PROJECT ______
LOCATION ______
SUBDIVISION 04200 - MASONRY

ESTIMATE No. 27/82
BY B.E.W. CHK'D ______
DATE ______

DESCRIPTION OF WORK	NO. PIECES	DIMENSIONS A	DIMENSIONS B	DIMENSIONS C	BLOCK 8" A×B	CAVITY INSULATION A×B	
CONCRETE BLOCK BACKING TO FACE BRICK & P.C. CONCRETE							
50.0							
2×1.0 (2.0)	2/	150.0					
48.0	2/	50.0	31.6		12600	Do.	
		(48.0)	(10.0)		(480)	Do.	
DEDUCT							
SPANDREL BEAM + SLAB EDGE	3/2/	(150.0)					
	3/2/	(50.0)					
		(100.0)	(2.8)		(3467)	Do.	
DRS. + W/W'S	2/2/	(137.9)					
		(89.7)					
	2/	(59.4)					
31.6	5/	(39.5)					
(7.0) 4" BRICK	2/	(10.0)	(4.6)		(4393)	Do.	
24.6 8" BLOCK		(10.0)	(8.0)		(80)	Do.	
12"	2/	(3.0)	(7.0)		(42)	Do.	
CORNERS	4/	(1.0)	(24.6)		(98)	Do.	
1 STOREY BLDG	3/	50.0	9.4		1400	Do.	
DEDUCT: DOORS/WINDOWS	2/	(29.6)	(4.6)		(266)	Do.	
	2/	(10.0)	(8.0)		(160)	Do.	
		(3.0)	(7.0)		(21)	Do.	
					4993 SF	4993 SF	
		× 1.13 =		5642		499	← 10% WASTE
		+5% WASTE		282		5492 PCS	
				5924 PCS			
					A		
DAMPCOURSE (16 oz.)							
	2/	150.0			300		
	5/	50.0			250		
					550		
				+10%	55		
					605 LF		

Figure 6.1. *(continued).*

QUANTITIES

SHEET No. 3 OF 6

PROJECT ____
LOCATION ____
SUBDIVISION 04200 - MASONRY

ESTIMATE No. 27/82
BY B.E.W. CHK'D ____
DATE ____

DESCRIPTION OF WORK	NO. PIECES	DIMENSIONS A	B	C	A.
FLASHINGS OVER WINDOWS & DOORS					
WINDOWS	2/2/	137.9			551
		89.7			90
	2/	59.4			119
	5/	39.5			197
	2/	10.0			20
	2/	29.6			59
O/HEAD DOORS	2/	9.10			20
SINGLE DOOR	2/	4.3			9
MAIN ENTRANCE		9.10			10
					1075 LF
ANCHOR SLOTS (SUPPLIED TO FORMWORK TRADE)					A
748.0					
297.0					
100.0					
1145.0					
÷2 = 573					
+ 5					
" 6					
" 1					
585	585/	2.8			1562
EXT. COLUMNS	12/	7.3			87
	2/3/	7.3			44
	2/12/	7.3			174
	2/2/4/	7.3			116
					1983 LF
DOVETAIL ANCHORS					
		585 × 2			1170
		58 × 7.25 / 2			210
					1380

SAY 1400 PCS

Figure 6.1. *(continued)*.

QUANTITIES

SHEET No. 4 OF 6

PROJECT
LOCATION
SUBDIVISION 04200 – MASONRY

ESTIMATE No. 27/82
BY B.E.W. CHK'D
DATE

DESCRIPTION OF WORK	NO. PIECES	DIMENSIONS A	B	C	6" BLOCK A×B	4" BLOCK A×B
INTERIOR CONC. BLOCK PARTITIONS						
150.0 − (2.0) = 148.0 − (54.0) = 94.0 − (5.0) = 89.0 ; 23.0 + 19.0 + 12.0 = 54.0						
GR. FL. CORRIDOR		94.0				
10.0 − (.8) = 9.4 ; 21.0		89.0				
26.0	2/2/	20.10				
3×6" 1.6	3/	5.0				
48.6	2/	48.6	9.4		3530	
DOORS	15/	(3.6)	(7.0)		(368)	
PARTITIONS	10/	20.10				
STAIR		14.10	9.4			2083
2nd & 3rd FLS	2/2/	148.0				
	2/2/	20.10	9.4		6301	
DOORS	2/15/	(3.6)	(7.0)		(736)	
PARTITIONS	2/8/	20.10	9.4			3111
					8727 SF	5194 SF
		X	1.13 =		9862	5869
			+ 5% WASTE		493	293
					10355 PCS	6162 PCS
EXTRA OVER – CONCRETE & RE-STEEL TO LINTELS					A	
	46/	5.6			253 LF	

Figure 6.1. *(continued)*.

QUANTITIES

SHEET No. 5 OF 6

PROJECT ______________ ESTIMATE No. 27/82

LOCATION ______________ BY B.E.W. CHK'D ______

SUBDIVISION 04200 – MASONRY. DATE ______

DESCRIPTION OF WORK	NO. PIECES	DIMENSIONS A	B	C	LINTEL BLOCK A	BULLNOSE UNITS A	
SPECIAL CONC. BLOCK UNITS							
	46/	5·6			253		
	5/	9·4				47	
					253	47	
						× 1·5	= 70 Pcs
				× ·75 =	190 Pcs		
EXPOSED BLOCK SURFACES					CLEAN BLOCK A×B		EXTRA FOR EXPOSED FACES
		19·0	9·4		177		
		(3·0)	(7·0)		(21)		
		9·10	9·4		92		248 × 1·13 = 280 Pcs
					248 SF		
SCAFFOLD FRAMES IN 5'·0" LIFTS							
1 STOREY – 2 LIFTS	3/2/	50·0			300		
HIGH – 7	7/	100·0			700		
5 "	5/	50·0			250		
INTERIOR (1 LIFT)		1030·0			1030		
					2280		
					÷ 7 =	326 FRAMES	
CAVITY WALL TIES							
10·0 − (1·4) SOLID = 8·8; + 1·6 = 10·2	3/	50·0	10·2		1525		
		100·0	22·0		2200		
		50·0	15·8		784		
					4509 SF		
					1 PER 2 SF =	4509 / 2	= 2255 = SAY 2300 Pcs

Figure 6.1. *(continued).*

QUANTITIES

SHEET No. 6 OF 6

PROJECT

LOCATION

SUBDIVISION 04200 – MASONRY

ESTIMATE No. 27/82

BY B.E.W. CHK'D

DATE

DESCRIPTION OF WORK	NO. PIECES	DIMENSIONS A	B	C	A				
EXTRA OVER – LABOUR TO BRICK SILLS									
	2/	137.9			276				
		89.7			90				
	2/	29.6			59				
					425 LF				
MORTAR (TYPE "N")									
BRICK FACTOR 8.06 CF/1000		=	$\frac{39 \times 8.06}{27}$		=	11.6			
CONC. BLOCK – 4" (1CY/1000)		= 6.1 × 1				6.1			
6" (1½CY/1000)		= 10.4 × 1.5				15.6			
8" (2CY/1000)		= 5.9 × 2				11.8			
						45.1			
					ADD 25% WASTE	11.2			
						56.3 CY			

Figure 6.1. *(continued).*

3. The factor to determine the number of bricks is obtained from Table 6.1.

4. The dimensions on the drawings are from corner to corner and are correct for the face brick measurements, but it should be noted that the block backup extends from the *inside face to inside face,* which would be 150 ft. (100 ft. + 50 ft.) less 2 × 4 in. = 8 in.

5. The anchor slots are measured the full depth of the spandrel beam at 24 in. on center, with extra slots allowed at the ends. The slots to the columns are measured for three sides.

6. The dovetail anchors are measured on the basis of two per anchor slot in the spandrel beams, and at 24 in. centers at the columns.

7. In this example the measurements for the interior concrete block partitions are developed from the dimensions noted on the drawings (with some overlapping at intersections, etc.). In practice, however, and particularly for a very large project with many floors and rooms divided by partitions, this is one item where time limitations ("there's only a week to go and there are extensions to be done and pricing . . .") would advocate the use of a scale or a "measuring wheel."

8. The length of the block lintels are developed as follows:

Width of opening	3 ft. 6 in.
Plus 2 × 1 ft.	2 ft. 0 in.
	5 ft. 6 in.

For the purpose of the estimate this is accurate enough, but it should be pointed out again that the dimension of 5 ft. 6 in. does not allow for the width of the door frame.

9. Only special jamb and bullnose units have been measured, although many other special shapes and sizes would be required. For bidding purposes it is sufficient to establish (by some method or another) an approximation of the premium cost of these items. On this example a linear measurement has been taken for the height of the jambs, and the lintel, and the number of units per foot established. A more detailed estimate of quantities of each type of unit would have to be made for actual purchasing purposes.

10. The extra cost of laying block which will remain exposed is measured as recommended in the schedule of items and measurements, that is, taking the "cleaning" area multiplied by the factor to establish the number of pieces, to which the estimated premium labor cost would be applied.

11. The scaffold frames are measured on the basis of linear feet per each 5 ft. *lift* of scaffold; the total length is then divided by 7 ft. to establish the number of scaffold frames to be erected and dismantled. (This is based on using 7 ft. braces.) The actual number of frames to be purchased or rented would be the minimum number required for the project according to the estimator's judgment.

12. The extra over for the brick sills is measured in linear feet and the cost will be based on three (3) bricks per foot.

13. The mortar quantities are based on the factors shown in Table 6.3. Note that 25 percent waste is added to the net quantity.

7

Take-off: Rough and Finished Carpentry, Miscellaneous Items

7.1 Rough Carpentry

The alternative wording for the term "rough and finished carpentry" would be the traditional "carpentry and millwork," and probably there are many places in Canada and the United States where these words still convey with more clarity the demarcation between these two divisions of the carpenter's trade.

Rough carpentry work as discussed in this book will be mainly concerned with those miscellaneous carpentry items most common to present-day buildings constructed of fire-resistant materials, such as steel, concrete, masonry, aluminum, and so on. Items pertaining to wood-framed structures will not be covered in any great detail; there are many excellent estimating text and reference books available that adequately cover this division of carpentry work.

The miscellaneous carpentry under review will include such items as blocking, furring, strapping, nailing strips, bearing plates, cant strips, and similar items. Stud partitions, floor, roof, and ceiling framing will also be considered.

The general purpose and function of most rough carpentry items is that other work will subsequently be fastened or attached to them; they exist for the purpose of *bearing or supporting something else*. Roof blocking and cant strips, for example, are usually covered by metal flashings; wall strapping or furring is installed to carry gypsum or other wallboards. Many *finished carpentry* items (particularly fitments) are fixed to wood blockings or bearers; therefore, it is reasonable to anticipate considerably more rough carpentry in buildings requiring a large amount of finished woodwork (*millwork*) such as schools, university buildings, residential buildings, hotels, hospitals and to some extent, research centers. Large speculative office buildings, industrial plant buildings, and warehouses normally require a minimum of finished carpentry, and therefore the rough carpentry items will often be limited to cant strips and blockings at roof areas, probably some nailing strips to structural steel, and miscellaneous furring and strapping inside certain areas of the building (offices in a factory or warehouse, for example).

Taking off the quantities for carpentry work in modern buildings can often be tedious and exasperating. A common complaint made by many estimators is that usually more time is devoted to searching the drawings to locate these items than in actually taking them off! This work is often delegated to junior or trainee estimators; and there is some merit in this, if only for the following two reasons:

1. This work usually demands keen and meticulous examination of the drawings, including much cross referencing between large-scale details and other drawings, all of which provide good training and experience to young estimators.
2. As the value of rough carpentry in modern construction represents a small percentage of the total overall cost, an error made in this take-off would not usually be so financially disastrous as an error made in the take-off for a more contentious trade, such as concrete or excavation work. (*Note:* The philosophy behind this is *not* that young estimators are more error-prone than their seniors, but that it is not good policy to burden them with responsibilities for which they are probably not being paid!)

It should not be inferred from the statement in the preceding paragraph proclaiming this work as representing "a small percentage of the total building cost" that it is *cheap* work. The material cost of lumber, plywood, hardware, and so on, might be moderate, but the labor cost of cutting and fitting miscellaneous pieces of blocking and furring can be excessively high. The cost per linear foot (meter) of fitting into place short pieces of 2 × 4 in. (50 mm × 100 mm) blocking can be three to four times greater than the cost of the same dimensioned lumber in large quantities of repetitive framing in walls, floors, and roofs.

The take-off can be facilitated by subdividing the rough carpentry work for a building into groups identifiable by location and/or function. These groups would include (although not be limited to):

1. Roof carpentry: blockings, cant strips, curbs, soffits, and the like.
2. Inside face of exterior walls: strapping, furring, and so on.
3. Windows: miscellaneous blocking to metal windows.
4. Interior partitions: structural walls, furring, strapping, and the like.
5. Blocking and furring to finished carpentry items.
6. Miscellaneous items to both interior and exterior of the building.

The number of these groups or categories could be further expanded (or condensed) according to the estimator's judgment. The advantage of this method is that when taking off the items in a particular category only certain drawings will usually be applicable to that division. Roof plans supplemented by large-scale sections will usually provide all the necessary information for carpentry items at that location. Exterior wall sections will supplement the floor plans regarding strapping and furring. Many architects confine the details of millwork fitments to certain drawings, and these will provide the base for taking off the blocking and bearing requirements for those items.

It is also recommended that estimators note the applicable drawing and detail numbers on both the take-off sheets and the summary sheets for pricing. This facilitates any rechecking required, and also simplifies the problem of adequately describing an item. "2 × 4 in. (50 mm × 100 mm) blocking as per detail A.6/21" is much simpler to locate and understand than, say, "2 × 4 blocking at perimeter ceiling recess for valance in gymnasium."

The quantities for the rough carpentry items that are applicable to or required for finished carpentry or millwork should be measured with those items. This will avoid the irritating chore of working twice through the same drawings and details.

7.2 Measuring Rough Carpentry Work

Despite the introduction of the metric system in Canada, at the present time lumber is still sold on the foot board measure (FBM) basis, with the existing Imperial dimensions expressed in "soft conversion" metric terms. The metric substitution for the foot board measure is the cubic meter (m^3). It is recommended that most items be measured and priced in linear or running feet; this applies particularly to the cost of installation, as will be demonstrated in Chapter 9. Exceptions to this rule might be for large quantities of structural framing (roofs, floors, walls, etc.) where it could be more realistic to establish unit costs per FBM for both material and labor.

All items should be measured net in place, but consideration must be given to basic construction requirements that are rarely shown or indicated on the drawings. These would include:

1. Allowances for bearing on walls, columns, beams, and the like.
2. Additional studs at corners, openings, and so on.
3. Diagonal bridging.
4. Studs and plates at partitions.
5. Overlapping of the various members.

All items should be kept separate according to lumber dimensions, classification, and grade, for example, "No. 2 Spruce, Construction Grade." The number of dressed sides should also be stated.

Items that require drilling for bolts or any system of fixing other than nailing, screwing, or gluing should be stated separately.

Adjustment factors should be applied to the net lumber quantities as allowances for cutting and waste. It was stated in Chapter 3 that most estimators do not have the time to accurately plan and categorize all the miscellaneous items of lumber into a practicable list of purchasable lengths. As long as good judgment is exercised in the assessment of each individual condition, these percentage factors can provide reasonably adequate gross and purchasable quantities.

Plywood and other wallboards should be measured in square feet and here again factors must be applied to allow for cutting and waste. (Items with very small quantities could be expressed in terms of the minimum number of sheets required.)

Lumber requiring pressure treatment should be kept separate, or, alternatively, the various items can be priced as "untreated" and then added and expressed in one single total as extra over in board feet ("extra over for pressure treatment—500 board feet")

All blockings and the like, which are in short pieces, should either be enumerated or the number stated in the description, for example, "2 × 4 in. blocking at metal windows (in 20 pieces) = 82 l.f." This enables the estimator to realistically price the cutting and fitting in place.

7.3 Schedule of Items and Measurements: Rough Carpentry

Item	*Comment*	*Unit of Measurement*
Miscellaneous roof carpentery	Keep separate for: • cants • blockings • curbs • copings and parapets • others (Built-up or laminated in place work to be identifed separately.)	Linear foot (m)
Strapping and furring	Keep separate for: • exterior walls • interior partitions • bulkheads • soffits • other surfaces	Linear foot (m)

Item	*Comment*	*Unit of Measurement*
Window blockings	If in short pieces less than 5 ft. (1.5 meters) long, state the number in the description. Include detail or section number with the item.	Linear foot (m)
Blocking and furring to finished carpentry work	Separate into categories such as: • paneling • counters and cupboards • shelving • railings • door frames • others	Linear foot (m)
Structural framing	Main categories: • roofs: rafters, ridges, eaves, ties • floors and ceilings: joists, bridging, plates, trimmers, girders, etc. • walls and partitions: studs, plates, lintels, etc. Allow for bearing into walls, beams. Extra members at the end of each span, "doubling" at corners, intersections, openings or under partitions, etc.	Linear foot (m) or Board foot
Wallboards	State: • thickness • material classification • number of finished (sanded) surfaces Keep separate categories for: • subfloors • wall sheathing • soffits • fascias • parapets • circular or sloping surfaces Wallboards in strips less than 12 in. wide should be stated in linear feet.	Square foot (m^2)
Boarding	Main categories: • floors • walls and partitions • roofs Keep diagonal work separate; add applicable waste factor to net quantities. State if tongued and grooved, rabbet edged.	Square foot (m^2)
Building paper	Describe material.	Square foot (m^2)
Roofing felt	Describe material.	Square foot (m^2)

Item	*Comment*	*Unit of Measurement*
Vapor barriers	Describe material.	Square foot (m^2)
Miscellaneous blockings	State location, function, and drawing detail numbers. Small quantities: state number of pieces.	Linear foot (m)
Rough hardware:		
anchor bolts,	State diameter and length.	Numerical
joist hangers, metal angles, brackets, etc.	State material, gauge, size, etc.	Numerical
Miscellaneous rough hardware	This includes nails, screws, spikes, etc. Usually the total weight is established by applying a factor based on the number of pounds per thousand board feet; this "rule of thumb" formula will usually provide an adequate sum of money to include in the estimate.	Pound (kilogram)

7.4 Finish Carpentry

The finish carpentry work reviewed here refers to the items in a modern building that are usually *supplied* by a millwork subcontractor; therefore, the estimating methods and procedures to be discussed will in most cases be restricted to the *receiving, handling,* and *installation only* of this work. It is not unusual for some subcontractors to quote this trade on the basis of both supply and on-site erection; but most contractors still take off and price finished carpentry work for the following reasons:

1. The estimated cost of installation can be added to a *supply-only* quotation to make a proper comparison with the complete package quotations.
2. There may be certain items excluded from the quotations, and by having a complete take-off and all work priced the contractor can estimate the value of these omissions. (The rough carpentry work to which this work is attached will also usually be excluded from these quotations.)

The Masterformat includes two divisions: 06200 Finish Carpentry and 06400 Architectural Woodwork. The distinction between these two divisions is best interpreted as one of quality. Cabinet work, for example, might be specified in both sections, but the specification in 06400 (Architectural Woodwork) would generally require the work to be custom-made and of a very high quality. This section is usually quoted by special subcontractors and is nearly always on the basis of complete supply and on-site erection in accordance with the specification.

There are no reliable shortcuts to estimating the cost of millwork or finish carpentry installation. Rule-of-thumb formulas such as allowing a percentage of the material cost to cover the cost of installation usually produce hit-and-miss results. All items should be measured and listed for pricing. However, it is possible to group items into categories that provide common cost factors.

A good example is fitments (counters, cupboards, storage units, etc.). One factor influencing the installation costs of these items is the amount of *cabinet hardware* required.

Example: Assume two counter units, each with similar dimensions and each with plastic laminate tops. Counter 1 has two cupboard doors, three shelves, and three drawers at one end. Counter 2 has two drawers, and two shelves open to view (no doors). The cost of installing this counter will be less than counter 1, because there is less hardware, such as hinges, knobs, shelf brackets, and drawer guides.

If categories are established such as these, the total length of all counter units pertaining to a selected category can be measured and summarized accordingly; this method should accelerate the "take-off" process considerably. The alternative is to take each counter or cupboard as a separate item, stating the dimensions. Whichever method is followed, the drawing or detail numbers should be shown on the summary sheets.

All other items (trim, stair rails, paneling, fascias, sills, etc.) should be taken off in detail. Specifications often contain items that some (or all) millwork suppliers will exclude from their quotations, and without a complete estimate it will be sheer guessing to evaluate the cost of the excluded items.

Estimators should also be alerted to the interface items that:

1. Form integral parts of specific finish carpentry or millwork units but are *specified under other divisions*, such as brackets, metal legs, glass shelves, angle supports, and stainless steel trim, or
2. Same type items as in item 1, but are included in the *finish carpentry specifications*, although local or regional trade practices might influence the *exclusion* of these items from subcontractors' quotations.

In both cases these items should be taken off, but consideration must be given as to the division in which they should be *summarized and priced*. If metal brackets for wood stair rails are included in the division for Miscellaneous Metals, for example, then the quantities of these brackets should be included in the list of items for that division (i.e., Miscellaneous Metals), as most subcontractors or suppliers bidding that trade will include these items in their quotations. If, however, contrary to normal trade practice, they have been included in the *finish carpentry* section of the specifications, then estimators can either list them under that division or under whatever division they consider as being the most likely to quote prices on these items.

All finish carpentry items located more than 10 ft above floor level should be measured and stated separately, and the average height stated. This would particularly apply to wood ceilings or valances.

The number of items included under the division of Finish Carpentry and Millwork is almost limitless, and the following Schedule of Items and Measurements covers only those items common to most buildings. The rules or measurement laid down can be followed for all other items not specifically listed. The function of the building (school, hospital, residential, etc.) dictates the items and quality of finish carpentry to be included.

7.5 Schedule of Items and Measurements: Finish Carpentry

Item	*Comment*	*Unit of Measurement*
Counters and cupboards	If by the linear foot (meter) then state width and height. If numerical then state all dimensions. State material for tops (plastic laminate, wood, linoleum, etc.) State whether floor or wall mounted, or ceiling hung. Open shelf units, or similar units requiring a minimum of hardware should be stated separately. Give drawing or detail numbers. State if "cut-out" for sinks required.	Linear foot (m) or numerical
Trim	State material, dimensions, location, and/or functions (to doors, windows, paneling, etc.).	Linear foot (m)
Paneling	Keep separate according to material classification. Soffits and sloping surfaces to be stated separately. State any requirements for grain or book matching.	Square foot (m^2)
Ceiling strips	State type and dimensions of the material, also the spacing centers and methods of fixing. Keep separate to sloping soffits.	Linear foot (m)
Stairs	Item to include treads, risers, nosings, wall strings, etc. State number of treads and risers, width, etc.	Numerical
Benches:		
Less than 6 ft. long	State width, height, and location.	Numerical
Longer than 6 ft.	State width, height, and location.	Linear foot (m)

Item	*Comment*	*Unit of Measurement*
Mop rails		Linear foot (m)
Base and nosing		Linear foot (m)
Sills, valances, wall or partition caps, copings, window stools, etc.	State material and dimensions.	Linear foot (m)
Shelving:		
Widths up to and including 12 in.		Linear foot (m)
Greater than 12 in. wide		Square foot (m^2)
Handrail	State separately for stairs. State all pertinent information re: • material • dimensions • fixing Keep laminated work separate.	Linear foot (m)
Glazed partitions	Item will include framing and trim. Partitioning greater than 10 ft. high to be stated separately.	Square foot (m^2)
Miscellaneous rough hardware	Includes for nails, screws, small bolts, brackets, etc. Keep separate any special requirements for stainless steel, brass, etc.	Pound (kilogram)

7.6 Doors and Frames

These can be taken off (counted) from the drawings or, preferably, from a "door schedule" where one is provided. These schedules will either be shown on the drawings or included in the specifications, or may even (particularly on a large project) be issued in a separate book.

General contractors usually only take off quantities for the doors and frames in order to establish the handling and installation costs of these items. Masterformat sections 08100 Metal Doors and Frames and 08200 Wood and Plastic Doors cover the items most applicable to this work. For many years it was customary for the millwork contractors to include the supply of wood and plastic doors in their quotations; many still maintain this custom, according to local or regional practice, or possibly because of a millwork supplier's belief that this could provide a marketing advantage. It is, however, becoming more common for the door manufacturers to quote directly to the general contractor. However, irrespective of who actually supplies the doors, the contractor still has to estimate the costs involved in receiving, unloading, storing, handling, and hanging them, including the preparation *for* and installation *of* the finish hardware.

The main concern to an estimator between these two sources of supply is that if the millwork supplier includes for the doors it will (invariably) be on a lump-sum basis, whereas the door manufacturer will usually only state a unit price for each type and size of door, to be multiplied by the estimated quantities to establish the total amount to be included in the bid.

The Masterformat sections 08250 Door Assemblies and 08300 Special Doors apply to specialized items where almost without exception the specialist companies undertake the responsibilities of fabrication, supply, and on-site installation. However, to be familiar with the requirements when checking the quotations, the total number and sizes of these door assemblies should be established. The door frames should be noted as separate items as they are often not included by the door manufacturers.

7.7 Miscellaneous Metals

The term "miscellaneous metals" is a time-honored expression for work that is now encompassed within the Masterformat sections of 05500 Metal Fabrications and 05700 Ornamental Metals, and also certain items that are now tabulated in Division 10000 Specialties.

This trade division requires a great amount of investigation and analysis by the estimator. Many items often appear on the drawings that are not clearly defined in the specifications as to which trade is responsible for their supply and/or installation; all the estimator knows with any certainty is that it is the contractor who must bear the responsibility of ensuring that the costs of these items are included in the bid total. The quotations for this trade also often differ in respect to which items will be *supplied only* and which will be both *supplied and installed*. Generally, most items of work that can be identified as "embedded" fall under the category of "supply only."

Some items may only be identified in the specification by an all-embracing label like "Miscellaneous Steel Angles, Channels, etc." or similar term, and there will be a brief description of the items followed by the statement "as shown and detailed on the drawings." This will entail an unavoidable meticulous examination of all the drawings (architectural, structural, mechanical, and electrical) to establish the location and quantities of such items. Estimators should examine details of metal window assemblies and work around escalators where it is quite common to find miscellaneous angles and the like, which may not be defined as being part of those particular trade divisions.

It is common practice for the subcontractor specializing in this work to provide the general contractors with a prebid proposal clearly listing all the items that will be included in their subsequent quotations, and noting those items that will be "supplied only." This practice is of great assistance to the contractor's estimator, who can prepare sheets for analyzing the different quotations and proceed to take off and price those items to be installed by the contractor. Even without these prebid proposal lists, an experienced estimator can identify most of the latter items; they usually apply to all items embedded in concrete or built in to masonry or woodwork.

THE X-B METALWARE COMPANY

5/23/82

Re: Research Building, Jackson University

The following outlines the items on which we shall be basing our quotation for the above-noted project.

Section 05510 - Steel Stairs and Railings — Supplied and Installed

Section 05999 - Miscellaneous Metals

a)	Ladder Rungs	Supplied
b)	Lintels	Supplied
c)	Vanity Support Brackets	Supplied
d)	Toilet Partition Supports	Supplied and Installed
e)	Gratings	Supplied
f)	Elevator Hoist Beams	Supplied and Installed
g)	Loading Dock Angles	Supplied
h)	Pipe Handrails	Supplied and Installed

Our price will be telephoned in prior to the bid-closing time.

The X-B Metalware Company

Figure 7.1.

It is recommended that estimators first list *all* the items noted in the specification for this trade; next measure and record the quantities of the "supplied" items; and then add to the list all those items that are detailed on the drawings but not identified in the specification. These should also be drawn to the attention of the trade contractors, although sometimes this process is reversed by the trade contractors alerting the general contractors!

Figure 7.1 shows a typical prebid proposal from a miscellaneous metal trade contractor.

7.8 Specialties

This trade division is not confined to a single trade contractor, but includes items that will be manufactured and supplied by certain companies specializing in these products; very large and specialized work will also have on-site erection performed by the specialist company (folding partitions, overhead doors, etc.).

The recommended method of establishing the total estimated cost of this work is the utilization of a *spread sheet* to list all the items noted in the specifications, with the applicable quantities. The names of the specified manufacturers or suppliers should be entered in an appropriate column (this will save a lot of rechecking on the specification). When the quotations are received from the various suppliers and/or contractors, the amounts will be entered in the "material" columns and the prices for installation for the materials that are only to be supplied. On some projects the aggregated total of this work can be a considerable amount of money. This is not a trade division that should be neglected until near the bid closing day and then put together with a flurry of quotations, rushed take-offs, and frantic stabs at installation costs with little knowledge about what is really involved in the work.

7.9 Miscellaneous Contractor's Work

Apart from the principal traditional contractor's trades already discussed, there are other items of work on most projects that require measuring or enumerating in the general contractor's office. These vary from project to project and locality to locality. Estimators must be prepared to take off quantities for the work, or portions thereof, of nearly all trades, if a particular condition arises which demands that necessity. Also, for certain trade divisions it is the general practice for the trade contractors to quote on a unit price basis. Asphalt paving, sodding and seeding, concrete floor finishes, sandblasting and bushhammering are some typical examples.

A list of some of these items with recommended rules for measurement are included in the following schedule of items and measurements.

7.10 Schedule of Items and Measurements: Miscellaneous Trades

Item	Comment	Unit of Measurement
Metal doors	State metal type and gauge. Keep in separate categories for: ● doors with fire underwriters labels ● metal-covered wood doors ● lead shielded doors For installation purposes only state doors in the following face area categories: ● up to and including 30 ft.^{2} (2.8 m^2). ● 30 ft.^{2} to 40 ft.^{2} (3.8 m^2). ● larger than 40 square feet State separately for any special hardware requirements.	Numerical
Metal door frames	Describe metal type and gauge. State separately for: ● door frames for more than a single door ● frames including transoms and/or sidelights ● lead-lined frames ● any other special features State if frames are to be installed in: ● concrete walls or partitions ● drywall or wood partitions ● other materials State as separate item any requirement for concrete or grout to door frames.	Numerical
Wood and plastic doors	State separately for plastic laminated doors. Keep separate according to the specified material classifications of wood doors, and describe. For installation purposes only, state doors in the face area categories as for metal doors. Where doors are to be supplied on a unit price base, state separately for each size and thickness of door. State if cut-outs for grilles, etc., are required. *Note:* The door grilles are usually specified in Division 10000 Specialities.	Numerical

Item	*Comment*	*Unit of Measurement*
	Keep in separate categories: • lead-lined doors • soundproofed • special-purpose doors with carvings, embellishments, etc. Folding or bifold doors to be stated as units of two, three, or more leaves.	
Wood door frames	State material and size. *Note:* Wood door frames are rarely quoted by door manufacturers or suppliers; they are usually included in the quotations from millwork contractors, and are often specified in that trade division. Door trim is included in the Finish Carpentry division.	Numerical
Miscellaneous metals	The following list represents those items most commonly considered as *embedded items,* or items usually quoted on a "supplied only" basis by the trade contractor. The method of fixing should be stated with each item. If sleeving is required, the sleeves should be enumerated and the material into which they are to be set described. (Strictly speaking, the setting of sleeves into the various materials should be transferred to and included with the applicable trade divisions.) *Note:* Check for sleeves embedded in concrete that might require fastening *to* and holes cut *in* the formwork. Recommended units of measurement are included with each item, along with alternative units.	
	Miscellaneous steel: angles, shelf angles, channels, plates, etc. State function and/or location, ("lintels to masonry," "loading dock nosings")	Linear foot (m) or Pound (kilogram)
	Covers and frames to: • manholes and catchbasins (state size, material) • trenches (state size, material) • sump and other pits (state size, material)	Numerical
	Sills, stools, thresholds	Linear foot (m)

Item	*Comment*	*Unit of Measurement*
	Miscellaneous brackets for the fixing of other items of work (wood railings, vanity units, etc.)	Numerical
	Expansion joint covers and assemblies	Linear foot (m)
	Corner guards (state all dimensions)	Numerical
	Gratings and frames	Square foot (m^2)
	Supports for ceiling-hung toilet partitions	Numerical
	Lateral supports for masonry partitions	Numerical
	Bollards (note if to be filled with concrete)	Numerical
	Channel door frames	Numerical
Specialties	It would not be practical to list all the items encompassed within this division of work. The following is a list of items common to most buildings. The unit of measurement will be on the basis of enumeration with suggested alternatives stated in brackets. All items should be fully described, including catalog numbers, specified manufacturers, etc.	
	Washroom accessories	
	Door grilles	
	Louvers	(Square foot)
	Roof hatches	
	Toilet partitions	
	Chalkboards and tackboards	(Square foot)
	Flagpoles	
	Overhead doors (sometimes specified under Division 8)	
	Vault doors (sometimes specified under Division 8)	
	Folding doors and partitions	
	Lockers	
	Shelving units	
	Directories	
	Access flooring	(Square foot)
	Prefabricated partitions	(Linear foot)
Miscellaneous Contractor's Work:		
Asphalt paving	State thickness of asphalt, material and thickness of subbases.	Square yard (m^2)
Concrete road curbs	State dimensions.	Linear foot (m)

Item	Comment	Unit of Measurement
Sodding	Give all details re classification, fertilizing, maintenance. State if topsoil is included. Keep sloping surfaces separate.	Square yard (m^2)
Seeding	Describe as for "Sodding."	Square yard (m^2)
Precast concrete paving	State details of underbed and grouting if applicable.	Square yard (m^2) or numerical, stating dimensions
Sandblasting	State if light, medium, or heavy. Keep separate for items with small surface areas.	Square yard (m^2)
Insulation	State all pertinent information relating to the material, and keep separate according to function and/or location, i.e., perimeter insulation at foundations, exterior walls, soffits, under slabs on grade, etc. Adhesive (where required) should be estimated on the basis of gallons (liters) per square foot (meter) area of the material.	Square foot (m^2)
Caulking	State location, function, and specified materials.	Linear foot (m)
Dampproofing	State location and function of surfaces to be coated, material, and number of coats.	Square foot (m^2)

7.11 Take-Off Example

Figure 7.2 provides an example of quantity take-off for rough and finish carpentry, doors and frames. Floor plans (Figure 3.4 and 3.5) show some of the information applicable to the trade take-off (door locations, for example), but most of the items which are recorded on the quantity sheets *do not appear on the drawings*. The examples are primarily intended to demonstrate methods and recording of measurements. The following brief specification notes are applicable to this take-off:

Framing lumber: No. 2 spruce (construction grade).
Blocking and cant strips at parapets and skylights.
Vanity units in washrooms.
Window stools and blocking.
Wood paneling in administrative offices.
Plastic laminated doors at interior partitions.
Hollow metal door frames.

QUANTITIES

SHEET No. 1 OF 2

PROJECT Research Centre ESTIMATE No. 27/82

LOCATION

BY B.E.W. CHK'D

SUBDIVISION 06100 Rough Carpentry 06200 Finished Carpentry 08100 Metal Doors & Frames 08200 Wood Doors DATE

DESCRIPTION OF WORK	NO. PIECES	DIMENSIONS A	B	C			
					Cant Strip A	Blocking 2"x4" A	Skylight Blocking 2"x4" A
No. 2 Construction Grade Spruce (unless noted otherwise)							
	2/	50.0			100	DO	
	2/	150.0			300	DO	
	4/	50.0			200	DO	
	3/2/	5.3					32
	3/2/	6.3					38
					600	600	70
				+5%	30	30	4
					630 LF	630 LF	74 LF
WD Stool & 1"x2" Blocking					Stool A	Blocking A	
	2/2/	137.9			551	Do	
		89.7			90	Do	
	2/	29.6			59	Do	
	5/	39.5			197	Do	
	2/	10.0			20	Do	
	2/	59.0			118	Do	
					1035 LF	1035 LF	
						52 ← +5%	
						1087 LF	
½" Plywood Panelling					Panelling A×B	1"x2" Strapping A	
50.0 / 2×1.0 (2.0) / 48.0	2/	48.0	10.0		960		
@ 16" c/c = 36 + 4	40/	9.0				360	
					960	360	
				+10% →	96	18 ← +5%	
					1056 LF	378 LF	

Figure 7.2.

QUANTITIES

SHEET No. 2 OF 2

PROJECT

LOCATION

SUBDIVISION 06100, 06200, 08100, 08200

ESTIMATE No. 27/82

BY B.E.W. CHK'D

DATE

DESCRIPTION OF WORK	NO. PIECES	DIMENSIONS A	B	C	EXT WOOD DOORS	PL. LAM DOORS	HOLLOW METAL DOORS	METAL DOOR FRAME INT	METAL DOOR FRAME EXT
DOORS + FRAMES									
		GR.	FL.		2	15	—	15	2
		2ND	FL.		—	14	1	15	—
		3RD	FL.		—	14	1	15	—
					2	43	2	45	2
PLASTIC LAM VANITIES TO WASHROOMS					VANITY A	2"x2" BLOCKING A			
	3/2/	6-6			39	DO			
	3/2/	1-6			9	DO			
					48 LF	48 LF			
					+5%	2			
						50			

Figure 7.2. *(continued.)*

Commentary on Take-off: Carpentry and Miscellaneous Items

1. These take-off examples include a number of items not shown on the drawings. For this type of a building the rough carpentry work would not be very extensive; it is assumed that, except for the roof cant strips and blockings, most of the rough carpentry would be miscellaneous blockings and furring for the fixing of millwork or other items. The take-off illustrates how certain finished and rough carpentry work can be taken off at the same time.

2. The applied percentage factors are intended to take into account cutting and wastage (which could be considerable for miscellaneous blocking) and overlapping where applicable.

3. The items shown would all be fixed with nails, spikes, screws, and so on. If, for example, the coping at the parapet wall had been in wood in lieu of stone, then the item would have been described as "drilled for bolting" and the number of bolts calculated.

4. The washroom vanities would probably require some fixing brackets, probably specified to be supplied by the miscellaneous metals subcontractor.

5. The doors and frames have been counted on the drawings, although a door schedule would be used for this purpose if one was provided. This take-off is made for the purpose of estimating the cost of *installing* doors and frames supplied and delivered to the site by the appropriate manufacturers, and is probably quoted on a lump-sum basis; however, a more detailed estimate would be required if the checking of fully itemized quotations was anticipated.

6. The paneling, wood stool, and vanity units are all assumed to be included in a quotation from a millwork subcontractor, the unloading and fixing in place to be done by the general contractor. If the contractor intended to purchase all these materials separately, a much greater detailed and itemized take-off would be essential. The vanity units are measured by the linear foot, but a count of these items would also be sufficient for pricing the cost of fixing.

8

Pricing the Estimate: Basic Principles

8.1 General

The pricing of an estimate falls into the following categories:

Material costs
Labor costs
Equipment costs and rentals
Unit rates (from subcontractors)
Firm price quotations from subcontractors

Each category demands special consideration be given by the estimator in regard to procedure and methodology, and the element of risk to the contractor also varies with each category. In the categories of *material costs* and *unit rates,* for example, the main risk is in the accuracy of the contractor's quantities to which the unit prices will be applied. The category of *labor costs* is vulnerable to both an error in the quantities plus the additional risk of an underestimated ("low") unit rate for the work. For example, the estimate includes an item of 3000 cubic yards of concrete with a strength mix of 3,000 p.s.i. The most competitive price received from a ready-mix concrete supplier is $50 per cubic yard, this price being guaranteed "firm" for 30 days. The estimated rate for *placing* this concrete is $5 per cubic yard. The material unit price ($50) is guaranteed providing a purchase order is issued within the stated time limitation; the unit rate for labor ($5) is an estimate of cost and *not* guaranteed. If the actual quantity of concrete proves greater than the estimated quantity, then both the material and labor costs will increase because of this error; however, the labor cost would be increased even further if the actual unit cost for placing the concrete was greater than the estimated cost. Assuming the actual quantity of concrete to be 3150 cubic yards and the reported placing rate to be $7, the following comparison between estimated and actual costs illustrates the differential in risk percentage between material and labor costs:

Estimate	Actual	Increase
Material:		
3000 c.y. at $50 = $150,000	3150 c.y. at $50 = $157,500	5%
Labor:		
3000 c.y. at $5 = $15,000	3150 c.y. at $7 = $22,050	47%

The risk in the category of *equipment costs and rentals* is one of judgment applicable to the selection of the type of equipment for a particular operation and also an over-optimistic assessment of the production output per hour or day to be anticipated from that piece of equipment. Also, a badly organized project often has items of equipment laying idle for long periods but still subject to rental costs.

8.2 Material Prices

Material prices are obtained from the following sources:

1. Quotations from material manufacturers and/or building supply companies. These quotations may be in the form of signed letters, or are telephoned into the contractor's office and (usually) confirmed in writing.
2. Catalog or price lists distributed to general contractors and up-dated periodically.

Whenever possible, and particularly for those materials where large quantities are applicable, competitive quotations should be solicited from a number of suppliers. Standard price lists are quite satisfactory for the less contentious items, but are usually higher than quotations prepared for a specific project.

The contractor's principal risk in the material prices in a bid has already been identified as relating to the estimated quantities. Other risks could evolve from lack of proper understanding or interpretation of the quotations (however bona fide) from reliable supply or manufacturing companies. The following are some points to be considered when checking quotations:

1. Ensure that the material quoted is in accordance with the specification requirements. If the specification for a particular material contains an amount

of technical data relative to weights, gauges, dimensions, and similar matters, and the quotation also contains such information, a careful check is essential to ensure that the data are the same in both instances; it is important to know that the apple as *quoted* is the apple as *specified!* Very often a specification will supplement the data with a manufacturer's catalog or model number, and even if this number is identified and repeated in a quotation, there could still be a problem if there are variations in the supporting technical data. The best thing to do here is to query both the architect and the supplier to clear up the discrepancy.

2. Check that the material will be delivered to the project site. Any wording other than "FOB Job Site" suggests that additional amounts for freight should be considered.
3. Check the supplier's time limitations on the placing of the order. The knowledge that a quotation is "good for 30 days" provides small comfort to an estimator if the bid itself has to remain open for the owner's acceptance for 60 days or longer. A query should be made immediately to the supplier; most firms are prepared to be reasonable about this matter when the problem is explained.
4. Check the quotation regarding sales or other taxes. Certain types of projects (hospitals, schools, and other public buildings) are often exempt from certain taxes, and the supplier should be queried if the status of the taxes in the price has not been clarified in the quotation.

B.X.N.W. BUILDING SUPPLIES CO. LTD.
PORT CRAGFIELD, ONTARIO

MATERIAL PRICES

Masonry Materials		
Concrete block:	*Price per Piece*	
	Standard	*Lightweight*
4 in. (10 cm)	.44	.48
6 in. (15 cm)	.50	.54
8 in. (20 cm)	.56	.60
10 in. (25 cm)	.70	.74
12 in. (30 cm)	.76	.80
Masonry Cement	\$2.66 per 66⅔-lbs. bag	
Dovetail brick anchors	\$120.00 per 1000 pieces	
Flashing (copper coated paper 2 oz.)	\$28.00 per 100 ft.^{2}	
Premixed grout	\$25.00 per 55-lbs. bag	
Rigid polystyrene insulation:		
1½ × 16 × 96 in.	\$5.75 per sheet	
2 × 16 × 96 in.	\$6.90 per sheet	
Brick sand	\$1.00 per 100-lbs. bag	
All prices include federal sales tax.		
Provincial sales tax extra.		

Figure 8.1.

Z-Y-X CONCRETE SUPPLY CO.

Ready-mix concrete delivered to the site.

Strength		Price
3000 p.s.i. (20 MPa)	-	$48.00 per c.y.
4000 p.s.i. (25 MPa)	-	$51.50 per c.y.
5000 p.s.i. (35 MPa)	-	$57.00 per c.y.

Extra for winter heating (November 1 to April 15)	-	$3.00 per c.y.
Extra for air entrainment	-	$1.50 per c.y.
Calcium Chloride (2%)	-	$1.00 per c.y.

Underload Charges:

5 c.y. and less than 7 c.y.	-	$10.00 per load
4 c.y. and less than 5 c.y.	-	$15.00 per load
3 c.y. and less than 4 c.y.	-	$20.00 per load
Less than 3 c.y.	-	$25.00 per load

Above prices are inclusive of Federal and Provincial Sales Taxes

Figure 8.2.

5. Check all the small print at the bottom or reverse side of a quotation for any other pertinent qualifications; these are often the "spooks" that will haunt the contractor later if not challenged and dispelled at the time of the bid.

Figure 8.1 shows a typical quotation from a building supply company covering a miscellany of items. Figure 8.2 is an example of a quotation from a ready-mix supplier.

8.3 *Labor Units*

Few general contractors would disagree with the statement that the estimated cost of labor in a bid signals the biggest exposure to risk. The only item that the contractor can predict with certainty is the prevailing hourly rate that has to be paid to the company's on-site labor force. Large projects of long duration will also require speculation regarding labor rate escalations that may occur during that period.

As already stressed in Section 8.1, the contractor is not only vulnerable to the risk of an error in the quantities (although proper adherence to good quantity surveying practices will temper this risk), but also to "tight" unit rates that reflect an output that may not *(or cannot)* be achieved. Cost reporting systems can provide useful information regarding the actual unit rates established on the site, but these unit prices are only *historical data;* they are not in the same category as material prices in a signed quotation from a supplier or a subcontractor. They are beneficial guides for subsequent estimating, but they carry no guarantee and they also need to be properly understood and interpreted. Also, where actual costs appear excessively high or low, the perennial problem of *misallocation of costs* has to be considered as a possibility.

An experienced estimator's leading question regarding a reported unit price for labor is always, What was the current labor rate at the time? Two similar projects might report a unit cost of $6.75 per cubic yard for placing concrete to foundation walls, but if these projects took place in different regions, or at different times, then the hourly labor rates would most likely also be different. Assuming the current labor rate in Project A is $12/hour, and on Project B it is $13/hour, the output per man-hour at each project would be:

$$\text{Project A} = \frac{\$6.75}{\$12} = 0.56 \text{ man-hour per cubic yard}$$

$$\text{Project B} = \frac{\$6.75}{\$13} = 0.52 \text{ man-hour per cubic yard}$$

Project B achieved a better output per man-hour for this labor item than did Project A. If Project A had attained the *same output* as the other project, the unit price reported would have been $6.24 ($12 × 0.52) and not $6.75.

Estimating the cost of labor is basically the assessment of the quantity of work that can be achieved by a worker or a crew of workers within a specific time span. The factors to be considered in making this assessment would include:

1. The size and mix (e.g., tradesmen, helpers, etc.) of the work crew.
2. The time duration to be considered (e.g., hour, day, week, etc.).
3. The total hourly (or daily) cost of the crew.
4. The anticipated output of work in that time duration.

Example: Crew composition: 6 laborers
Hourly rate per laborer: $13
Time duration: 8 hours (48 man-hours)
Productivity for 8 hours: 160 units

$$\text{Unit rate: } \frac{48 \times \$13.00}{160} = \$3.90 \text{ per unit}$$

This could also be expressed as a man-hour factor:

$$\frac{48 \text{ man-hours}}{160 \text{ units}} = 0.3 \text{ man-hour per unit}$$

With this information, an estimator can establish a unit price by multiplying the hourly labor rate by the man-hour factor.

Example: Labor rate = \$13.75
Unit rate = \$13.75 × 0.3 = \$4.13 per unit

Competency (and also *confidence!*) in computing the estimated labor costs is attained by the development of the following knowledge and skills:

1. Familiarity with the methods and systems used for the various construction operations and, most important, an appreciation of how such methods and systems relate to and influence costs.
2. Analytical on-the-spot observation of construction operations, checking crew sizes, equipment, and approximate assessment of output.
3. Understanding the factors that limit productivity in some items of work while promoting it in other items. For example, placing concrete to large repetitive floor slabs in a multistoried structure can be organized to provide a high output per man-hour, while the footings in the substructure will be limited to a much lower output however economically the work is planned and carried out.

A label with the one word "Experience" can be affixed to all those three prerequisites, but *how to channel that experience effectively* is equally, if not more, important when estimating the cost of labor. This applies also to how such methods relate to and influence costs. Possessing know-how about the methods of specific construction operations is one thing, but this know-how is useless to estimators if they cannot translate it into the language of costs.

Some other factors that influence productivity are:

1. *Climatic conditions:* Inclement weather can seriously impair productivity, and the time of the year in which certain work will be carried out must be taken into consideration, as well as the geographical location of the project. Northern Manitoba in January provides a different open-air work environment from California during the same month, yet the working conditions in July for *both* regions might not be dissimilar. Extremes in heat or cold, rain, snow, gusting winds, all have an effect on workers' output and proficiency.
2. *Labor conditions:* In certain regions there may exist a shortage of skilled or semiskilled construction tradespeople; also the experience of those workers who are available may be limited to small projects with less scheduling pressures and requirements than the larger jobs. Both factors can retard productivity, and estimators should investigate the local labor situation when bidding on projects in new and unfamiliar locations.
3. *Supervision:* Intelligent planning and good organization of a project always open the way to optimum output from the labor force, and these elements are provided by the superintendents, project managers, foremen, and other supervisory personnel. Inefficient supervision will usually result in bad planning accompanied by a drop in productivity, but construction companies do not usually retain inefficient supervisors on their payrolls for a very

long period! Many successful contracting companies adhere to the philosophy that it is foolhardy to bid on a project if there is no experienced superintendent available for the job. The situation could exist, however, of the availability of a seasoned superintendent with an excellent company record of profitable projects, but without experience on the kind of building for which the bid is being prepared. ("Jake's topnotch at schools or hospitals; no one to touch him! But he's never done a large industrial plant like this.") In this case a factor for supervision might be advisable, but this is a decision that should be made after discussion with company management. Generally, estimators should think positively and base their estimates on the ready availability of first-class supervision.

One essential truth to be hammered into young estimators when they first start pricing estimates is that they are not expected to accurately predict the actual field unit cost down to the last cent for each item in the bid. If and when there is an exact match between estimated and actual unit rates, it is often due to either coincidence (luck!) or some fancy "juggling" with figures!

There will usually be a fluctuation of rises and falls in all the unit rates, but everyone—field personnel, management, and estimators—always look hopefully toward the final cost as representation of a victory of the falls (cost underruns) over the rises (cost overruns).

Another harsh truth for neophyte estimators is that, in the opinion of the field personnel who have to build the structure, *all* estimates (and estimators) fall into two categories: bad! and very bad!! The distinction between these two categories is that, in the first case the estimated cost was met or improved upon *only by the good organization and hard work of the site personnel;* in the second case the estimated cost was so ridiculous and impossible to achieve that it was not the fault of the field staff that money was lost!

These statements may seem facetious, but one point should be emphasized seriously: the category designated in the field as "bad" pinpoints the target at which estimators should be aiming when computing prices. This target is the maximum output that is possible, feasible, and reasonable for any given operation, dependent on the necessary ingenuity and effort of the work crew. An experienced estimator attempting to assess the quantity of units (for whatever) that could be installed by a worker in an 8-hour day would consider the options this way:

- 160 units: reasonable, quite possible
- 200 units: optimum, not impossible
- more than 200 units: unreasonable, unrealistic

With the exception of uncontentious items of small quantities, estimators would usually opt for the second option as the target to be considered. The name of the game is always to be competitive, but at the same time to be also practical and constructive. After analyzing previous costs, preparing some price buildups, and testing the results by discussion with other people (estimators, managers, superintendents, etc.), the estimator may decide that 190 units per 8-hour day is the best that could be achieved, and the unit price would be based on that output factor.

Estimators should always attempt to strip unit costs back to this essential factor of output. To retain a catalog memory of hundreds of unit prices for various items can be very impressive (and also useful if suddenly requested to provide some quick "ball-park" guesstimates in a short amount of time), but it is more important to know what these units actually mean and what items of work they actually include. Two estimators from different companies talking "shop" might remark that $10 a cubic yard is a good average unit price for placing concrete to a floor slab on earth, but the system in the one company might be to include the screeding and troweling of the slab in that unit, and the second company's system might treat these operations as separate cost items; in other words, apples are not being compared with apples! One company's units might include equipment costs, and the second company might consider these under separate headings.

Where labor unit prices are concerned, estimators must seek out the man-hour productivity that lies behind them. Mention was made of the usefulness of on-the-spot analytical time and method studies. These studies can pinpoint the methods used, the crew composition, and the output accomplished within a certain time. Experienced estimators form the habit of doing cost checks like this anytime they see a particular operation in progress. Any number of "sidewalk superintendents" can gawk incomprehensibly through an opening in a hoarding at what appears to be a chaotic muddle of men, dirt, and equipment; estimators discipline themselves to quickly identify the various activities, to note the number of workers involved and the equipment used, and to assess the quantity performed in the time duration of the observation.

A more constructive observation on-the-spot method and system, covering a time duration of 4 hours, would be reported down as follows:

Operation:	Place concrete to suspended slab and beams
Method:	Mobile crane and buggies
Crew:	8 laborers, 1 foreman
Equipment:	Mobile crane
Buggies:	4 hand-powered type

Average time cycle for buggying (loading, wheeling, depositing, reloading) = 3 min
Concrete delivered by ready-mix truck: 8 cubic yard capacity
Number of trucks observed in 4-hour period = 10 = 80 cubic yards.

This type of record is useful for future estimating purposes, but it must be remembered that this particular observation study covered only 4 hours of the whole operation and did not reflect any initial setting up time, cleanup at completion, and any lost-time factors; it may also have been taken at the peak period and did not reflect a possible lower *average output*. The productivity reported for that specific time cycle was 80 cubic yards averaging 20 cubic yards per hour. An adjustment factor would be necessary to reduce the *optimum output* down to the *average output* for the entire operation. Assume this factor to be 10 percent; the observed output would be modified to

	80 cubic yards
Less 10%	8
Average	72-18 cubic yards per hour

This information can be reduced to a single man-hour per unit factor:

$$\frac{9 \text{ man-hours}}{18 \text{ cubic yards}} = 0.5 \text{ man-hour per cubic yard}$$

With a current laborer's rate of $13/hour, the estimated unit price per cubic yard would be $13 × 0.5 = $6.50. Considerable time can be saved if these man-hour factors are used for pricing rather than building up a detailed analysis in the same manner as the observation report, particularly if only a single category of workers is being considered (e.g., laborers).

What about a mixed crew? Consider a crew of six carpenters and two laborers, or eight bricklayers with five helpers—the tradesmen's rates are higher than the laborer's rates of pay. Except for large, highly contentious items in an estimate, when the prices should be tested by using two or three different approaches or methods to compute the costs, it will generally be sufficiently realistic and accurate to consider the tradesmen-to-laborers mix in a crew as coming under these categories:

1. Ratio of 1:1: one tradesman, one helper
2. Ratio of 2:1: Two tradesmen, one helper (or four tradesmen, two helpers, and so on). This could also be expressed as two-thirds skilled labor, one-third semiskilled.
3. Ratio of 3:1: Three tradesman, one helper (or six tradesmen, two helpers, etc.) This could be expressed as three-quarters skilled labor, one-quarter semiskilled.

There are obviously more possible mixes than the three stated, but for estimating purposes these will be sufficient; a more in-depth price buildup would be recommended for a large item of work with excessive quantities where every cent in a unit rate could make a significant change in the total cost. To use single man-hour production factors for mixed crews requires the establishment of *composite rates*.

Example: Tradesman's rate = \$15/hour
Laborer's rate = \$13/hour

The composite hourly rate for the ratios stated would be:

$$1{:}1 = \frac{15 + 13}{2} = \$14/\text{hour}$$

$$2{:}1 = \frac{2 \times 15}{3} + \frac{13}{3} = \$14.33/\text{hour}$$

$$3{:}1 = \frac{3 \times 15}{4} + \frac{13}{4} = \$14.50/\text{hour}$$

To compute the unit rate cost of an operation where a crew of, say, four carpenters and two helpers would be reasonable, the estimator would identify an appropriate man-hour/output factor and multiply the factor by a composite rate for a 2:1 ratio.

Estimators should build up their own tables of labor factors for the various construction operations. The source of information to prepare these tables would be observation studies, cost reports, or discussions with field supervisors, foremen, tradesmen, and the like. There are many excellent books on the market that also provide much useful data, and some are listed in the Introduction.

The following examples illustrate different formats for these tables, all based on formwork to foundation walls, and all assuming the same output and crew composition.

Method 1: Output per Specific Time Cycle

Specific time:	8 hours	
Crew:	2 carpenters at \$14	= \$28
	1 helper at \$13	= \$13
		\$41
Average output:	175 square feet	

Computation: $\frac{\$41 \times 8}{175} = \$1.87$ per s.f.

2 Carp @ 30/HR = 480
÷ 320 S/F = 1.50 ¢

Method 2: Time Cycle per Specific Quantity

Specific quantity:	100 ft.^{2}
Average time:	9.2 hours for carpenter
	4.6 hours for helper

Computation: $\frac{(9.2 \times \$14) + (4.6 \times \$13)}{100} = \$1.88/\text{ft.}^2$

2.5 HRS × 30 × 2 = 150
÷ 100 = 1.50 ¢

Method 3: Man-hour Factor/Composite Rate

Using data from Method 2:	
Crew ratio:	2:1 (two carpenters, one helper)
Composite rate:	$\frac{2}{3} \times \$14 = \$\ 9.33$
	$\frac{1}{3} \times \$13 = \underline{\$\ 4.33}$
	$13.66 (say, $13.67/hour)
Man-hour factor:	$\dfrac{13.8 \text{ (total man-hours)}}{100} = .138 \text{ man-hour/ft.}^2$
	(using composite rate for 2:1 ratio)
Computation:	$.138 \times \$13.67 = \$1.88$

It will be noted that there is a difference of one cent between the unit price in method 1 and methods 2 and 3, which is not significant unless it was to be applied to an exceedingly large quantity.

Estimators can prepare tables or price analyses in any format they choose or prefer. The advantage of method 3 is that a lot of data can be included in a small space, and these reference tables, once compiled, enable estimators to make quick computations. If these man-hour factors are further divided and grouped into categories according to low, average, or optimum productivity, the estimator can exercise judgment on each item according to its merits. Using the same example of formwork to a foundation wall, the table would show the item in this fashion:

			Productivity		
Item	*Crew Ratio*	*Per*	*Average*	*High Decrease by:*	*Low Increase by:*
Formwork to foundation walls	2:1	$ft.^2$	.167	10–20%	10–15%

Note: The man-hour factors, whether designated average, high, or low, are all-inclusive of setup time, peak output, and down time. The categories low, average, and high refer to the conditions imposed by the influences of repetitive work, climate, supervision, and so on. The estimator will take these factors into consideration and use judgment in regards to the adjustments. In the example shown, the judgment might be to consider a factor between average and high, and the *mean* of these two factors would be used.

Unit rates given in project cost reports can be used to calculate these man-hour factors, but it must be stressed that these unit rates do not provide the information regarding a mixed trade crew; this can only be obtained by actual observation or after discussion with the site personnel. Man-hour factors derived from these costs can be achieved by dividing the hourly rate of the *principal trade* into the unit price:

Example: Unit price in cost report = \$2.25 per ft.^{2}
Carpenter's rate = \$14

$$\text{Computation: } \frac{\$2.25}{\$14} = .16 \text{ carpenter hours/ft.}^2$$

If this factor is to be used in future estimating, it must only be applied to the *current hourly rate for a carpenter*. If the applicable rate for a carpenter is \$14.75, then the revised unit rate will be \$14.75 × .16 = \$2.36. If a crew ratio was assumed as 2:1 and an existing composite rate established as \$13.50, then the factor would be $\frac{\$2.25}{\$13.50} = .167$ man-hour per s.f. and this would be applied against the revised composite rate.

A contentious item with a large quantity, say several hundred thousand square feet of formwork or more than 5000 cubic yards of concrete, should be first computed with the man-hour factor per square foot or cubic yard, and then tested with other methods such as:

1. Preparing a detailed price buildup for a typical day, assessing crew requirements, output, and other factors.
2. Calculating the cost of the completion operation, say for a typical "pour," from start to finish, including setting up, cleanup, and so on.

These check methods will probably produce different unit prices; the estimator is then confronted with a decision-making process as to which to select for use in the bid. Discussion with other people (estimators, managers, superintendents) will be required.

The hourly rates used for pricing labor items in a bid should be the *basic* rate (i.e., exclusive of labor premiums such as unemployment insurance, vacation pay, welfare). These vary from trade to trade and region to region. They are best calculated as a percentage to be added to either the: 1. Total labor cost of each trade summary (i.e., excavation, concrete, etc.), or 2. Total labor cost for complete project as shown in the main bid summary.

The advantage of method 2 is that the estimator has only to make this adjustment *once* rather than five or six times on the individual trade summaries, with the chance of forgetting to do it on one of them. Also method 2 permits the use of a specific item on a standard printed general estimate summary, which would eliminate the possibility of the item being overlooked.

8.4 Equipment

Certain items of construction equipment may be contractor-owned and other equipment rented as and when required. The examples given in this book will be based on the assumption that *rental rates* will apply to *both categories* (i.e., rented or owned).

Most construction equipment companies distribute lists or books outlining the equipment available, accompanied by a schedule of rental rates on an hourly, daily, weekly, or monthly basis. (*Note:* Many companies list a *four-week* rental in lieu of monthly rate, and estimators should not confuse the two as being the same thing.)

The following are some points that should be checked when assessing an equipment company's schedule of rental rates:

1. Do the rates include operators where applicable (e.g., excavation equipment, cranes)?
2. Do the rates include for repairs or fuel?
3. What is the minimum rental period? (This is usually a minimum of 4 hours.)
4. Are there any additional pickup and/or delivery charges?
5. What accessories are included or will be an additional charge (hoses, conduits, etc.)?
6. What taxes are included or must be added?

Making the best possible decision regarding the choice of equipment for specific uses on the project is something estimators should not hesitate to discuss with job superintendents and other field personnel. Practical experience can foster good advice and second or third (or fourth) opinions are invaluable, especially from people who are continually exposed to these matters. Sometimes, and particularly if opinions differ greatly about the pros and cons of certain equipment, the estimators may have to make the final decision themselves. Also, the equipment companies can provide a lot of data regarding the suitability of certain equipment for the various operations, output, fuel requirements, and so on. Most important, never base any decisions regarding equipment solely on the optimistic "rose-colored" statements in promotional literature! Production factors in such literature are often applicable to only peak periods of highly repetitive work under ideal conditions.

Sometimes before a decision is made regarding the choice of equipment, an analysis will be necessary showing comparative evaluation of costs. This particularly applies to items where the use of equipment could reduce the crew size and, at the same time, increase output, but estimators must convince themselves that the comparative cost will be economical.

Example: Placing concrete to concrete walls where it is not possible to chute directly from the ready-mix truck.

Method 1: Buggy the concrete into place.

Size of crew: 1 at truck
3 wheeling
1 vibrating
1 spading
Total: 6
Average output: 10 cubic yards/hour
Cost: 6 laborers at $11 = $66
3 buggies at $0.67 = $ 2
Total: $68
$68 ÷ 10 = $6.80 per cubic yard

Method 2: Place concrete with mobile crane and bucket directly into walls.

Size of crew: 1 at truck
1 vibrating
1 spading
Total: 3
Mobile crane (incl. operator, fuel, etc.) = $50
Average output = 16 cubic yards/hour
(peak period might be 20 to 25 cubic yards)
Costs: 3 laborers at $11 = $33
Mobile crane = $50
Total: $83
$83 ÷ 16 = $5.19 per cubic yard

Obviously, method 2 provides the most economical solution. Apart from cheaper unit cost for placing the concrete, the crane could also be used for hoisting reinforcing steel, formwork, and other items. When it is decided to perform all the main concrete placing items in the structure (that is, excluding floor toppings, equipment bases, curbs, etc.) with the use of a mobile crane, the crane cost should be computed on a monthly rental basis for the scheduled duration of the structural operations. This will be more accurate than assessing the rental period on the basis of hours per cubic yards of concrete.

8.5 Subcontractors' Unit Prices

Most subcontractors prepare lump-sum quotations for the work of their specific trades, but there are certain trades where some quotations should be anticipated as being submitted on a unit-price basis. These trades would include (but not necessarily be limited to):

Excavation and grading (including backfilling operations)
Asphalt paving and concrete curbs
Sodding and seeding
Concrete floor finishing

In some cases the subcontractors bid on this basis as a declared and fixed trade practice, but sometimes it is only lack of sufficient time to prepare a lump-sum quotation, or difficulties in procuring the drawings for take-off purposes, that prompt trade contractors to provide only unit rates for the work of their trades.

As has already been stated, the principal risk to general contractors with this type of quotation is the same as with material prices, that is, the possibility of a serious error in the quantities. However, with these unit prices there are some other hazards to be considered. Quotations for construction materials can be checked against the specification and the prices confirmed as representing the specified requirements. Unit prices for subtrade work usually include the cost of materials, equipment, and labor, and cannot always be so readily identified with the specifications.

Estimators should check closely with subcontractors as to what is and what is not included in their unit prices if they choose this method of submitting a quotation. For example, an excavation subcontractor who quotes a rate for bulk excavation may have to be queried regarding the disposal of the excavated material; does the rate include for trucking away, or for spreading on the site, or just "sidecasting"? Equally, unit rates for backfill operations should be explicit regarding compaction and that the fill material corresponds to what is demanded in the specification. Also, even if the subcontractor has been pressed for time to prepare a proper take-off and estimate, his unit prices should be received with caution if he cannot demonstrate that he has seen the drawings and properly read and understood the specification.

The subcontractor may query the general contractor regarding the quantities applicable to the items of work on which he intends to quote. This information should be given when requested, and even it if is not requested it is a good idea to check that the subcontractor is aware of the magnitude of the quantities involved. They do have an impact on the estimated rate; a postbid written confirmation from a subcontractor stating that a unit rate for "bulk excavation by machine" was applicable only to a *minimum quantity* of 100,000 cubic yards is unlikely to soothe the feelings of an estimator who has estimated the maximum quantity to be 70,000 cubic yards!

8.6 Examples of Pricing

The following chapter will provide examples of pricing the estimates for the various trade divisions already considered in the quantity take-off examples.

A schedule of man-hour/output factors is provided for each trade as background to the pricing demonstrated. Also, basic labor rates are provided for the applicable trades, which will remain consistent throughout the various examples; also, the additional payroll charges, fringe benefits, and the like, are shown.

9
Pricing the Estimate: Examples

9.1 *General*

The examples of pricing estimates of selected trades as demonstrated in the following pages are in accordance with the principles and methods discussed in the last chapter. The purpose is to display some of the options and methods an estimator would consider when determining unit rates that are competitive but also realistic.

The prices shown are applied to Imperial units, and appropriate factors are presented for conversion to metric units. Each specific trade specimen is supplemented by explanatory comments where some additional clarification appeared necessary.

The quotations from the various material suppliers are not illustrated; it is to be assumed that the material rates noted on the estimate sheets were the most competitive received from a number of suppliers. For the most part, the unit prices for labor are based on *average productivity per man-hour* as shown on supplied schedules; comment is made on operations where output might be above or below the average. For certain major items where large quantities and repetition of work prevail, a more in-depth analysis of the crew makeup and production is discussed in the supplementary comments for each trade section.

9.2 *Labor Rates*

The following are the hourly labor rates used to establish the unit prices and from which the composite rates are developed. Also shown are the various labor charges applicable to each trade. These include ***statutory labor charges*** (unemployment insurance, workmen's compensation, and so on) and some typical ***benefits*** as defined in union agreements according to trade and locality. The estimated unit costs reflect only the ***basic hourly rate for each trade;*** the labor burdens will be expressed as a premium percentage on the total estimated cost of labour.

Carpenter

Basic rate	$15.00
Vacation pay, 10%	1.50
Payroll charges, 9%	1.35
Welfare	0.65
Pension fund	0.60
Total projected rate	19.10
Basic rate	15.00
Total burdens	4.10

Premium on basic rate: 27.3%

Bricklayer

Basic rate	$14.50
Vacation pay, 10%	1.45
Payroll charges, 9%	1.31
Welfare	0.65
Pension fund	0.60
Total projected rate	18.51
Basic rate	14.50
Total burdens	4.01

Premium on basic rate: 27.6%

Laborer

Basic rate	$13.00
Vacation pay, 10%	1.30
Payroll charges, 9%	1.17
Pension fund	0.90
Training fund	0.10
Total projected rate	16.47
Basic rate	13.00
Total burdens	3.47

Premium on basic rate: 26.7%

Labor rates for other trades are noted on the estimate sheets where applicable.

9.3 Composite Labor Rates

The pricing examples include many items where mixed crews of tradesmen and helpers would be required. In these instances "composite rates" have been established and used. The schedules of man-hour factors (Section 9.4) show some suggested crew ratios on which the following composite rates are based.

1. *Crew ratio 1:1.* The composite rate will be the *average* of the aggregated rates of the tradesmen and helper:

Carpenter	$15
Laborer	13
Total	28
Composite rate = $14.00	

2. *Crew ratio 2:1.* The composite rate represents two-thirds of the tradesmen's rate plus one-third of the helper's rate:

Carpenter:	⅔ × 15	10.00
Laborer:	⅓ × 13	4.33
	Composite rate =	$14.33

3. *Crew ratio 3:1*

Carpenter:	¾ × 15	11.25
Laborer:	¼ × 13	3.25
	Composite rate =	$14.50

A word of caution: the anticipated productivity for each operation as expressed in terms of man-hours per unit of measurement is always related to the output by the principal tradesmen in the crew (e.g. carpenters, bricklayers, electricians). The helper's role is supportive to the work of the craftsmen; some operations require more support than others, which is indicated by the crew ratios. However, in some regions, union agreements demand certain operations of work to be performed by *craftsmen,* which in other areas would be performed by *helpers;* stripping of formwork would be a good example. Normally, the greater proportion of carpenters in a crew signifies a higher output of production; but where additional carpenters are only *replacing* helpers or laborers, there will be no improvement in production. The additional cost of using carpenters in lieu of laborers increases the amount of the composite labor rate, but usually not more than about 2%.

A more significant factor to be considered is the hourly cost of a foreman, where one is required. Most construction companies include the foreman's time as a direct labor cost, and the composite rates would require adjustment to reflect the foreman's hourly rate. The suggested adjustment factors to be applied to the composite rates are:

1. *Working foreman* (i.e., one who will also be using his tools): add 1 to 2 percent to the composite rate, or divide the *extra* hourly cost of the foreman by the number of workers in the crew, *including* the foreman.

Example:	Foreman's premium rate	\$1.50/hour
	Total crew	8 people
	Premium on composite rate	\$1.50/8 = \$0.19

2. *Nonworking (general) foreman:* increase the composite rate by 12 to 15 percent, or divide the full hourly rate paid to the foreman by the number of workers in a crew *excluding the foreman*.

Example:	Foreman's rate	\$16.50/hour
	Total crew	7 people
	Premium on composite rate	\$16.50/7 = \$2.35

Note: More than likely the foreman would be responsible for the supervision of more than one crew, in which case his time could be spread over a greater number of workers, reducing the premium on the composite rate.

9.4 Schedules of Man-hour Factors

The following schedules show the man-hour factors applicable to a series of construction operations for selected trades. These are provided to illustrate the data on which the estimated labor units in the pricing examples are founded, and also as a suggested format for estimators to produce within their individual company organizations to be based on cost records and analytical on-site observations.

The factors shown against each operation are based on *average output* per man-hour. Where production output could be anticipated to be greater or less than the average applicable percentages, adjustment factors are shown. The supplementary comments following each trade schedule define the conditions whereby production would be either improved or retarded.

The suggested crew ratios are shown to establish the appropriate composite rate for each item. If different crew compositions are contemplated, not only will the composite rate be revised but consideration should also be given to the man-hour factor. As a general rule of thumb, if the principal trade proportion *increases*, the man-hour factor could be *reduced* to allow for greater output; however, this would usually be a very nominal adjustment of less than 2 percent.

Crew ratios are not shown for those trade divisions where the work will be performed solely by laborers, excavation and concrete placing, for example. (In certain areas union agreements require a premium on the basic rate for concrete and other operations.) Also, some trade sections are based on using the full-hourly rate for a carpenter, and allowance for the supportive work by a helper is included in the man-hour factor. The adjustment to a composite rate was not considered to be significant for these items. The man-hour factors include for unloading and handling of materials, and also allowances for lost or nonproductive time.

TABLE 9.1 Schedule of Man-hour Factors: Excavation and Fill

Metric Conversion Factors	*Multiply by:*
Linear feet to meters =	3.28
Square feet to square meters =	10.764
Cubic yards to cubic meters =	1.308

				Adjust for Higher or Lower Productivity	
Item	*Per (unit)*	*Crew Ratio*	*Average Productivity*	*High, Reduce Factor by:*	*Low, Increase Factor by:*
1. Hand excavation, light soil	yd.^{3}	Lab.	2.3	—	20–30%
2. Hand excavation, medium soil	yd.^{3}	Lab.	2.7	—	25–35%
3. Hand excavation, heavy soil	yd.^{3}	Lab.	4.2	—	25–35%
4. Hand trim bottom of excavations, earth	ft.^{2}	Lab.	0.007	—	25–35%
5. Hand trim bottom of excavations, shale	ft.^{2}	Lab.	0.023	—	25–35%
6. Hand trim to spread footings, earth	ft.^{2}	Lab.	0.018	—	—
7. Hand trim to spread footings, shale	ft.^{2}	Lab.	0.07	—	—
8. Hand rock excavation	yd.^{3}	Lab.	5.6	—	20–25%
9. Place and compact backfill	yd.^{3}	Lab.	0.48	—	20–25%
10. Trim and compact backfill placed by machine	yd.^{3}	Lab.	0.18	20–30%	25–35%

TABLE 9.1 *(continued)*

Metric Conversion Factors	*Multiply by:*
Linear feet to meters =	3.28
Square feet to square meters =	10.764
Cubic yards to cubic meters =	1.308

				Adjust for Higher or Lower Productivity	
Item	*Per (unit)*	*Crew Ratio*	*Average Productivity*	*High, Reduce Factor by:*	*Low, Increase Factor by:*
11. Underfloor fill, stone	yd.^{3}	Lab.	0.65	15–25%	25–35%
12. Underfloor fill, granular	yd.^{3}	Lab.	0.58	20–30%	25–35%
13. Weeping tile and fittings	ft.	Lab.	0.09	25–30%	25–35%
14. Bed and surround to weeping tile	yd.^{3}	Lab.	0.65	—	25–35%
15. Concrete sewer pipe and fittings (av. 6 in. dia.)	ft.	Lab.	0.16	—	—
16. Bed and surround to sewer pipe	yd.^{3}	Lab.	0.56	—	20–30%
17. Sand cushion on underfloor fill	yd.^{3}	Lab.	2.12	—	—

Notes:

1. Low productivity for hand excavation should be anticipated in small isolated items such as curbs and bases, work in wet weather conditions, and in deep excavations where double-handling of material would be necessary.
2. The hand-trimming items apply to the fine-grading of surfaces after excavation by machine. *Note:* If the estimate for this work is to be based on unit rates quoted by an excavation subcontractor, it will be advisable to ascertain if these unit rates include the cost of a *grade man* working along with the machine; if so, this item for trimming may not be necessary.
3. Item 9 refers to backfill that is almost wholly to be placed, spread, and compacted by hand. Small quantities, isolated locations, difficult access, and very often environmental conditions, all these circumstances will reduce output.
4. Item 10 refers to the spreading and compacting *by hand* of backfill materials pushed or dumped into place by machine. Large quantities of backfill at the exterior side of perimeter foundation walls could provide better-than-average production and also where moderate compaction requirements are specified.
5. The man-hour factors reflecting average output for the placing of underfloor fill are based on the material being wheeled into place with hand buggies or barrows, usually after the building is closed in. Where machine assistance is provided, the man-hour factors would be reduced.
6. The factor for the placing of weeping tile includes for any necessary wrapping with building paper.

TABLE 9.2 Schedule of Man-hour Factors: Perimeter Shoring and Underpinning

Metric Conversion Factors	*Multiply by:*
Linear feet to meters =	3.28
Square feet to square meters =	10.764
Cubic yards to cubic meters =	1.308

Item	*Per (unit)*	*Crew Ratio*	*Average Productivity*
1. Place steel walers, struts, etc.	ton	2:1	19.50
2. Wood lagging	ft.^{2}	Lab.	0.20
3. Remove wood lagging	ft.^{2}	Lab.	0.16
4. Sand fill behind lagging	yd.^{3}	Lab.	1.75
5. Concrete fill to H-piles	yd.^{3}	Lab.	3.65
6. Pockets for rakers, formwork	ft.^{2}	2:1	0.28
7. Pockets for rakers, concrete	yd.^{3}	Lab.	0.41

TABLE 9.3 Schedule of Man-hour Factors: Demolition

Metric Conversion Factors	*Multiply by:*
Linear feet to meters =	3.28
Square feet to square meters =	10.764
Cubic yards to cubic meters =	1.308

Item	*Per (unit)*	*Crew Ratio*	*Average Productivity*
1. Break up and remove interior masonry	ft.^{3}	Lab.	0.17
2. Break up and remove exterior masonry	ft.^{3}	Lab.	0.19
3. Strip existing roofing and flashings	ft.^{2}	Lab.	0.04
4. Remove plaster ceilings	ft.^{2}	Lab.	0.03
5. Remove acoustic ceilings	ft.^{2}	Lab.	0.02
6. Break up and remove terrazzo	ft.^{2}	Lab.	0.08
7. Break up and remove glazed wood partitions	ft.^{2}	Lab.	0.06
8. Remove existing doors and frames	ea.	Lab.	2.60
9. Remove existing windows	ea.	Lab.	3.50

TABLE 9.3 *(Continued)*

		Metric Conversion Factors	*Multiply by:*
		Linear feet to meters =	3.28
		Square feet to square meters =	10.764
		Cubic yards to cubic meters =	1.308
Item	*Per (unit)*	*Crew Ratio*	*Average Productivity*
10. Remove counter and cupboard units	ft.	Lab.	0.95
11. Break up and remove concrete	$ft.^3$	Lab.	0.32
12. Load debris into trucks or containers	$yd.^3$	Lab.	0.86
13. Remove metal roof or floor decks	$ft.^2$	Lab.	0.03
14. Remove resilient tile and base	$ft.^2$	Lab.	0.03
15. Dust screens, fabricate and erect	$ft.^2$	Carp	0.07
16. Dust screens, relocate	$ft.^2$	Carp	0.06

Notes on Pricing: Earthwork

The unit prices for machine excavation are based on the table of factors in Table 9.4 as applied to the following equipment rental rates:

1½ $yd.^3$ shovel	$57/hour (fuel and operator included)
¾ $yd.^3$ shovel	$52/hour (fuel and operator included)
½ $yd.^3$ shovel	$47/hour (fuel and operator included)
Bulldozer	$50/hour (fuel and operator included)
Trucks (tandem 9 $yd.^3$ bank measure)	$30/hour (fuel and operator included)

Float charges = $160 for a maximum of 4 hr.

The item for mass excavation to the building is computed as follows:

Using a 1½ $yd.^3$ shovel and assuming an average productivity of 50 $yd.^3$/hour:

Shovel	$57 × 1.15 =	$ 65
Trucks	$30 × 3 =	90
		$155

÷ 50 $yd.^3$ = $3.10/$yd.^3$

PAGE 1 OF 1

GENERAL ESTIMATE

PROJECT Research Centre LABOUR RATES Lab. $13.00 QUANTITIES B.E.W.

ESTIMATE NO 27/82 EXTENSIONS J.M. CHECKED

TRADE SECTION 02200 - Earthwork DATE PRICED N.G.

DESCRIPTION	QUANTITY	UNIT	MATERIAL U.P.	MATERIAL TOTAL	LABOUR U.P.	LABOUR TOTAL	TOTAL
Strip topsoil (av. 6") & Stockpile on site	350	c.y.	3.00	1050		✓	1050
Bulk Excavation to Building (2 mile haul)	4104	c.y.	3.18	13051		✓	13051
Trench Excavation to Foundations	764	c.y.	5.00	3820		✓	3820
Excavation for Interior Column Footings	160	c.y.	5.00	800		✓	800
" " Interior Trenches (Mechanical Trade)	554	c.y.	5.00	2770		✓	2770
Hand Trim to Surface (After Machine Excavation)	12479	s.f.		✓	0.09	1123	1123
Hand Trim to Trench Bottoms	2346	s.f.		✓	0.23	540	540
Hand Trim to Interior Col. Footings	80	s.f.		✓	0.23	18	18
Backfill Perimeter Foundation Walls (Excav. Material)	993	c.y.	3.00	2979	2.35	2334	5313
" " " " (Imported Granular)	604	c.y.	7.00	4228	2.35	1419	5647
Backfill Int. Col. Footings " "	186	c.y.	7.00	1302	2.35	437	1739
Backfill Mech. Trenches	665	c.y.	7.00	4655	6.25	4156	8811
Stone Fill to Underside of Concrete Slab	280	c.y.	12.50	3500	8.45	2366	5866
Weeping Tile - 6" dia. (Perforated Plastic)	209	l.f.	1.50	314	1.17	245	559
Weeping Tile - Extra for Special Fittings	10	pcs	10.00	100		✓	100
Pea Gravel Surround to Weeping Tile	154	c.y.	13.00	2002	7.30	1124	3126
Equipment Rentals - Bulldozer (Placing Backfill)	2442	c.y.	1.64	4005		✓	4005
- Compaction Equipment	2	mos.	350.00	700		✓	700
				45276		13762	59038

Figure 9.1.

Multiplying this unit by the total estimated quantity:

$$
\begin{array}{lr}
4003 \text{ yd.}^3 \times \$3.10 = & \$12{,}409 \\
\text{Add float charges} & \underline{320} \\
 & \$12{,}729 \\
\div\ 4003 = \$3.18/\text{yd.}^3 &
\end{array}
$$

The following computation applies to the three items of excavation for footings and mechanical services. It is assumed the same 1½ yd.^{3} shovel will be used but the hourly productivity is now assessed as 25 yd.^{3}:

$$
\begin{array}{llr}
\text{Shovel} & \$57 \times 1.15 = & \$\ 65 \\
\text{Trucks} & \$30 \times 2 \quad = & \underline{60} \\
 & & \$125 \\
\div\ 25 = \$5/\text{yd.}^3 & &
\end{array}
$$

The estimated unit rate for placing the backfill with a bulldozer is computed as follows:

$$
\begin{array}{l}
\text{Total rental period} = 2 \text{ weeks} = 80 \text{ hours} \\
@\ \$50/\text{hr} = \$4{,}000 \div 2{,}442 \text{ yd.}^3 \\
\quad = \$1.64/\text{yd.}^3
\end{array}
$$

Note that a quantity of excavated material has to be retained for backfilling to perimeter foundation walls. The quantities and unit price for excavation

TABLE 9.4 Machine Excavation

Probable Output/ Hour (yd.^{3})	Equipment Hours (incl. loss time factor)	Number of Trucks per Hour (Avg. speed 15 MPH) 1-Mile Haul	2-Mile Haul	3-Mile Haul
20–50	1.15	2	3	4
60–90	1.15	3	4	5
100–115	1.15	4	5	7
115–125	1.15	5	6	8
130–150	1.15	5	7	10

Note: The factors given provide for loading time and depositing at dump.

Example: Assume a production rate of 100 yd.^{3}/hour, using a 1½-yd.^{3} shovel; the excavated material is to be hauled to a dump 2 miles from the site.

$$
\begin{array}{lrr}
\text{Shovel} & 1.15 \text{ hr. at } \$57 = & \$65 \\
\text{Trucks} & 5 \text{ hr. at } \$30 = & \underline{150} \\
 & & \$215 \\
\div\ 100 = \$2.15/\text{yd.}^3 & &
\end{array}
$$

included the hauling away of this material, and it has been assumed that this unit price would also cover the cost of hauling it to and from a stockpile. The material unit rate against this item is for the cost of digging and hauling the material from the stockpile.

Labor Costs. In this example all the items are based on the man-hour factors reflecting *average* productivity. Medium soil conditions are anticipated. The items for backfill are based on the material being pushed into place by the bulldozer, with trimming and compaction performed by hand, with the exception of the pipe trenches where the backfill is entirely hand-placed and compacted.

TABLE 9.5 Schedule of Man-hour Factors: Concrete Placing and Finishing

Metric Conversion Factors	*Multiply by:*
Linear Feet to Meters =	3.28
Square Feet to Square Meters =	10.764
Cubic Yards to Cubic Meters =	1.308

			Adjust for Higher or Lower Productivity	
Item	*Per (unit)*	*Average Productivity*	*High, Reduce Factor by:*	*Low, Increase Factor by:*
1. Isolated (column) footings	yd.^{3}	0.48	15–20%	25–35%
2. Pile and caisson caps	yd.^{3}	0.53	15–20%	25–35%
3. Wall footings	yd.^{3}	0.55	10–15%	25–35%
4. Foundation walls and pilasters (perimeter)	yd.^{3}	0.75	15–25%	25–35%
5. Foundation walls (interior)	yd.^{3}	0.78	15–25%	25–35%
6. Retaining walls	yd.^{3}	0.80	15–25%	25–35%
7. Columns and piers	yd.^{3}	0.96	15–20%	25–35%
8. Pits (walls and slabs)	yd.^{3}	0.85	—	—
9. Slabs-on-grade	yd.^{3}	0.54	20–30%	25–40%
10. Raft slabs	yd.^{3}	0.36	20–25%	—
11. Skim (mud) slab	yd.^{3}	0.80	—	—
12. Skim coat to underside of footings	yd.^{3}	0.95	—	—
13. Suspended slabs (slab and beam)	yd.^{3}	0.85	25–40%	15–30%
14. Suspended slabs (flat slab)	yd.^{3}	0.80	25–40%	20–35%

TABLE 9.5 *(Continued)*

Metric Conversion Factors	*Multiply by:*
Linear Feet to Meters =	3.28
Square Feet to Square Meters =	10.764
Cubic Yards to Cubic Meters =	1.308

			Adjust for Higher or Lower Productivity	
Item	*Per (unit)*	*Average Productivity*	*High, Reduce Factor by:*	*Low, Increase Factor by:*
15. Suspended slabs (metal pan/joist)	yd.^{3}	0.83	25–35%	20–35%
16. Slabs on V-rib forms	yd.^{3}	0.65	—	—
17. Miscellaneous (small) suspended slabs	yd.^{3}	1.20	—	—
18. Fill to metal deck	yd.^{3}	0.83	—	—
19. Isolated beams	yd.^{3}	0.80	—	—
20. Upstand beams	yd.^{3}	1.40	—	—
21. Floor toppings (separate)	yd.^{3}	1.45	—	25–35%
22. Floor toppings (monolithic)	yd.^{3}	1.86	—	30–40%
23. Fireproofing structural columns and beams	yd.^{3}	1.70	—	—
24. Stairs and landings	yd.^{3}	1.80	—	30–45%
25. Exterior walks	yd.^{3}	0.96	—	—
26. Equipment bases	yd.^{3}	2.80	—	30–50%
27. Interior curbs	yd.^{3}	1.65	10–15%	20–40%
28. Exterior curbs	yd.^{3}	0.86	15–20%	—
29. Shear and core walls	yd.^{3}	0.62	15–25%	—
30. Lightweight roof fill	yd.^{3}	1.70	—	—
31. Clean, patch, and rub exposed concrete surfaces (vertical)	ft.^{2}	0.053	5–10%	10–15%
32. Clean, patch and rub exposed concrete surfaces (horizontal)	ft.^{2}	0.042	5–10%	10–15%
33. Set anchor bolts (structural steel bases)	Pcs	0.75	—	—

TABLE 9.5 *(Continued)*

		Metric Conversion Factors		*Multiply by:*
		Linear Feet to Meters =		3.28
		Square Feet to Square Meters =		10.764
		Cubic Yards to Cubic Meters =		1.308
			Adjust for Higher or Lower Productivity	
Item	*Per (unit)*	*Average Productivity*	*High, Reduce Factor by:*	*Low, Increase Factor by:*
34a. Grout column base plates (not exceeding 24 in square)	Pcs	0.95	—	—
34b. Grout column base plates (exceeding 24 in square)	Pcs	1.50	—	—

Notes:

1. Better-than-average productivity in placing footings and foundation walls would be possible in conditions where the concrete could be chuted directly from the truck, and also with very large spread footings where almost the entire contents of the truck could be discharged into one, two, or at the most three footings.

2. Foundation walls that extend above grade would probably require the use of mobile cranes, and if the concrete is placed directly from the bucket into the forms, an improvement in average productivity could be anticipated.

3. Large-sized columns will provide better output than those with slender dimensions, particularly if placed with crane and bucket (as opposed to buggying into place).

4. Suspended slabs and beams will reflect the highest output per man-hour when the labor crew is supported by concrete-placing equipment such as a crane or concrete pump. Multistory buildings with repetitive slabs and providing large quantity "pours" will lend themselves to maximum output. The man-hour factors for average productivity are applicable to wheeling and placing with hand-propelled buggies. Thin slabs usually mean lower output per hour, as do slabs where the wheeling distance is greater than 80 feet.

5. Placing floor topping is not usually an operation that yields any great output, particularly if the partitions extend down to the structural slab, and the concrete topping has to be placed between the partition walls.

Notes on Pricing: Concrete

1. The ready-mix concrete prices are presumed to be the most competitive received from a number of suppliers. The premium charges for winter heat are applied to the quantities of items scheduled to be performed during the winter months. The item "miscellaneous charges" is a contingency amount to cover incidental charges for underloads and the like.

2. *Labor costs:* All items are priced on the basis of "average" productivity as noted on the man-hour schedules with the exception of the following:

Column footings: The total quantity for this item being very small the average factor has been increased by 35 percent.

$$0.48 \times 1.35 = .65 \text{ man-hour/yd.}^3$$
$$= \$8.45$$

PAGE ______ OF ______

GENERAL ESTIMATE

PROJECT Research Centre LABOUR RATES Lab. $13.00 QUANTITIES J.D.

ESTIMATE No 27/82 EXTENSIONS J.M. CHECKED ____

TRADE SECTION 03300 - Concrete DATE ______ PRICED N.B.G.

	DESCRIPTION	QUANTITY	UNIT	MATERIAL U.P.	MATERIAL TOTAL	LABOUR U.P.	LABOUR TOTAL	TOTAL
	Ready-Mix Materials:							
1.	3000 P.S.I. (25 MPa) - 3/4" Stone (5% Waste)	41	c.y.	48.00	1968			1968
2.	4000 P.S.I. (30 MPa) - 3/4" Stone (2% Waste)	1148	c.y.	51.50	59122			59122
3.	Lightweight Concrete	32	c.y.	59.00	1888			1888
	Premium Charges: Air Entrainment	1189	c.y.	1.15	1367			1367
	Winter Heat	300	c.y.	3.00	900			900
	Misc. Charges	Item			300			300
Strength Mix	Placing to:							
1	Isolated Column Footings	4	c.y.			8.45	34	34
1	Wall Footings	25	c.y.			9.65	241	241
2	Foundation Walls and Pilasters	153	c.y.			9.75	1492	1492
1	Piers (Pedestals) Below Grade	1	c.y.			17.00	17	17
2	Columns	18	c.y.			12.50	225	225
2	Suspended Slab (Flat Plate)	62	c.y.			10.40	645	645
2	Suspended Slab (Incl. Beams)	687	c.y.			8.32	5716	5716
3	Fill to Metal Deck (L/Wt. Conc.)	30	c.y.			22.00	660	660
2	Slab on Grade	204	c.y.			7.00	1428	1428
2	Stairs and Landings	2	c.y.			33.00	66	66
1	Equipment Pads (18 ea.)	2	c.y.			53.00	106	106
1	Fill to Metal Stair Pans (32 ea.)	39	c.f.			3.50	137	137
1	Sump Pits (Incl. Base and Walls)	5	c.y.			11.00	55	55
	Rub Exposed Conc. Surfaces - Walls and Columns	2847	s.f.	0.03	85	0.70	1993	2078
	" " " " - Soffits	2352	s.f.	0.03	71	0.55	1294	1365
	Asphalt Impregnated Expansion Joint - 6" wide x ½" thick	610	l.f.	0.36	220	0.47	287	507
	Grout Column Base Plate	1	ea.	12.00	12	15.00	15	27
	Misc. Runways, Scaffolds and Ladders	Item			500		1000	1500
	Concrete Placing Equipment:							
	Mobile Crane (25 tons)	200	hrs.	65.00	13000			13000
	Buggies (2 x 6 mos.)	12	mos.	85.00	1020			1020
	Vibrators (2 x 6 mos.)	12	mos.	175.00	2100			2100
					82553		15411	97964

Figure 9.2.

PAGE 1 OF 1

GENERAL ESTIMATE

PROJECT Research Centre LABOUR RATES ____ QUANTITIES J.D.

ESTIMATE Nº ____ EXTENSIONS J.M. CHECKED ____

TRADE SECTION 03300 Concrete Floor Finishing DATE ____ PRICED ✓

DESCRIPTION	QUANTITY	UNIT	MATERIAL U.P.	MATERIAL TOTAL	LABOUR U.P.	LABOUR TOTAL	TOTAL
Unit Prices by "L.P.N. Concrete Floors Ltd."							
Machine Trowel (Plain)	24,200	s.f.	0.18	4356		✓	4356
" " (Hardened)	2,352	s.f.	0.52	1223		✓	1223
Wood Float at Roof	10,000	s.f.	0.12	1200		✓	1200
Membrane Curing	36,522	s.f.	0.04	1461		✓	1461
Finish to Equipment Bases (Hand Trowel)	79	s.f.	0.45	36		✓	36
" " Sump Pit Base " "	81	s.f.	0.45	37		✓	37
" " Stairs & Landings	122	s.f.	0.80	98		✓	98
" " Cement Fill to Metal Stair Pans	229	s.f.	0.85	195		✓	195
				8606		✓	8606

Figure 9.3.

Wall footings: Another low production operation, and the average factor is increased by 35 percent.

$$0.55 \times 1.35 = 0.74 \text{ man-hour/yd.}^3$$
$$= \$9.62, \text{ say } \$9.65$$

Piers or pedestals: The average factor increased by 35 percent.

$$0.96 \times 1.35 = 1.3 \text{ man-hours/yd.}^3$$
$$= \$16.84, \text{ say } \$17.00$$

Suspended slab and beams: With the use of a mobile crane to place the concrete, and allowing for a minimum amount of buggying to those locations that could not be reached directly by the crane, it is considered that the average factor could be improved by approximately 15 percent.

$$0.75 \text{ less } 15\% = 0.64 \text{ man-hour/yd.}^3 = \$8.32$$

Stairs and landings: Always a costly operation and in this case the small quantity would result in very low production. The average factor is escalated by 40 percent.

$$1.8 \times 1.40 = 2.52 \text{ man-hours/yd.}^3$$
$$= \$32.76, \text{ say } \$33.00.$$

TABLE 9.6 Schedule of Man-hour Factors: Formwork

Metric Conversion Factors:	Multiply By:
Linear Feet to Meters =	3.28
Square Feet to Square Meters =	10.764
Cubic Yards to Cubic Meters =	1.308

				Adjust for Higher or Lower Productivity	
Item	Per (unit)	Crew Ratio	Average Productivity	High, Reduce Factor By:	Low, Increase Factor by:
1. Spread (column) footings	ft.^{2}	1:1	0.16	10–15%	15–25%
2. Pile or caisson caps	ft.^{2}	1:1	0.18	10–15%	15–25%
3. Wall footings	ft.^{2}	1:1	0.192	10–15%	15–25%
4. Foundation walls not over 12 ft. high	ft.^{2}	1:1	0.13	10–15%	15–25%
12 ft. to 18 ft.	ft.^{2}	1:1	0.14	10–15%	15–25%
Over 18 ft.	ft.^{2}	1:1	0.145	10–15%	15–25%
5. Interior walls (hand-placed)	ft.^{2}	1:1	0.12	20–30%	20–25%

TABLE 9.6 *(Continued)*

			Metric Conversion Factors:		*Multiply By:*
			Linear Feet to Meters =		3.28
			Square Feet to Square Meters =		10.764
			Cubic Yards to Cubic Meters =		1.308
				Adjust for Higher or Lower Productivity	
Item	*Per (unit)*	*Crew Ratio*	*Average Productivity*	*High, Reduce Factor By:*	*Low, Increase Factor by:*
6. Shear walls (gang-formed)	ft.^{2}	3:1	0.086	25–30%	—
7. Pilasters	ft.^{2}	1:1	0.165	—	—
8. Columns and piers:					
Rectangular	ft.^{2}	1:1	0.16	15–20%	20–25%
Shaped	ft.^{2}	1:1	0.185	—	—
9. Pit walls	ft.^{2}	1:1	0.19	—	—
10. Suspended slabs (hand-placed)	ft.^{2}	1:1	0.115	10–15%	15–20%
Shoring height over 12 feet	ft.^{2}	1:1	0.135	—	15–25%
Using crane	ft.^{2}	3:1	0.085	15–25%	—
11. Miscellaneous suspended slabs	ft.^{2}	1:1	0.145	—	—
12. Beams (interior)	ft.^{2}	1:1	0.182	10–15%	20–25%
13. Beams (spandrel)	ft.^{2}	1:1	0.19	10–15%	20–25%
14. Drop slabs (edges and soffits)	ft.^{2}	1:1	0.21	10–15%	20–25%
15. Isolated beams	ft.^{2}	1:1	0.20	—	—
16. Upstand beams	ft.^{2}	1:1	0.195	—	—
17. Fireproofing steel columns	ft.^{2}	1:1	0.187	—	—
18. Fireproofing steel beams	ft.^{2}	1:1	0.23	—	—
19. Stairs and landings	ft.^{2}	1:1	0.31	—	25–40%
20. Slab edges	ft.^{2}	2:1	0.19	—	35–45%
21. Slab edges (suspended)	ft.^{2}	2:1	0.27	-	35–45%
22. Bulkheads to construction joints	ft.	2:1	0.23	—	25–35%
23. Keys	ft.	3:1	0.115	—	25–30%
24. Keys (continuous to footings)	ft.	3:1	0.07	—	—
25. Chamfer strips	ft.	3:1	0.05	—	—
26. Boxings	ft.^{2}	2:1	0.28	—	25–35%
27. Circular columns (fiber tubes)	ft.	1:1	0.70	—	—
28. Equipment bases	ft.^{2}	2:1	0.32	—	30–40%
29. Interior curbs	ft.^{2}	2:1	0.29	—	30–40%

TABLE 9.6 *(Continued)*

	Metric Conversion Factors:			*Multiply By:*	
	Linear Feet to Meters =			3.28	
	Square Feet to Square Meters =			10.764	
	Cubic Yards to Cubic Meters =			1.308	
				Adjust for Higher or Lower Productivity	
Item	*Per (unit)*	*Crew Ratio*	*Average Productivity*	*High, Reduce Factor By:*	*Low, Increase Factor by:*
30. Exterior curbs	ft.^{2}	2:1	0.22	—	30–40%
31. Set screeds	ft.^{2}	3:1	0.001	—	—
32. Prefabricate gang forms	ft.^{2}	2:1	0.014	—	—
Install Miscellaneous Items:					
33. Waterstops	ft.	1:1	0.13	—	—
34. Anchor slots	ft.	1:1	0.026	—	—
35. Expansion joints	ft.	1:1	0.11	—	15–25%
36. Anchors for precast concrete	Pcs	Carp.	0.42	—	—
37. Inserts for shelf angles	Pcs	Carp.	0.46	—	—
Forms to Architectural Concrete:					
38. Board finish	ft.^{2}	1:1	0.25	—	—
39. Smooth finish	ft.^{2}	1:1	0.21	—	—
40. Grooved finish	ft.^{2}	1:1	0.24	—	—

Notes:

1. Improved productivity will always be achieved with a large quantity of items that are repetitive in size and shape (column footings, columns, piers, etc.), particularly where the forms can be prefabricated and then reused a large number of times.

2. Long straight walls of consistent height and with a minimum of pilasters or other projections will also provide good productivity. Prefabricated wood panels or metal forms will also assist output, but the estimator must always check that the cost of renting or purchasing special panels, be they wood or metal, does not offset any decrease in labor costs. (Even so, these could still affect savings by shortening the schedule.)

3. Circular work; surfaces with offsets, recesses, haunches, and similar; walls with fluctuating changes in height—all such conditions will impair productivity.

4. Suspended slabs in multistory buildings, particularly where "flying" forms can be constructed and handled with a tower crane, will provide the optimum output per man-hour. Hand-placed formwork to repetitive floor slabs will also achieve excellent productivity if a system of metal (usually aluminum) joists is used. The aluminum joists and trusses are very light to handle and, except for the plywood soffits, a minimum of lumber is required. However, as these form systems are often rented from a specialist company, estimators should ensure that they will be put to continuous work during the course of the project; bad weather, strikes, sheer bad planning, all these could result in the sad situation of paying monthly rentals for items that do not get put to consistent use. Companies specializing in these systems will usually provide assistance in estimating a contractor's requirements.

5. Forms to slab edges (particularly when "suspended") and bulkheads at construction joints are always costly items, and very often the productivity will be less than average. The same applies to small equipment bases and interior curbs, particularly if scattered around a structure in various locations.

PAGE ______ OF ______

GENERAL ESTIMATE

PROJECT: Research Centre — LABOUR RATES: Carp. $15.00 — QUANTITIES: J.D.

ESTIMATE Nº: 27/82 — Lab. $13.00 — EXTENSIONS: J.M. — CHECKED: ______

TRADE SECTION: 03100 - Formwork — DATE: ______ — PRICED: N.G.

DESCRIPTION	QUANTITY	UNIT	MATERIAL U.P.	MATERIAL TOTAL	LABOUR U.P.	LABOUR TOTAL	TOTAL
Isolated Column Footings	112	s.f.	1.25	140	2.30	258	398
Wall Footings	818	s.f.	0.46	376	2.75	2250	2626
Foundation Walls (Not exceeding 12'0" high)	8084	s.f.	0.52	4204	2.42	19563	23767
Pilasters (Projections and Face)	202	s.f.	0.52	105	2.30	465	570
Piers (Below Grade)	110	s.f.	1.35	149	2.70	297	446
Columns	1936	s.f.	0.48	929	2.30	4453	5382
Beams - Spandrel Incl. Slab Edges	6691	s.f.	0.70	4684	2.72	18200	22884
- Interior	3607	s.f.	0.70	2525	2.60	9378	11903
Soffit of Suspended Slab (Flat Plate)	2500	s.f.	0.70	1750	1.67	4175	5925
Soffit of Suspended Slab (Beam/Slab Construction)	19411	s.f.	0.70	13588	1.67	32416	46004
Stairs and Landings	165	s.f.	2.40	396	4.45	734	1130
Equipment Pads (18 ea.)	103	s.f.	1.40	144	4.65	479	623
Sump Pits (Incl. Walls and Base)	306	s.f.	1.20	367	2.70	826	1193
Key at Wall Footings (2" x 4")	581	l.f.	0.15	87	1.05	610	697
Construction Joints (Vertical) - Bulkheads	86	l.f.	0.85	73	3.36	289	362
- Key (2" x 4")	86	l.f.	0.15	13	1.70	146	159
- Waterstop	86	l.f.	1.10	95	1.85	159	254
Construction Joints (Horizontal) - Bulkheads	388	l.f.	0.85	330	3.36	1304	1634
- Key (2" x 4")	388	l.f.	0.15	58	1.70	660	718
Slab Edges (Not Exceeding 12" wide)	312	l.f.	0.85	265	2.80	874	1139
Masonry Shelf - 4" x 6"	150	l.f.	0.90	135	4.00	600	735
Shelf Angle Inserts (at Spandrel Beams)	206	pcs.	10.00	2060	7.00	1442	3502
Set Anchors for Precast Conc. Panels (Suppl. by P.C. Subcontractor)	200	pcs.		✓	6.30	1260	1260
Anchor Slots	1983	l.f.	0.35	694	0.40	793	1487
Set Screeds	36552	s.f.	0.01	366	0.015	548	914
Formwork Hardware and Accessories	Item			4000		✓	4000
Form Oil	Item			300		✓	300
Misc. Small Tools and Equipment	Item			400		✓	400
				38233		102179	140412

Figure 9.4.

Equipment pads: There are only 18 of these pads located in various parts of the average building. A factor of 4.06 man-hour/yd.^{3} is used (an increase of 45 percent over the average man-hour factor).

Fill to metal stair pans: This item does not appear on the man-hour factor schedule, and is one of those items that can be more realistically priced by the cubic foot:

$$0.27 \text{ man-hour/ft.}^3 \times \$13 = \$3.50$$

or price by the number of treads.

Notes on Pricing: Formwork

The following are some of the factors which contribute to formwork material costs:

- Size and spacing of studs, bracing, and the like
- Grade and thickness of sheathing (usually plywood)
- Cost and spacing of form ties
- Shores and/or scaffold frames (usually a rentable item)
- Form oil
- Rate of pour per hour

As stated in the schedule of items and measurements for formwork, the items for formwork "hardware and accessories" and form oil are recommended to be treated separately, as they are not subject to "re-use" adjustment factors.

The quantity of plywood sheathing required per square foot of formwork will be the formwork contact area plus a percentage to cover cutting and wastage. The lumber quantities of studs and walers, etc. are usually calculated with the use of prepared tables of factors showing the number of board feet of lumber required per square feet of formwork. Estimators can prepare their own tables or use ready-made tables available in text or reference books on estimating; however, these ready-made tables should be checked to establish knowledge and understanding of the data used in their preparation.

Table 9.7 shows a table of factors for wall forms based on various stud and waler sizes and spacing. It will be noticed that miscellaneous lumber for stakes and bracing is excluded from this table, but a percentage factor is suggested.

The factors do not include an allowance for reuse, which is usually achieved by dividing the established unit price by an assessed number of times that the material will be used. This is quite sufficient for most items, particularly if the quantities involved are not excessive; however, for more contentious items a more constructive approach would be to assess the minimum quantity of plywood and lumber to be purchased for a specific operation.

In the example of a priced estimate for formwork, the item for materials to

TABLE 9.7 Formwork to Walls: Lumber and Plywood Quantities per Square Foot

Stud Size and Spacing	*Waler Size and Spacing*	*Board Feet of Lumber (per ft.²)*	*Plywood ⅝ in. Square Feet*
2 × 4 in. 12 in. O.C.	Double 2 × 4 in., 30 in. O.C.	1.2–1.3	1.05–1.10
2 × 4 in. 14 in. O.C.	Double 2 × 4 in., 30 in. O.C.	1.15–1.25	1.05–1.10
2 × 6 in. 12 in. O.C.	Double 2 × 6 in., 36 in. O.C.	1.7–1.9	1.05–1.10
2 × 6 in. 10 in. O.C.	Double 2 × 6 in., 30 in. O.C.	2.0–2.3	1.05–1.10

Notes:

1. The selection of factors applies to walls not exceeding 12 ft. in height. For walls from 12 ft. to 20 ft. in height, add 3 to 5 percent. For walls greater than 20 ft. in height, add 5 to 10 percent.
2. Hourly rise of pour up to 5 ft. at 68° F.
3. Miscellaneous stakes and bracing not included; add 5 percent.

the foundation walls was calculated as follows: The total contact area quantity is 8084 ft.^{2}. It is assumed that a purchased quantity of materials sufficient to form 120 linear feet of walls would be sufficient. This indicates a quantity of approximately 2900 ft.^{2} of contact area.

$$\text{Cost of form plywood} = 0.85/\text{ft.}^2$$
$$\text{Cost of lumber} = \$400 \text{ per thousand board feet (\$0.40/board foot)}$$

The forms will be constructed with 2 × 4 in. studs at 12 in. centers and double 2 × 4 in. walers at 30 in. centers, which according to the table indicates a factor of 1.2 board feet/ft.^{2}.

$$\text{Plywood} = \frac{2900 \text{ ft.}^2 \times 0.85 \times 1.05 \text{ (5\% for waste)}}{8084 \text{ ft.}^2 \text{ (Total quantity)}}$$
$$= \$0.32$$
$$\text{Lumber} = \frac{2900 \text{ ft.}^2 \times 1.2 \times 0.40}{8084 \text{ ft.}^2}$$
$$= \$0.17$$
$$0.17 + 0.32 = 0.49.$$

Add 5 percent for miscellaneous braces, and so on, and the total cost per square foot is $0.514, say $0.52.

Table 9.8 shows a table of factors for other items of formwork. These factors have been used in the pricing examples, and for most items, because of the small quantities, only one reuse of material has been considered and, in some instances, *no reuse at all*.

TABLE 9.8 Formwork: Lumber and Plywood Quantities

	Lumber bd.ft./ft.^{2}	Plywood (5/8 or 3/4 in.) ft.^{2}
Column footings	1.2–1.5	1.05–1.10
Wall footings	2.2–2.8	
Columns	1.3–1.6	1.05–1.10
Suspended slabs (hand-placed)	2.1–2.6	1.05–1.10
Beams	2.5–3.5	1.05–1.10
Stairs and landings	4.5–5.0	1.10–1.15

Note: The suspended slab factor is based on:
4 × 4 in. joists at 12 in. O.C.
Three 2 × 10 in. beams at each shore head (two per frame)
Sills, 2 × 12 in.
Scaffold frames at 5 ft. O.C., with 5 ft. cross braces

The price for materials to the suspended slabs was computed as follows:

Purchase quantity: Plywood and lumber for one complete floor, equal to approximately 7500 ft.^{2}. The total *gross area* of all suspended slab soffits is 2500 + 19,411 = 21,911 ft.^{2}.

$$\text{Plywood: } \frac{7500 \times 1.05 \times 0.85}{21{,}911} = 0.305$$

$$\text{Lumber: } \frac{7500 \times 2.1 \times 0.40}{21{,}911} = \frac{0.29}{0.595}, \text{ say } \$0.60/\text{ft.}^2$$

To this unit price must be added the cost of shoring. It is calculated that 220 scaffold frames will be required to form one floor. The rental for each frame is $4 per month. Allowing a cycle of 1½ weeks per each half of the main building slabs yields 1.5 × 6 = 9 weeks, or say, a 2-month rental period. This calculates out as:

$$\frac{220 \times 4.00 \times 2}{21{,}911} = 0.08/\text{ft.}^2$$

The total unit price =	$0.60
	0.08
	0.68
Add for reshoring	0.02
Cost per square foot	$0.70

Formwork Labor Costs. Average productivity has been considered for all items except as follows. An allowance of 2 percent has been added to the composite rates for the working foreman's time (approximately \$0.29 for each rate).

Wall forms: man-hour factor is reduced by 10 percent as these walls have generally repetitive heights (except at stepped footings): 0.13 less 10 percent = 0.117/ft.^{2}.

Piers below grade: this quantity is very small and the factor is increased by 20 percent.

Suspended slabs: consideration was given to a 10 percent reduction in the average man-hour factor = 0.104 man-hours/ft.^{2}. This factor computed by the composite rate of 14.29 = \$1.49/ft.^{2}. However, this is a major item in the estimate and needs to be checked out more practically:

Assume a crew of 6 carpenters and 5 laborers, including a working foreman:

Foreman	\$16.50 × 1 =	\$16.50
Carpenters	15.00 × 5 =	75.00
Laborers	13.00 × 5 =	65.00
Total hourly cost of crew	=	\$156.50

If one-half of a typical floor slab (3750 square feet) could be formed and stripped in five days = 40 hours, the estimated rate would be:

$$\frac{\$156.50 \times 40}{3750} = \$1.67/\text{ft.}^2$$

This indicates that the rate of \$1.49 is probably too optimistic and would be difficult to achieve, and therefore the rate of \$1.67 is used in the estimate. In practice, some discussion with a superintendent or carpenter foreman could provide further considerations on this operation, with a resultant increase or decrease in the estimated unit.

All major and contentious items should be subjected to alternating methods of establishing estimated costs, with the estimator using the best possible judgment after reviewing all the options and alternatives.

Notes on Pricing: Masonry

1. All the items in this section have been priced on the basis of average productivity with the exception of the following:

Face brick: Except for the window openings, the wall surfaces are straightforward and a little better-than-average productivity would be possible; therefore, the average man-hour factor is reduced by 10 percent.

TABLE 9.9 Schedule of Man-hour Factors: Masonry

Metric Conversion Factors:	*Multiply by:*
Linear feet to meters =	3.28
Square feet to square meters =	10.764
Cubic yards to cubic meters =	1.308

Item	Per (unit)	Crew Ratio	Average Productivity	*Adjust for Higher or Lower Productivity* High, Reduce Factor by:	Low, Increase Factor by:
1a. Facing brick (stretchers)	1000 pcs	2:1	22.00	10–15%	15–20%
lb. Facing brick (6 course, headers)	1000 pcs	2:1	22.80	10–15%	15–20%
1c. Facing brick (full English bond)	1000 pcs	2:1	24.00	5–10%	15–20%
1d. Facing brick (Flemish bond)	1000 pcs	2:1	23.50	5–10%	15–20%
1e. Common brick	1000 pcs	2:1	19.00	5–10%	15–20%
2a. Concrete block 2 in. (5 cm)	piece	1:1	0.06	—	10–15%
2b. 4 in. (10 cm)	piece	1:1	0.07	5–10%	10–15%
2c. 6 in. (15 cm)	piece	1:1	0.075	5–10%	10–15%
2d. 8 in. (20 cm)	piece	1:1	0.095	5–10%	10–15%
2e. 10 & 12 in. (25 and 30 cm)	piece	1:1	0.125	—	10–15%
2f. Extra for exposed block faces	piece	1:1	0.01	—	—
2g. Extra for special units	piece	1:1	0.01	—	—
2h. Extra for block lintels	ft.	1:1	0.08	—	—
3a. Glazed concrete block: 2 to 6 in.	pcs	1:1	0.105	—	—
3b. 8 to 12 in.	pcs	1:1	0.15	—	—
3c. Special units	pcs	1:1	0.25	—	—
4a. Structural clay tile 2 in. furring	pcs	1:1	0.035	5–10%	10–15%
4b. 4 in. backup	pcs	1:1	0.04	5–10%	10–15%
4c. 6 in. backup	pcs	1:1	0.045	5–10%	10–15%

TABLE 9.9 *(Continued)*

	Metric Conversion Factors:	Multiply by:
	Linear feet to meters =	3.28
	Square feet to square meters =	10.764
	Cubic yards to cubic meters =	1.308

Item	Per (unit)	Crew Ratio	Average Productivity	*Adjust for Higher or Lower Productivity* High, Reduce Factor by:	Low, Increase Factor by:
4d. 8 in. backup	pcs	1:1	0.06	5–10%	10–15%
4e. 10 to 12 in. backup	pcs	1:1	0.075	—	10–15%
4f. 4 in. partition	pcs	1:1	0.038	5–10%	10–15%
4g. 6 in. partition	pcs	1:1	0.042	5–10%	10–15%
4h. 8 in. partition	pcs	1:1	0.058	5–10%	10–15%
4i. 10 to 12 in. partition	pcs	1:1	0.073	5–10%	10–15%
5a. Structural glazed tile 2 to 6 in.	pcs	1:1	0.10	—	—
5b. 8 to 12 in.	pcs	1:1	0.15	—	—
5c. Specials	pcs	1:1	0.25	—	—
6. Dampcourses and flashings	ft.	2:1	0.04	—	—
7. Clean down masonry	$ft.^2$	Lab.	0.005	—	—
8. Rake out and point	$ft.^2$	2:1	0.02	—	—
9. Masonry reinforcement	$ft.^2$	3:1	0.004	—	—
10. Expansion joint	$ft.^2$	3:1	0.06	—	—
11. Cavity wall insulation	$ft.^2$	2:1	0.035	—	—

Notes:

1. The man-hour factors include for the unloading and site handling of materials, mixing of mortar, and normal cutting of masonry units. The factors applicable to "average productivity" allow for masonry construction up to a height of 30 ft. *Note:* The man-hours applicable to erection and dismantling of scaffolding are shown separately.

2. Large wall surfaces with a minimum of corners and openings will improve on the average productivity, while the reverse must be expected with walls that are chopped up with openings, projections, recesses, decorative features, and so on. Also, cavity wall construction should be considered as slightly slower than solid masonry.

3. Furring around columns and pilasters is low-productivity work.

4. Only average productivity should generally be considered for structural glazed tile and glazed block units. This work demands high-quality workmanship and is not usually a high-production operation. The exceptions would probably be large areas of furring to concrete or masonry walls unbroken by openings or projections, and requiring a minimum of "special" units.

GENERAL ESTIMATE

PAGE 1 OF 1

PROJECT Research Centre — LABOUR RATES Bricklayer $14.50 — QUANTITIES B.E.W.

ESTIMATE NO 27/82 — Lab. (Helper) $13.00 — EXTENSIONS J.M. — CHECKED

TRADE SECTION 04000 - Masonry — DATE — PRICED H.G.

DESCRIPTION	QUANTITY	UNIT	MATERIAL U.P.	MATERIAL TOTAL	LABOUR U.P.	LABOUR TOTAL	TOTAL
Face Brick to Exterior Walls - 6th course headers, modular size, red rug, 3/8" mortar joints	39	M.pcs	190.00	7410	293.00	11427	18837
Extra Over - Labour to Brick Sills	425	l.f.		/	0.90	383	383
Concrete Block, Lighweight - 8" back-up to Brick & P.C.Panels	5924	pcs.	0.60	3554	1.26	7464	11018
" " " - 6" Interior Partitions	10355	pcs.	0.54	5592	1.05	10873	16465
" " " - 4" " "	6162	pcs.	0.48	2958	0.98	6039	8997
" " Extra Over - Specials: Lintel Blocks	190	pcs.	0.12	23	0.14	27	50
" " " " " Bullnose	70	pcs.	0.12	8	0.14	10	18
" " " " Labour only to Exposed Faces	280	pcs.		/	0.13	36	36
3000 P.S.I. Conc. & 2 #4 reinf. bars to block lintels	253	l.f.	1.55	392	1.10	278	670
Stone Coping at Parapet (Fasten) with Anchors-Measured sep.	550	l.f.	11.00	6050	2.90	1595	7645
Anchors to Stone Coping	282	pcs.	0.75	212	3.75	1058	1270
Dampcourse (2 oz. copper laminated paper) - 18" wide	605	l.f.	0.42	254	0.55	333	587
Flashings at Window Heads	1075	l.f.	0.42	452	0.60	645	1097
Cavity Wall Insulation (1" Polystyrene Type 4)	5492	s.f.	0.53	2911	0.48	2636	5547
Clean Down Face Brick	3936	s.f.	0.03	118	0.07	276	394
Clean Down Exposed Surfaces of Conc. Block	248	s.f.	0.03	7	0.10	25	32
Mortar (Type "N" - Masonry Cement)	56.3	c.y.	44.55	2508		/	2508
Cavity Wall Ties - Z Bars 3/16" Steel Wire	2300	pcs.	0.20	460		/	460
Dovetail Anchors (Hot-Dipped Galvd. 16 Ga. - 1" x 3½" x 3/8")	1400	pcs.	0.12	168		/	168
Scaffold Frames - Erect and Dismantle	326	ea.			4.25	1386	1386
Masonry Equipment: Mortar Mixer	3	mos.	250.00	750		/	750
Fork Lift	3	mos.	900.00	2700		/	2700
Brick Buggies	3	mos.	85.00	255		/	255
Masonry Saw & Blades	Item			1000		/	1000
Scaffolds (Frames, Braces, etc.)	320	mos.	5.00	1600		/	1600
Scaffold Plank	Item			300		/	300
Misc. Small Tools & Equipment	Item			200		/	200
				39882		44491	84373

Figure 9.5.

$$22.80 - 10\% = 20.52 \text{ man-hour/1000 pieces}$$

Remember the crew ratio is 2:1, which provides a composite man-hour rate of $14, which is adjusted by 2 percent to allow for a working foreman:

$$\begin{aligned} \$14.00 \times 1.02 &= \$14.28 \times 20.52 \\ &= \$293/1000 \text{ pieces} \end{aligned}$$

2. The "extra over" item for brick sills is calculated as 10 percent of the basic rate of $297 per 1000 pieces, or $0.30 per piece, multiplied by three pieces per linear foot equals $0.90.

3. The composite rates for concrete block are for a 1:1 ratio = $13.75/hour, plus 2 percent for the foreman = $14.02. The factor for the backup block to face brick and precast concrete has been decreased by 5 percent = 0.09 man-hour/block.

4. A 10 percent increase over the basic unit price has been allowed for the additional labor to exposed concrete block faces.

5. The cost of the concrete and reinforcing bars in concrete block lintels is

TABLE 9.10 Schedule of Man-hour Factors: Rough Carpentry

Metric Conversion Factors	*Multiply by:*
Linear feet to meters =	3.28
Square feet to square meters =	10.764
Cubic yards to cubic meters =	1.308

				Adjust for Higher of Lower Productivity	
Item	*Per (unit)*	*Crew Ratio*	*Average Productivity*	*High, Reduce Factor by:*	*Low, Increase Factor by:*
1. Blocking to roof	ft.	Carp.	0.08	15–25%	—
2. Roof cants	ft.	Carp.	0.055	15–25%	—
3. Blocking around metal windows	ft.	Carp.	0.11	—	20–25%
4. Miscellaneous blocking	ft.	Carp.	0.12	—	20–25%
5. Wall strapping	ft.	Carp.	0.06	15–25%	15–20%
6. Nailing strips to structural steel	ft.	Carp.	0.096	—	—
7. Grounds	ft.	Carp.	0.11	—	—
8. Plywood to parapets, soffits, etc.	$ft.^2$	Carp.	0.12	—	—
9. T & G roof/floor decks	FBM	Carp.	0.025	—	—

stated as a linear foot item based on previous costs. The premium cost of the special lintel block is shown separately under "specials."

6. The cost of the mortar material is computed as follows:

Masonry cement	31.33 lbs. at \$0.027 =	\$0.85
Sand	80.00 lbs. at \$0.01 =	0.80
		\$1.65 × 27

= \$44.55/yd.^{3}

Notes on Pricing: Rough and Finish Carpentry

In the examples given only the factors for average production have been selected, with the exception of the following:

Curbs at skylights. These would be short pieces, with very little total quantity. There is no specific item for these curbs on the man-hour schedule, so 15 percent is added to the average factor for roof blocking: 0.26 × 1.15 = .30.

TABLE 9.11 Schedule of Man-hour Factors: Finish Carpentry (Millwork)

	Metric Conversion Factors:		*Multiply by:*
	Linear feet to meters =		3.28
	Square feet to square meters =		10.764
	Cubic yards to cubic meters =		1.308
Item	*Per (unit)*	*Crew Ratio*	*Average Productivity*
1. Counter units (incl. doors, drawers, trim)	ft.	Carp.	1.30
2. Kitchen counters and cupboards (floor mounted)	ft.	Carp.	0.56
3. Kitchen overhead cupboard units	ft.	Carp.	0.43
4. Open shelf units	ft.	Carp.	0.40
5. Miscellaneous trim	ft.	Carp.	0.08
6. Wall battens	ft.	Carp.	0.09
7. Ceiling battens	ft.	Carp.	0.10
8. Handrails	ft.	Carp.	0.32
9. Base (incl. nosing)	ft.	Carp.	0.09
10. Paneling (moderate quality)	ft.^{2}	Carp.	0.09
Paneling (top quality)	ft.^{2}	Carp.	0.15
11. Vanity units (plastic lam. tops)	ft.	Carp.	0.60
12. Window stools	ft.	Carp.	0.156

TABLE 9.12 Schedule of Man-hour Factors: Doors, Frames, Screens

Metric Conversion Factors	*Multiply by:*
Linear feet to meters =	3.28
Square feet to square meters =	10.764
Cubic yards to cubic meters =	1.308

Item	*Per (unit)*	*Crew Ratio*	*Average Productivity*	*Adjust for Higher or Lower Productivity* *High, Reduce Factor by:*	*Low, Increase Factor by:*
1. Metal door frames installed in masonry	each	3:1	2.30	10–15%	15–25%
2. Metal door frames installed in concrete	each	3:1	3.25	—	—
3. Handle only frames to be installed by subcontractor	each	Lab.	0.20	—	—
4. Metal doors	each	3:1	4.20	—	15–25%
5. Wood doors: interior, hollow core	each	3:1	2.30	5–10%	15–25%
6. Wood doors: interior, solid core	each	3:1	3.50	5–10%	15–25%
7. Plastic laminate doors	each	3:1	4.80	—	15–25%
8. Doors, exterior	each	3:1	4.60	—	—
9. Lead-lined doors	each	3:1	16.20	—	—
10. Hollow metal screens	ft.^{2}	3:1	0.11	—	—
11. Borrowed lights	each	3:1	2.15	—	—
12. Soundproof doors	each	3:1	5.80	—	—
13. Sliding closet doors	pair	3:1	4.00	—	—
14. Bifolding doors	unit	3:1	1.80	—	—
15. Wood door frames	unit	3:1	2.50	—	—
Miscellaneous Door Hardware:					
16. Kickplates	each	Carp.	0.25	—	—
17. Door closer	each	Carp.	0.75	—	—
18. Door stops or holders	each	Carp.	0.20	—	—

GENERAL ESTIMATE

PROJECT Research Centre
ESTIMATE NO 27/82
TRADE SECTION 06100 - Rough Carpentry
LABOUR RATES Carp. $15.00
DATE
QUANTITIES B.E.W.
EXTENSIONS J.M.
CHECKED
PRICED N.G.

	DESCRIPTION	QUANTITY	UNIT	MATERIAL U.P.	MATERIAL TOTAL	LABOUR U.P.	LABOUR TOTAL	TOTAL
	The following in No. 2 Spruce (Construction Grade)							
	unless stated otherwise							
A-4	Roof Carpentry: 4" X 4" Cant Strips	630	l.f.	0.50	315	0.83	523	838
	2" X 4" Blocking	630	l.f.	0.24	151	1.20	756	907
	2" X 4" Curbs at Skylights	74	l.f.	0.24	18	1.40	104	122
6/1001	Blocking at Window Stools - 2" X 4"	1087	l.f.	0.24	261	1.80	1957	2218
	" " Vanity Units - 1" X 2"	50	l.f.	0.08	4	1.80	90	94
A-6	1" X 2" Wall Strapping to Receive Panelling	378	l.f.	0.08	30	0.90	340	370
8/1001	Misc. Blocking - 2" X 4" at Counter Units	66	l.f.	0.24	16	1.80	119	135
	- 2" X 6" at Misc. Fixtures	40	l.f.	0.43	17	1.80	72	89
	Rough Hardware	Item			50		--	50
					862		3961	4823

Figure 9.6.

PAGE 1 OF 1

GENERAL ESTIMATE

PROJECT Research Centre LABOUR RATES Carp. $15.00 QUANTITIES B.E.W.

ESTIMATE NO 27/82 EXTENSIONS J.M. CHECKED

TRADE SECTION Miscellaneous Contractor's Work DATE PRICED N.G.

	DESCRIPTION	QUANTITY	UNIT	MATERIAL U.P.	MATERIAL TOTAL	LABOUR U.P.	LABOUR TOTAL	TOTAL
	06200 Finish Carpentry							
Detail 6/1001	Window Stool	1035	l.f.	) Supplied by		2.35	2433	2433
8/1001	Washroom Vanity (Fixed to Brackets - Supplied by Others)	48	l.f.	) Millwork		9.00	432	432
9/A/10 1001	Wood Panelling (Fixed to Wood Strapping)	1056	s.f.	) Subcontractor		1.35	1426	1426
4/1002	Counter Units - Av. 2'6" wide x 3'0" high	37	l.f.	) - Firm Price		20.00	740	740
7/1002	Cedar Battens at Ceilings - 1½" x 1"	600	l.f.	) Quotation		1.50	900	900
9/1002	Laminated Wood Handrails to Metal Stairs	210	l.f.	)		4.80	1008	1008
	Rough Hardware	Item			100		—	100
					100		6939	7039
	08100 - Metal Doors and Frames							
	Metal Door Frames - Av. 3'0" x 7'0" Set in Block Partitions	45	ea.		—	33.00	1485	1485
	" " " - " " " " to Exterior Wall	2	ea.		—	38.00	76	76
	Metal Doors - Av. 3'0" x 7'0"	2	ea.		—	60.00	120	120
	Misc. Rough Hardware, Braces, etc.	Item			100		—	100
					100		1681	1781
	08200 - Wood and Plastic Doors							
	Exterior Wood Doors - Oak 3'6" x 7'3"	2	ea.		—	66.00	132	132
	Plastic Laminated Doors at Interior Partitions	43	ea.		—	70.00	3010	3010
							3142	3142

Figure 9.7.

10
Estimating Site Overhead Costs

10.1 Definitions

Site overhead costs are also termed *indirect costs* by some general contractors because they refer to items of work that, although necessary to the construction, are not identifiable with the work of specific trades. They also represent the cost (a significant cost, anywhere from 6 to 15 percent) of items that do not become functional parts of the completed building and visible to the building users, as do doors, windows, floors, ceilings, and so on. However, without these indirect items of work, the building would not, and in fact could not, be constructed. Although termed "indirect," these costs are chargeable to the project.

Specifications give various labels to this classification of work: General Conditions, Temporary Facilities, Contractor's Work, and so on. Masterformat Divisions 0 Bidding and Contract Requirements and 1 General Requirements state most of the applicable items. They differ from direct trade items, inasmuch as they are intangibles and not detailed on the drawings, with the possible exception of perimeter hoardings and covered ways, and occasionally site offices. Certain items will be clearly specified and detailed, but generally the requirement is stated in terms of a desired performance or result. For example, the contractors are told the building must be maintained at a minimum temperature of 50° F (10° C) in cold weather, and there may be some specified restraints regarding the type of heating equipment to be used; otherwise, it is left to the contractors to evaluate and decide on the methods and systems to satisfy the specified requirements.

Although few of these items will form part of the finished building, this does not mean that they will not be visible *during construction*. Site offices, hoardings, cranes, hoists, pumps, wheelbarrows, rubbish containers, temporary piping—all these are very evident to a building owner when visiting the site!

Because only a few of these items appear on the drawings, the methods of estimating these costs will be different from the direct trades. With the exception again of hoardings and fences, any take-off work will be confined to things that, although *not actually shown on the drawings*, the drawings can still be used to establish their scope and measurements. For example, most specifications include a requirement for temporary doors and windows. These temporary items will not actually be detailed on the drawings (or very rarely so), but the *permanent* doors and windows will be shown and can be measured or counted.

Temporary access roads are sometimes shown on the drawings, but usually the drawings will only be used to plot and measure the extent of necessary access routes. Other items in this category would be temporary barricades around floor openings or the perimeter of suspended floor slabs, temporary stairs and ladders, areas for final cleanup, and rubbish chutes.

Obviously, some sort of planning and decision-making processes have to function before many of these items can be measured. The matter of who should make such decisions varies from company to company. Some construction firms consider it to be a normal function of an estimating department, others consider it to be a managerial responsibility; and there are many who consider the best results are achieved when this part of the estimate requires the involvement of both estimators and construction managers, working together as a team. Whoever is going to shoulder the responsibility of running the project should have some input into the estimate of these indirect cost items. A criticism sometimes expressed against this arrangement is that it can provide the opportunity for estimated costs to be escalated up to a comfortable level, where a supervisor would subsequently have little difficulty in improving on them and looking rather smug about it at the completion of the project! This, of course, is in a sense Catch-22; if the estimated costs are too high, there will probably be no project to be smug about!

The combination of estimating skills and managerial or supervisory input will usually bring the most benefits. A good supervisor can provide sound practical suggestions based on experience with similar projects. Existing cost records are invaluable for this division of the estimate, but estimators should always aggressively seek out the background story to such reported costs. To be informed that on a certain project the cost of temporary heating totaled $25,000 does not tell the estimators very much unless they are also provided with more detailed information regarding the methods and equipment employed for this operation. Contacting the superintendent for this particular project will usually pay dividends to the estimator in obtaining this kind of background information.

10.2 Schedule

Before proceeding with the estimate of job overheads, a project schedule should be prepared. For the purpose of the bid, this schedule will usually be a simple (time-honored) bar chart. Certain complex projects might be better serviced at the bidding stage with a more sophisticated diagrammatic (critical-path method) type of schedule; however, there is usually insufficient time available to prepare this type of schedule in any great detail.

Many items pertaining to job-site overheads are time related, and the preparation of this schedule is essential for the purpose of assessing the anticipated total time duration. To arrive at this requires the calculation of start and completion dates for each major division of work, which in the aggregate will provide the total duration period. This schedule will also be useful in pinpointing the extent of the work being performed during the winter months, particularly excavation, concrete, and masonry. Also, the duration period for certain equipment (hoists, cranes, compactors, concrete placing equipment, etc.) can be assessed with the use of this schedule.

This schedule should not be prepared until quantities for key trades such as excavation and concrete (if applicable) are completed. The extent of these quantities will assist in assessing the time duration for these operations.

Figure 10.1 is an example of a schedule prepared for bidding purposes. It indicates the start and completion times of the major trades, and also shows which trades will be working during the winter months. If the bid is successful, then a more refined and detailed schedule is prepared for the project.

10.3 Site Visit

A familiar clause in many bid forms is the one which states that "the contractor is deemed to have visited the site and made a thorough examination of all existing conditions." Irrespective of the existence or nonexistence of such a clause, it is doubtful if an experienced estimator would ever prepare a bid without visiting the site of the proposed construction.

Many estimators make more than one prebid site visit, and this is a good idea. An early (and probably *brief*) visit shortly after the receipt of the drawings will assist an estimator to "get a feel" for the project. At a later date, when more knowledge has been assimilated about the project's complexities, and prior to the preparation of the site overhead or indirect costs, a second visit will be necessary for a more in-depth investigation to establish firsthand information relative, although not limited, to the following items:

1. Existing structures (or portions thereof) requiring demolition.
2. Proximity of existing buildings, presenting possible requirements for underpinning and/or perimeter sheeting and shoring.

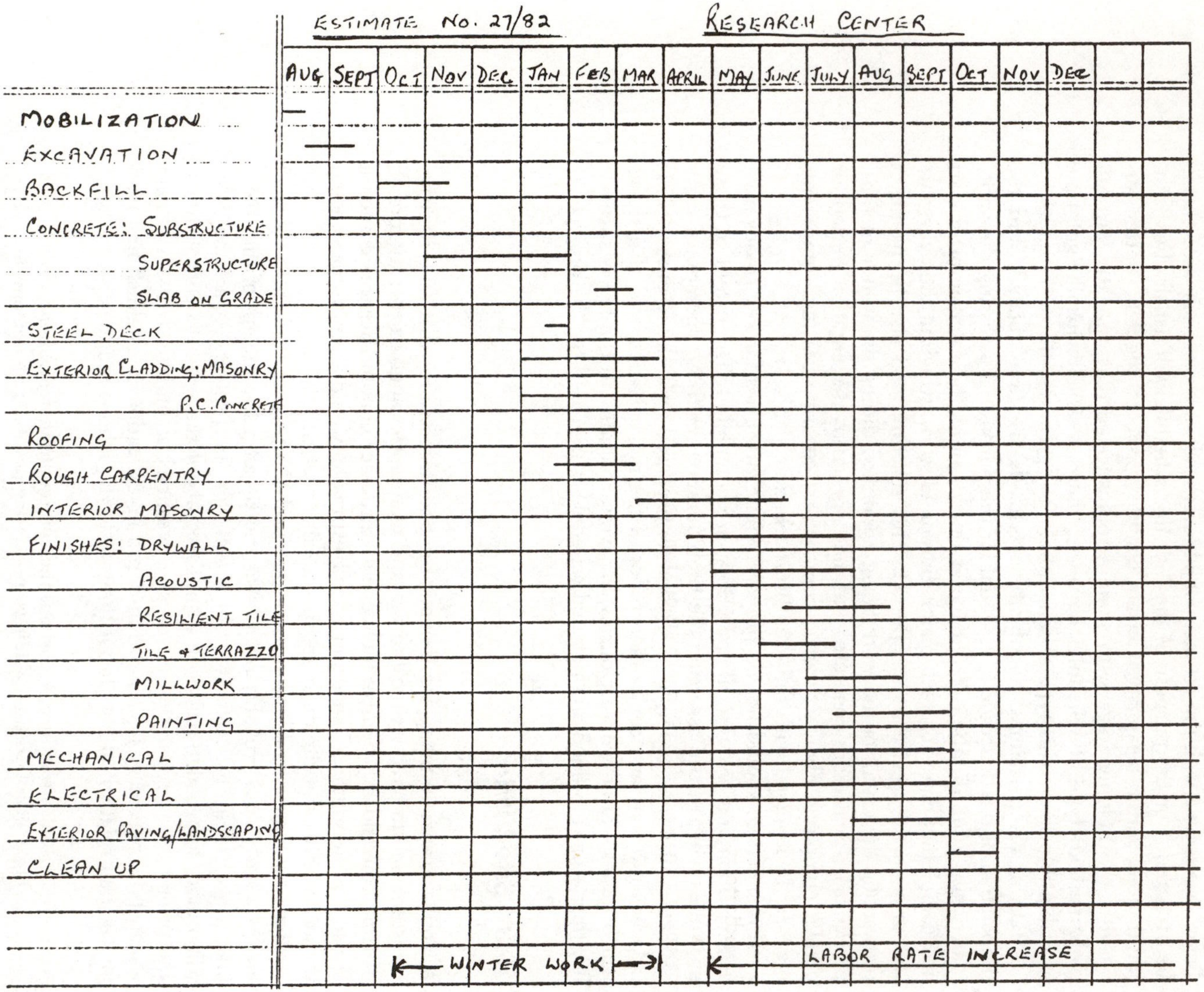
ESTIMATE NO. 27/82
RESEARCH CENTER
AUG SEPT OCT NOV DEC JAN FEB MAR APRIL MAY JUNE JULY AUG SEPT OCT NOV DEC
MOBILIZATION
EXCAVATION
BACKFILL
CONCRETE: SUBSTRUCTURE
SUPERSTRUCTURE
SLAB ON GRADE
STEEL DECK
EXTERIOR CLADDING: MASONRY
P.C. CONCRETE
ROOFING
ROUGH CARPENTRY
INTERIOR MASONRY
FINISHES: DRYWALL
ACOUSTIC
RESILIENT TILE
TILE & TERRAZZO
MILLWORK
PAINTING
MECHANICAL
ELECTRICAL
EXTERIOR PAVING/LANDSCAPING
CLEAN UP
WINTER WORK
LABOR RATE INCREASE

Figure 10.1.

3. Availability of utilities: water, electric power, gas lines, sewer, telephone service, and so on.
4. Availability and extent of space for storage, site offices, trailers, parking, hoists, and similar equipment.
5. Obstructions to be removed: overhead wires and lines (intended use of a mobile crane or similar equipment would call for temporary removal and subsequent reinstallation), poles, fences, transformers, and so on.
6. Trees and brush to be removed.
7. Existing work requiring protection during construction; requirements for dust screens for interior renovation work.
8. Site access, temporary road, traffic congestion problems.
9. Soil and groundwater conditions.
10. Other pertinent information according to the nature and complexity of the project.

The use of a camera is highly recommended. It should preferably be a Polaroid-type camera to avoid an unnecessary return visit because the prints were not good and failed to provide a satisfactory picture of the site conditions. Views should be taken from a number of angles and a sketch provided to indicate the location of these views.

A site visit for a project in an out-of-town location, particularly in remote or country areas, will require additional information, including such items as:

1. Existing labor rates, union agreements, availability of existing trades.
2. Board and lodging facilities.
3. Travel factors: distances, public transportation facilities.
4. Well digging, access road construction, pole lines for power transmission.
5. Local building bylaws; building and other permits.

It is recommended that estimators prepare a standard company form for use on these site visits, which could be conveniently attached to a clipboard. This form would be in effect a check or "reminder" list of all items common to most projects, with space (on additional paper if necessary) for any additional information to be reported. Figure 10.2 shows an example of a standard prebid site visit form.

10.4 Categorizing Site Overhead Items

The various indirect items should be grouped and classified in certain categories. This will enable the estimator (also a construction manager or project supervisor) to consider together a number of items whose individual functions aggregate to a specific functional category.

PRE-BID SITE VISIT REPORT

PROJECT: THOMPSON ROAD HIGH SCHOOL DATE: AUG 10/1982
LOCATION: CENTERVILLE ONTARIO ESTIMATE NO: 15/81

1. Existing and Adjacent Work (Demolitions, underpinning, perimeter shoring)

REMOVE EXISTING GARAGE (WOOD FRAMED)
" EXISTING CHAIN LINK FENCE (APPROX. 65'.0")

2. Access and Site Restraints

(a) Temporary Road PAVED ROAD AT NORTH, GRAVEL AT EAST - GOOD ACCESS
(b) Space for Storage, Offices, etc. O.K.
(c) Disposal of Excavated Materials HAUL OFF SITE (5 MILES)
(d) Other information

3. Existing Trees

(a) Removal THREE @ 24"Ø; TWO @ 18"Ø — MISC. BUSHES
(b) Protection FIVE MAPLE TREES AT NORTH END OF SITE

4. Soil and Water Conditions REFER SOIL REPORT

5. Utilities

(a) Electric Power AVAILABLE
(b) Water ✓
(c) Sewers ✓
(d) Gas BEING INSTALLED
(e) Telephone AVAILABLE

6. Other Information CLOSE TO HOSPITAL — MAY BE NOISE RESTRICTIONS ?
GOOD CLEAN SITE

Report Prepared By: B.E.W.

Figure 10.2.

Example: "Hoisting." By combining all the items pertaining to cranes, material and personnel hoists, derricks, temporary elevators, conveyors, and the like, in one group, the estimator can concentrate on this category as a whole before considering another category.

The following pages show some suggested categories, and the items applicable to each category. Some construction companies will probably have standard lists of items either longer or shorter than those shown here. It does not matter what sort of format an estimator decides to use—whether broken down into a larger number of items or reduced to a few specific classifications—as long as all the work required by the specification is accounted for and a proper understanding prevails of *what* and *why* certain items have to be included in this part of the estimate.

The following are the principal categories of site overheads:

1. Project supervision.
2. Offices and administrative requirements.
3. Site access, protection, and security.
4. Temporary utilities.
5. Construction facilities and services.
6. Hoisting: materials and personnel.
7. Small tools and equipment.
8. Permits, insurances, and bonds.

10.5 Category 1: Project Supervision

This applies to personnel working directly and exclusively on a particular project. Personnel to be considered would include:

Item	*Comment*
Project managers	
Superintendents	On large projects these would include general superintendents, assistant superintendents, mechanical and electrical superintendents, and so on
Engineers	Project, field, office engineers, etc.
Estimators, quantity surveyors, and cost engineers	
Accountants and timekeepers	
Safety supervisors	This could be a mandatory requirement in the specification
Instrument men	
Secretarial and clerical	
Purchasing and expediting	

Each member of the project staff will be listed separately, stating the estimated time (usually in months) of duration and the salary. Fringe benefits and labor burdens should also be included, usually by the addition of an applicable percentage factor to the total sum of the salaries.

10.6 Category 2: Offices and Administrative Requirements

Temporary Offices and Buildings

These would include on-site offices, storage sheds, temporary wash houses, lunchroom or canteen facilities, and other buildings as required by the specifications. A frequent specification clause is one that asks for the provision of a separate office facility for the sole use of the architects or engineers or their site representatives. A minimum floor area is often stated for this item. On large projects a separate facility for the storage of finish hardware materials may also warrant consideration.

If rented or purchased office trailers are to be used, they should be stated separately.

When the construction of a building is sufficiently advanced, and providing the specification endorses the arrangement, general contractors often take a section of a floor and utilize this space for site office purposes. All costs should be included for the provision of temporary partitions, doors, shelving, cupboards, and similar items.

Large projects of long duration, and particularly those located in the downtown areas of cities, will often require rented office space in buildings adjacent to the site. This would be in addition to the on-site offices and trailers for field superintendents and engineers. Costs would include rent (or even purchase, a small house for example) and all necessary renovations and partitioning.

Costs must always be included for such items as:

1. Heating, ventilating, air conditioning, sanitation and lighting.
2. Painting of temporary buildings, allowing also for any necessary repainting during construction.
3. The dismantling and removal of temporary buildings at completion of the project.
4. Office furniture: desks, tables, chairs, drawing racks, storage cabinets, conference tables, and other similar items. The specifications will probably state some minimum requirements for the architects' site office; sometimes this will be a complete inventory of items coupled with the request that all furniture and equipment is to be new (often office furniture catalog numbers will be quoted!). For the contractor's office the normal procedure is to move existing furniture from another (completed) project or place of storage to the new project, and purchase or rent additional items as required.

Estimators should also check the specifications regarding temporary buildings for the use of subcontractors. For major subtrades (mechanical and electrical, for example) it is usually specified that these contractors include the cost of all temporary buildings in their quotations; sometimes, however, this is specified to be a cost carried by the general contractor; and more ominously, some specifications remain silent on the matter. To avoid possible conflicts about this matter at a later date, it is best to solicit prebid clarification from the architect on this item.

Secretarial Supplies and Equipment

Include for the cost of items such as:

Stationery and miscellaneous office supplies
Writing and printing materials
Typewriters, calculators, adding machines
Photocopying equipment
Postal equipment
Drafting supplies
Bookkeeping, accounting, time-keeping supplies

A monthly cost should be established to cover these items. Previous cost information will be useful. Certain of the more specialized items (photocopiers, postal equipment, special drafting equipment, for example) should probably be identified as separate costs. An experienced office manager would be able to advise the estimator on all these items and costs.

Janitorial Services

This service may be stated in the specification as a mandatory weekly requirement for the architect's office, and the contractor will either hire a specialist company or perform the work with direct labor. This facility is sometimes included in the rental charges for temporary offices in existing buildings.

The estimate should include a lump-sum total or weekly cost as quoted by a janitorial service company. If the work is to be performed with direct labor, an estimated number of man-hours will be given.

10.7 Category 3: Site Access, Protection, and Security

Temporary Roads

This will vary according to the type and location of the project. Some projects will require special roads for construction purposes to be brought into the site from existing main access roads, and the drawings and specifications will provide detailed information regarding construction of such roads. However, for most projects the specifications will only stipulate the *requirement* for this work; the estimate of cost will be based on standard construction practices applicable to the locality or region. This estimate will usually be confined to the rental of equipment to rough grade, spread, and compact purchased granular materials, and possibly the labor costs of any necessary hand trimming.

Some specifications allow the early placement of the stone or gravel subbases for the permanent access routes to be used for temporary road purposes, with the final asphalt coating to be applied at the completion of the project. As this permanent paving work will usually be a subcontract item, the paving trade contractors will have to be consulted about this arrangement; the estimate should also include an allowance for "making good" to this subbase before the paving work is completed.

Apart from major access roads into the site, the estimate should also allow for temporary roadwork around the structure and into storage areas and hoist locations.

Available cost information from other projects might be useful in establishing unit prices (per linear or square foot), which could be updated to reflect current material and labor costs. It is important on projects of long duration to allow for some maintenance work to these temporary roads. Also check if the specifications make reference to any special requirements for dust control.

Fences, Hoardings, and Covered Walkways

The specifications will often contain definitive instructions about these items. They are usually noted on the site plot plans, enabling the total length to be measured with reasonable accuracy. A typical specification item for a perimeter hoarding might read:

> Provide hoarding at property line constructed with 4 × 4 in. studs at 2 ft. centers, ½ in. fir plywood good 1/side. Allow for gates. Paint hoarding two coats, color to be approved by the architect. Maintain and repair during construction; dismantle and remove from site at completion.

It is recommended that a unit price per linear foot (or meter) be established by taking off the materials in detail for a specific length of the hoarding (say 10 ft.) and then applying this unit price to the total length measured on the drawings. However, some specifications may refer the estimator to a "suitable hoarding to be constructed in accordance with local municipal regulations" or similar phraseology; in this case, other authoritative literature will need to be examined.

This applies particularly to covered walkways. Although, like the hoarding, this item may be specified in detail, very often the estimator will be referred to local regulations regarding not only the construction but also for information as to *the conditions that make the provision of a covered way mandatory*.

When standard details of hoardings and covered ways exist, the materials could be taken off for a specific length and a factor established indicating the number of board feet of lumber per linear foot of hoarding or covered way. This would simplify the task of estimating the material costs for these structures; there would be no necessity to build up prices from scratch for every estimate. Cost records would be the best source of information regarding the installation, maintenance, dismantling, and removal of these structures.

Sometimes a snow fence is specified around the perimeter of the site or a portion thereof. This should also be priced by the linear foot, and this cost will include both the fence material *and* the metal posts, which are usually sold separately. Also, as in the case of hoardings and covered ways, the item must include for subsequent dismantle and removal.

An item that can be overlooked is lighting in the covered ways. Some estimators may consider that this cost is applicable to the item for "temporary wiring and lighting"; the most important thing is to ensure it is included somewhere in the estimate!

Other items that relate to access would be:

1. Stairs and ladders to projects with deep excavations. These are usually wood-constructed structures designed and built to meet local or regional safety requirements. This item should be measured and priced on the total board feet of lumber required.
2. Temporary stairs and ladders in the structure required before the installation of the permanent stairs.
3. Temporary (wood) treads to metal stairs. This could be an enumerated item.

Protection

This requirement will vary according to different conditions and specifications. It usually refers to the protection during construction of adjacent structures, roads, walks, curbs, landscaping, and so on. The estimator is usually faced with the choice of being realistic and allowing a single sum of money to cover this item, or being optimistic that any damage occurring during the course of construction will not be the fault or to the cost of the contractor. The following are two specific items that should be identified and priced individually:

1. Protection of existing trees on the property. This will usually entail a physical count at the site. Close boarding or snow fencing is usually specified and can be an onerous item, particularly where the specification warns about a penalty sum for every tree damaged by construction.
2. Protection of finished floors. This should be taken off in square feet and priced according to the material specified (usually plywood).

Watchman and/or Security Services

A typical specification clause will state that a watchman's services will be required at all times *outside regular working hours*. It is usually included in the estimate as an hourly cost. The number of hours can be calculated by establishing the total number of hours for the period when the watchman will be required and deducting from this the number of regular working hours.

Example: A watchman is required for a 12-month period. The total number of hours for that period is 365 × 24 = 8760 hours. The number of *regular* working hours for the same period (based on an 8-hour day = 40 hours per week) would be 52 × 40 = 2080 hours. Therefore, the watchman would be required for 8760 − 2080 = 6680 hours.

If a specification requires the employment of a professional security agency, a quotation should be obtained from the applicable companies. This will usually be on a weekly or monthly basis. If the project is within a large industrial plant complex, the specification might state that the permanent plant security staff will be responsible for the construction site area.

Temporary Parking Areas

This could be stated as a separate item or included with the item for temporary access roads. This is another item where the updating of a basic unit price per square foot will be useful. Some projects may permit the use of permanent parking spaces for *a limited number of cars;* if the contractor's requirements are for more than that number, the additonal parking spaces will be subject to a stated monthly cost, which should be included in the estimate.

10.8 Category 4: Temporary Utilities

General

Some of the items in this category can run to fairly excessive costs, particularly on large projects. Temporary heat, light, and power can run into large sums of money. They are difficult to estimate and, if not properly planned and controlled at the project level, can soon exceed the budgeted costs.

For most of these items, historical data should be the basis for a realistic estimate of related costs. Previous cost records, the advice of project supervisors, debate and discussion, and comparative cost studies relative to the choice of methods and equipment, all these things will assist the estimator to produce intelligent cost planning.

Water

This item would normally include the following work:

1. Provision of temporary water lines, including excavation and backfill. This could be priced as a cost per running foot of water line, using either an updated unit cost from a previous project or soliciting a price from a plumbing subcontractor.
2. Connections to an existing water main.
3. Payment of local authorities' fees for water consumption, or metered costs if so specified. (*Note:* The specification might signify the building owner's intention of supplying water to the contractor *without charge*.)
4. Specifications usually obligate the general contractor to provide hoses for the use of subcontractors.
5. Well drilling may be necessary on projects in isolated or rural areas.

This item could be shown in the estimate by a single sum of money or it could be split into two items: (1) the total cost of providing the service lines, branches, connections, and the like, and (2) the water supply, shown as a cost per month.

Temporary Electrical Work

This should be considered in terms of three subdivisions:

Power
Electrical service
Distribution and lighting

These can be included in the estimate under one item of cost, or shown separately. Some estimators might prefer to show the first separately, but to combine the second and third into one item.

The most costly item would probably be power, although this could vary from project to project. Hoists, climbing cranes, temporary elevators, and similar equipment, all have an obvious influence on the demands for electrical power. If the specification states that the owner will supply the temporary power to the contractor, then only the costs of lighting and electrical service will have to be considered; but estimators should always confirm that such a clause also means that it will be supplied *free of charge to the contractor*.

Allow for metering costs. Temporary electrical power should be stated in the estimate as a *cost per month*. Check the specification carefully regarding such time as when the owner will take over and pay for operation.

Temporary electrical work can range from connections to existing services, to the more costly construction of pole lines into the site, particularly in rural or isolated areas. An electrical subcontractor should be consulted on this work. Allow for extension cords, outlets, transformers, panels, overhead cables, and so on. The cost of this work on a previous project of a similar size and function would provide a good base that could be updated and developed accordingly. The total estimated cost should be established as one lump-sum amount.

Distribution and lighting has reference to such items as wiring, panels, lights, lamps, transformers, and so on, everything to distribute the power *brought into the site by the electrical services*. This has to be a single amount item, and again a similar project's cost records will be helpful. In all temporary electrical work, make proper allowance for local charges where applicable.

Temporary Heat

This should be subdivided into two divisions:

1. Heating for specific construction purposes (concrete, masonry, defrosting frozen ground, etc.)
2. Heating within an enclosed structure.

The first category applies to the heating necessary for the cold-weather placing of concrete or masonry work, and the following items should be considered:

1. Purchase or rental of heaters, stating type (gas, oil, or propane) and capacity.
2. Estimated fuel requirements, stating estimated gallons, liters, pounds, kilograms.
3. Labor for handling the equipment and fuel, estimated on an hourly cost basis.

Some construction companies may consider that the estimated heating costs pertaining to concrete placing or masonry work should more correctly be included as part of the estimates for those trades, and there is a lot of merit in this consideration. They still remain indirect items, whether tacked onto specific trades or not, and for the purpose of this book have been included with general site overhead items. Also, it is very doubtful if many subcontractors for masonry or concrete work would include such items, and there would be a risk of them being accidentally overlooked in the analysis of subtrade bids.

Heating an enclosed building will be accomplished with either portable heaters (using oil, gas, or propane) or by using the permanent heating system. The second method can only be used if the specification condones it. A typical specification clause for this item would read:

> The permanent heating system may be used for temporary heating purposes, subject to the Architect's approval, etc.

Where a project is an addition to an existing building, or is an additional building within a complex of existing buildings (say a large hospital or university), the specification may state that steam will be available from an existing boiler room and will either be supplied free of charge or at cost to the contractor. If the last condition exists, the estimator will have to contact the maintenance engineer at the existing building to obtain a unit cost per pound (kilogram) of steam. The cost of a meter will also have to be included. Other items to be considered when using the permanent heating system would include:

1. Attendance on equipment (check local union regulations, which may demand the use of skilled operators for this work). This item should be given in total estimated man-hours.
2. Refurbishing and cleaning at completion (lump-sum item).
3. Temporary unit heaters and piping (rental or purchase).
4. Fuel consumption (or steam as already mentioned).

If the permanent system is not used, the estimate will have to be based on portable heating units, including for the same items as outlined for heating to concrete or masonry work.

On very large projects, estimators should check with a reliable mechanical contractor regarding this heating, particularly if the permanent system can be used. This contractor will be able to offer expert advice and might even be prepared to submit a quotation for this work. However, this quotation would be conditional upon his also being the successful bidder for the permanent mechanical work in the project, which is not unreasonable.

The cost of temporary heating (both for enclosed structures and specific trade operations) can be very excessive, depending upon the number of winter months in the project duration, and also according to the geographical location. Northern provinces or states will be very contentious areas in this respect.

Sanitary Facilities

Specifications require the provision of temporary toilets, usually of the portable chemical type. These are generally rentable, and the estimator should assess the number required (usually based on 1 unit per 30 employees) and the anticipated duration. The rental rate usually includes the servicing.

Specifications also usually allow for the use of permanent plumbing services when these are installed and to which contractors may connect temporary water closets and wash basins. A sum of money to cover the supply and installation costs of water closets, toilet bowls, and sinks (often "second quality") will be established for this item. Some sort of enclosure may have to be considered if the permanent cubicles are not installed; also cleaning and maintenance should be taken into account.

Temporary Telephone Service

There is usually a specification requiring the general contractor to provide temporary telephone service for the duration of the project. On small projects this service might be stipulated as being for the use of the contractor, the subcontractor, and the architect. (This usually means the architect's site representative, i.e., clerk of works.) On large projects the requirement is for the on-site architect (or representative) to have a separate telephone, and this is very often specified in the section dealing with the architect's site office.

The estimator should use up-to-date charges obtained from the local telephone company office for:

Installation costs (per telephone)
Number of extensions and push buttons
Number of lines required

An allowance should be made for the additional cost of long-distance calls *initiated by the contractor*. Normally, the specifications decree that long-distance calls by subcontractors, architects, or other people outside the contractor's organization will be charged to the parties originating the calls.

Telegrams and Telex

On major projects of long duration it would be advisable to anticipate the frequent occasions when conditions of urgency or crisis warrant the dispatching of telegrams to expedite materials or equipment, very often in the form of ultimatums to subcontractors or suppliers who have fallen behind schedule! A contingency sum of money should be provided for this item.

Major projects in the multimillion dollar range, where completely equipped offices will be provided for a duration of two, three, or more years, will often have a telex service installed. The local telphone company should be contacted for applicable costs for installation, monthly rental, servicing, and so on. Also, where the telex traffic might be excessive, the cost of a permanent operator should be contemplated.

Public Address, Paging Systems

Large multistory buildings, or projects with various buildings under construction spread over a large site, usually mean key supervisory personnel need a fast means of communicating with the main project office, and vice versa. This will rarely be a specification requirement; it is something on which a contractor would make an in-house decision in the interests of all-round efficiency. If it is decided that the project warrants these requirements, then reputable audiovisual companies should be contacted for proposals. Intercom systems, two-way radios, pocket pagers, all serve useful functions, and any reluctance to include this additional item of cost in the bid should be balanced against the costs involved in the nonproductive time of people looking for people! (Charlie searching the site with an urgent message for Joe and finally locating Joe in Charlie's office!) Telephone installation in a senior manager's car might also deserve some serious consideration.

Quotations from audiovisual companies should be checked carefully for any possible exclusions, such as wiring, repairs, or maintenance fees.

10.9 Category 5: Construction Facilities and Services

Layout and Surveys

A typical specification clause requires the contractor to be responsible for all layout, lines, levels, and grades, with the possible exception of the lot lines, which are often established by the owner.

This item should include the costs of stakes, batter boards, lines, and so on. The purchase or rental of surveying instruments is another applicable cost to be considered and either included with this item or identified separately. The labor cost will be shown as the estimated number of man-hours pertaining to carpenters, helpers, and rodmen. An instrument man would either be shown as a separate item or included with the item for the salaried or supervisory and technical personnel.

If the specification requires the services of a professional land surveyor to check and verify the layout and provide a necessary certificate, the fee for this service should be obtained from a land surveyor's office.

Trucking

This item could refer to either the hourly costs of company-owned trucks or the rental of vehicles from a truck-hire company. Some construction companies do not own any trucks, or only own one or two, and make use of hired trucks to meet additional demands.

The trucking allowance in an estimate of site overheads is to cover the costs applicable to the pickup and delivery of miscellaneous materials and the transfer of tools and equipment between projects within a specific area or between the site and a company equipment storage yard. A contractor doing formwork with direct labor will incur considerable trucking costs for the pickup and delivery of form lumber, scaffold frames and shores, metal form panels, joists and trusses, and similar items.

The cost of company-owned trucks should be computed as an hourly, weekly, or monthly rental cost, including fuel, lubrication, and repairs. The truck driver's time and rate should be given as a separate item. If a truck-hiring facility is used, the driver's time might be included in the rental rate.

Cleanup during Construction

Most specifications call for the site to be maintained free from excessive accumulation of debris and rubbish, something that most construction sites can provide without any apparent effort! The estimate should include costs of rubbish chutes, built either with lumber or metal chutes can be rented.

The costs of garbage containers are obtained from companies specializing in this service. These containers vary from 14 to 40-yd^3 capacities, and the charge (per container) will vary with the size. Estimators should check that the charges include the removal of a loaded container to the dump.

If the specifications make the general contractor responsible for providing these containers for *all* trades, at the *contractor's cost*, then the estimator should allow for loading the contractor's own debris into the containers; the subcontractors will be responsible to load their own rubbish. In many instances the contractor will do this work and *back-charge* the subcontractor with the cost. (Back-charges for cleanup are the cause of a perennial war between general contractors' and subcontractors' supervisors, which can only be tempered with good organization and straightforward handling, although, in a dispute, each side will claim sole ownership of both these virtues!)

Final Cleanup

This cost is usually estimated on the basis of separate unit prices for material and labor to be applied to the *total gross floor area of the project*. Although applied to a floor area, this unit should cover all items of final cleaning to all floors, walls, ceilings, and partitions in the finished project.

Some contractors include the cost of cleaning the glass areas with this item, while others prefer to measure and price it separately. It is usually estimated as a unit cost per square foot of *glass area* (i.e., the unit cost provides for cleaning two sides of the glass).

Sometimes architects request that these final cleaning operations must be carried out by approved specialist cleaning companies, in which case quotations should be solicited from these companies.

Modern high-rise structures with large areas of glass and aluminum require this work be done by a cleaning company with the staff and equipment to perform such work. Such a company will usually quote as a cost per square foot of gross wall area; estimators should question these companies carefully about the computation of this area, as it will be the basis of payment.

Construction Safety Requirements

Safety regulations demand that guard rails be provided at slab perimeters, around openings in floors and roofs, and at other locations that are 10 ft. or more in height from the ground. The perimeter of the floor slabs and slab openings should be measured in linear feet (meters) and separate unit prices established for material and labor costs. These rails usually have a minimum height of 3 ft., and can be built with 2 × 4 in. lumber, or purpose-made metal and wire mesh perimeter barricades are often acceptable. If lumber is to be used, estimators should allow approximately 1.8 FBM of lumber per linear foot of perimeter. Installation (and final removal) costs should be allowed as approximately 8 to 10 carpenter hours per 100 linear feet of railing. (*Note:* This does not allow for any temporary removal and reinstallation of sections to allow necessary access for material handling or other operations.)

An allowance should be included to cover the estimated material and labor costs of other miscellaneous barricades, platforms, runways, ramps, and similar structures whose scope and extent is difficult to determine on the drawings.

Snow and Ice Removal

This could apply both to access roads and to the structure under construction. Snow and ice removal to the structure should be estimated as a man-hour cost. For the larger areas of roads and parking lots, the rental costs of bulldozers, graders, and similar equipment should be assessed, plus any applicable hand labor costs.

The cost of snow and ice removal will naturally vary according to the geographical location of the project, from zero costs in Los Angeles to the other extreme in the Yukon or Alaska. Previous data will be valuable as a guide. Estimators can only resort to a "crystal ball" to predict the number of heavy snow or ice storms that might occur in a winter season (again depending on location), and then allow for so many hours of clearance work per occurrence. For example, an average of five storms per winter month, assuming four months would yield (5 × 4) 20 incidents. Snow-removal equipment might average 4 hours each time; therefore, at least 80 hours of equipment rental should be allowed. The number of man-hours for manual shoveling and icebreaking could run to 8 hours per occasion (8 × 20) or 160 hours. Chipping ice from parts of the structure could be a costly labor item under certain conditions.

Broken Glass

It happens on all projects! On small jobs it may not be a significant item, and if the culprit responsible for the breakage was a subcontractor, then (theoretically) there will be no costs accruing to the general contractor. On major projects it can be a very contentious item. The cost should include the cleaning up and removal of the broken glass and also the material and labor costs of glass replacement.

Temporary Enclosures

This item is specified for protection against the environment and also vandalism or crime. Temporary doors and windows are usually priced separately and estimated on the basis of total square feet of openings to be enclosed, or the items could be enumerated. Temporary doors will be necessary on all projects, but the need for temporary windows can be eliminated (or reduced to a minimum) if the permanent windows can be scheduled for installation before the arrival of inclement weather.

Attention should be paid to any large items of equipment—boilers, chillers, storage tanks, refrigeration equipment, switchgears, and other large size items—that may require portions of exterior wall being left out to provide access into the building. These temporary openings will also require enclosures during cold weather.

Enclosures for maintaining heat during the construction of the structure are usually made with tarpaulins or polyethylene, often attached to a framework of lumber. The net area in square feet of the area to be enclosed should be measured, and either priced at a unit cost per square foot or at a unit cost per tarpaulin. Make all necessary adjustments to the measured surfaces for overlapping.

In some areas complete enclosures will be necessary for the placing of concrete or masonry. Where possible, these should be prefabricated in pieces light enough to be moved by hand, or crane if necessary. These are best estimated as a cost per each section, with an allowance for repairs. The labor cost will be per number of times installed and removed. (Sometimes these might be built on skids and could be pulled horizontally, say for a tunnel or duct.)

Dust screens are usually specified where demoliton or renovation work is to take place in an existing building. Sometimes they will be required at an opening in walls where the new structure "ties in" to the existing. These can be simple enclosures of wood framework and tarpaulins or polyethylene, or soundly constructed partitions faced at one or both sides with either plywood or gypsum board. Insulation may also be specified. It is recommended that estimators build up a price based on the specification for a particular length, 10 linear feet, to establish a unit cost per running foot. The full extent of dust screen requirements can then be measured in linear feet. (If the screens can be relocated several times during the course of the work, then it is recommended that *two* items be measured:

1. The maximum length of screens to be fabricated. The labor unit will provide for the first in place, including the cost of dismantling.
2. The subsequent relocation costs, including dismantling at the balance of the necessary locations.

Progress Photographs

A common specification requirement is for the contractor to arrange for progress photographs to be taken, usually at monthly intervals. The number of different viewpoints will be stated and also the number of prints required. (Usually these photographs are stated to be in black and white, but sometimes there will be a requirement for a special colored set at the completion of the project.) Photographic agencies who specialize in taking progress pictures of construction projects should be contacted for the monthly cost of photographs and prints.

Scheduling Costs

This refers to a specific requirement for computerized preparation and updating of a schedule (usually CPM), and would include a consultant's fees (where applicable), drafting, computer, and printing charges. A total cost should be built up and included in the estimate as a single-sum item.

10.10 Category 6: Hoisting, Materials and Personnel

The word "hoisting" can be something of a misnomer. A crane can be used for both raising and lowering, and a project starting at a depth of 30 to 40 ft. below street level will have certain materials or equipment that have to be *lowered* to the required location. However, it is normal to refer to cranes, elevators, hoists, and the like, as "hoisting" equipment.

The shape and height of a building influence the requirements for hoisting. A building of only one to three stories spread over a large area would influence a contractor's choice toward a mobile crane, or a material hoist at a central location, or two hoists, or a hoist plus a crane, and so on. High-rise structures constitute an automatic demand for climbing cranes; they will probably also require material and personnel hoists, usually after the structural framework is completed and the climbing cranes dismantled and removed.

Many companies own their own hoists, towers, and cranes, but (and this applies to all equipment discussed in this book) these items should still be considered as rented or purchased for the project. Proposals from equipment rental companies will usually assist the estimator to establish an all-inclusive estimate of costs by highlighting all those items of work or equipment to be provided by the contractor.

Mobile Cranes

These can be rented by the hour, week, or month. If small-sized cranes are only required at certain intervals, estimators should consider hourly rental. Established crane rental companies should be contacted for applicable rates. These rates will vary according to the weight and capacity of the crane. Quotations should be checked carefully regarding:

Minimum rental period (usually 4 hours)
Transportation time (usually 1 to 1½ hours each way)
If operator is included
Costs of premium time for operator

Boom trucks usually have different rental rates from mobile cranes. If the mobile crane is to be used solely for the purpose of placing concrete, lifting and moving formwork, and hoisting reinforcing steel, these costs should more properly be included with the estimate for that division of work; and this practice is followed by some construction companies. In this book, *all* equipment is being considered with the site overhead estimates, but sufficiently identified as to function to be transferred to another division if required. This would be essential if a proper comparison had to be made against a quotation for this work from a subcontractor that included all hoisting costs.

Estimators should study the drawings carefully (also the site) regarding access for the crane. For example, it may only be possible to properly service two sides of a structure. This will mean horizontal transportation across the floor with buggies to place concrete or other materials to the inaccessible locations. Also will hydro wires and the like have to be relocated?

Tower Cranes

These fall into three categories: (1) climbing, (2) stationary, and (3) traveling. In high-rise buildings the climbing crane is the type universally selected for the construction of a reinforced concrete structural frame. Positioned in the center of the structure, or as close to the center as possible, it can provide maximum coverage to the building area. Smaller buildings, where the reach is not excessive, can be serviced either by a stationary crane or a traveling crane may be a feasible solution in some instances.

On the assumption that the climbing crane is the feasible selection, the estimator must check the drawings to see whether an elevator shaft can be utilized (if reasonably close to the desired location), or if openings need to be provided in each successive floor slab. This will mean allowances for bulkhead forms, possible additional reinforcing steel (for structural reasons), and a premium cost of placing the concrete when the crane is removed.

The selection of the size and capacity of the crane will be based on the manufacturer's data regarding lifting capacity at the maximum reach radius. For example, if the crane is to be used for the hoisting of precast concrete panels, each weighing 3 tons, and the minimum distance from the crane position to the point of hoisting is 170 ft., then the crane selected will be the one that can lift that weight with the trolley and hook extended to that distance. To maximize on the use of this equipment, the selected crane must have the capacity to hoist concrete, prefabricated "gang" forms, flying shores, and the like, at the maximum radius location.

A number of circular cut-outs can be made with stiff paper or cardboard scaled in size to the maximum radius of each size of crane and with the lifting capacities graduated on the surface. These can be laid on the drawing (the scale will of course have to be identical) with the center at the intended crane position, and it will be a simple matter to check the capacity at the longest reach.

Climbing cranes are either purchased or rented (or even acquired by a rental–purchase arrangement). Some manufactureres or equipment rental companies also provide additional services such as erection, dismantling, and raising; or these will be done by the general contractor. There are also companies who specialize in crane erection and dismantling, servicing, repairs, inspection, and so on.

When the size and capacity of the crane have been determined, the items to be considered in the estimate will include:

Rental (or purchase price)
Erection and dismantling
Raising
Maintenance, servicing, repairs
Electrical work (hookup, transformers, cable, etc.)
Concrete bucket
Freight (if excluded from rental or purchase costs)
Miscellaneous items: wire rope, guying, inspection
Operator's hours, including premium and shift time
Outer tower charges, where applicable

Items that will most certainly have to be provided by the general contractor would include:

1. Concrete foundation pad. A recommended size will be given on the manufacturer's data sheets (although this may have qualifications regarding soil conditions). A detailed estimate could be prepared of all applicable items, but to save time it is recommended that only the cubic volume of the concrete be measured and priced at a single unit price inclusive of the supply, placing, and finishing of concrete, formwork, reinforcing steel, and anchor bolts. This unit price could be updated for each bid.
2. Additional reinforcing steel might be necessary at any special openings made in the concrete slabs; also, shoring may be necessary here.

Many projects will provide conditions where concrete is required at some locations that extend beyond the reach of the crane, but where the concrete quantities are insufficient to justify a second climbing crane. Estimators should allow for some miscellaneous rental time of mobile cranes to service these locations.

Material Hoists and Towers

These will be used for the hoisting of all materials, including concrete, if a crane is not considered practicable. On large high-rise projects, the cranes will usually be dismantled when the structural work is complete, and the balance of the hoisting accomplished with material hoists. These towers will be either single or double well. They are usually located giving easy access by trucks hauling the material into the site.

Items to be allowed in the estimate will include:

1. The cost of the tower (single or double well), including repairs.
2. The cost of the hoist (state number of drums), including repairs.
3. Erection and dismantling costs of the tower (per linear foot).

4. Installation and removal of the hoist.
5. Landings and gates: one per floor.
6. Freight (if excluded from manufacturer's charges).
7. Wire rope, signals, and so on.
8. Electrical hookup.
9. Cost of the operators: man-hours, including premium time.

Note: if the tower is to be used for hoisting concrete, special handling equipment should be allowed for, such as bucket, hopper, and loading chute. Also, a Chicago boom will be an additional item that might be required. An enclosure for the heat may also be necessary during inclement weather.

Personnel Hoists

These will be necessary on high-rise buildings where many workers (both general and subcontractors' employees) will be engaged at different levels. The items noted for the material hoist will apply to this equipment, except of course for the special items (i.e., Chicago boom, concrete handling equipment, etc.).

Forklift

This is rather a modest piece of hoisting equipment after considering tower cranes and material hoists, but it serves many useful functions. It is limited to the reachable heights, approximately 25 feet, and is very much in evidence in masonry work. This is usually an hourly rentable item.

Temporary Elevators

This applies to the use of permanent elevators for temporary construction purposes, if permitted in the specifications. The estimator should allow for protection to the cab (tarpaulins or polyethylene), temporary shaft partition, and the hourly cost of skilled operators.

10.11 Category 7: Small Tools and Equipment

Most construction companies have a standard (typed or printed) list of items to be included in this category, and they can vary from reasonably condensed lists to sheets of paper cataloging just about every tool or piece of equipment in the book.

The following is a modest schedule of the items to be considered, either as purchases or rentals:

Small tools: This refers to hand tools, and some companies express it in two categories: expendable and nonexpendable. Usually, a sum of money, based on past cost records, is placed against this item.
Concrete equipment: buggies (hand- or motor-powered)
vibrators
machine trowels
elephant trunks
grinders
Skil saws
Radial saws
Electric drills
Compressors and air tools
Hose and cable (water hoses, extension cables, etc.)
Scaffold frames and plank
Compaction equipment: tampers
vibratory plates
Electric generators
Pumping equipment

Separate allowances should be made against these items (where applicable) for repairs, fuel and lubrication.

As already stated, some companies might lean toward including these items with the appropriate trade estimates, such as concrete, excavation, and so on.

10.12 Category 8: Permits, Insurances, and Bonds

The estimate should include for all permits required by authorities having jurisdiction. Some specifications state that the building permit will be paid for by the owner, in which case the cost will be excluded from the bid. It is a good idea for estimators to prepare a schedule of all permits and rates pertinent to different localities within a region and update this schedule periodically. It will serve as a good checklist and also save a lot of unnecessary telephoning for each bid.

Insurances

The most common are fire (builder's risk), public liability and public damage (PL and PD), and automobile and vehicle. The specification should be checked as to which have to be carried by the contractor and which are paid for by the owner. Most contractors deal with a selected insurance company who will provide the rates to be used in a bid to cover these requirements.

Bonds

Specifications often require the contractor to provide in the bid the cost of a 50 or 100 percent performance bond. A construction company usually has a bonding or surety company who will supply the cost of these bonds. They are quoted at a cost per thousand dollars per annum.

Example: The bond cost is \$5 per \$1000. The estimated value is \$2,000,000 with a duration of one year. The premium amount will be 2000 × 5 = \$10,000.

Some general contractors consider it prudent to include in their bids the premium costs of bonding major subtrades. This is rarely a specification requirement, because this bond is only a protection for the contractor against the financial failure of a subcontractor. The building owner is already protected by the performance bond from the contractor. In effect, the general contractor is asking and *paying* for the same protection from a subcontractor that the owner is receiving from the general contractor by virtue of the performance bond. Of course, as this amount is included in the bid, the owners do in fact pay this cost, and some owners get disgruntled at what they consider is *double bonding*. Indirectly, the owner is receiving some additional protection because the bankruptcy of a major subcontractor can delay the project and nearly everyone gets hurt, and particularly so if there was no bond on the subcontractor.

10.13 Review

It is difficult to define the limitations of items and work that qualify for inclusion in this category of site overhead or indirect costs. Specifications differ regarding the allocation of items to this division or to some other trade division. Various general contractors tend to hold conflicting views as to the extent and limitations of standard company checklists of related items; too often such lists can grow uncontrollably and very often additional items are created as a result of some isolated incident that happened on one particular project. "Better put that on the list," someone will growl. "Might happen again." Other contractors may consider such out-of-the-way incidents as part of the "risk" syndrome to which all contractors are exposed, believing it more important to consider ways to prevent such recurrences rather than putting additional sums of money in a bid that is intended to be competitive.

Estimators should prepare notes from the specifications, writing down all the items properly identified. The standard checklists should then be consulted for all other items that are included in the specifications by inference, or what would be dictated by standard practice. Because there is no specified reference to the services of a watchman, this does not mean a watchman is not required. A clause holding the contractor responsible for "the protection and security of the site at all times" is contractually sufficient to bind a contractor to provide the services of a watchman or equivalent.

Equally, if a contractor decides to provide a watchman service for valid reasons of company security, he can do so (and include the cost in the bid) even though there may be no contractual requirement for this service. There will be other similar items that although not asked for by the owner will still be necessary for the contractor's operations.

11 Closing the Bid

11.1 General

The day when the bid must be finished and submitted to the owner is always an ominous one for estimators. At a certain hour on this day, the brakes are applied and the whole bid process grinds to a halt, and whatever has been forgotten or omitted, or was not properly checked, or could (or should) have been done differently—with the striking of that hour it is too late for regrets or second thoughts. A well-known verse from Edward Fitzgerald's translation of the "Rubaiyat of Omar Khayyam" is a grim reminder:

> The Moving Finger writes; and having writ,
> Moves on: nor all thy Piety nor Wit
> Shall lure it back to cancel half a Line,
> Nor all thy Tears wash out a word of it.

Most estimators would sympathize with the urge to "lure it back to cancel half a line"! Bid-day tensions can bring a series of problems, and even the bid that has been well preplanned and superbly organized can come apart at the seams in the final closing hours. The atmosphere in a general contractor's office on the final day usually appears to be one of turmoil and confusion. The closest comparisons might be the backstage of a theater on opening night of a new show or a newspaper office going to press. Telephones ring, calculators rattle, blood pressures ascend, heartbeats accelerate, and things that seemed certainties two days ago now whisper alarming doubts!

Did I take off the concrete fireproofing in the penthouse?
Did I allow a compaction factor?
We should've figured *eight* space heaters, not *six!*

Venerable estimators will entertain their grandchildren with enthralling tales about some of their most memorable bid-closing experiences, and featured in these stories will usually be the one about the bid "When Everything Went Wrong"; the favorite will probably be "When Everything Went Wrong but We Got the Job Anyway!" (Whether any money was made on that job never comes into the story!)

It is difficult to avoid a bid-closing day without some snags or problems cropping up, particularly in those areas where it is the rule rather than the exception for 80 percent of the quotations to be telephoned into the contractor's office within the short span of about 3 hours! Good organization and forethought can assist in reducing problems, or at least eliminating those that only *became problems because they were left until the last day*.

Apart from the obvious advantages of having all quantity take-offs and pricing completed beforehand (and often that is painful enough), there are a number of items that experienced estimators usually write into a checklist and try to do two days ahead, or the day before, or, failing that, at least early in the morning of bid day. Many of these are simple routine matters that can be accomplished easily and quickly in advance, and it is usually because they seem so mundane that *they get pushed temporarily to one side*. The next section provides a checklist of some such items to be considered.

11.2 Bid-Closing Checklist

1. Has the bid form been signed (by an officer of the company with signing authority) and witnessed or sealed?
2. Has the bid bond (if applicable) been processed and signed and is it ready at hand? (Not stuck away in someone's drawer!) Has the certified check been arranged for? This can be a problem where the amount is to be a specified percentage of the bid total, the actual amount of which is not known until near the final hour. However, at the earliest opportunity a reasonable assessment should be made (leaning toward the "high" side as a precaution) and the check processed.
3. Bid envelope? The "Instructions to Bidders" will most probably provide instructions regarding the name and address to be typed on the envelope and also the format of the envelope. Some bid-calling authorities provide special preaddressed envelopes for the bid. (Someone should know where this was filed when it arrived with the other documents!)
4. Some bids require a statutory declaration to be included with the bid documents. Has this been processed? and where is it?

5. Has someone ascertained whether telephones are available at the place where the bid is to be delivered? Most bids are completed by telephone communication between the estimating office and the person delivering the bid, and it is strongly recommended that a prebid reconnaissance be made to locate the proximity of the public telephones. If the nearest public telephone is a mile or so down the road, then contact should be made with nearby gas stations or restaurants, or there may be adjacent private offices where some sort of a "deal" could be made for a half-hour use of a telephone. Failing that, send a hefty-size courier and have him (or her) "gate-crash" someone's office for a telephone! Get the bid in, argue later!
6. If the normal mail delivery to a contractor's office is late in the day, arrangements should be made with the nearest post office for a mail pickup on bid day. This particular day's delivery will probably include quotations from subcontractors and suppliers, which the estimator needs to see as early as possible.
7. Have the Agreements to Bond (if pertinent) been received from the surety company?
8. Miscellaneous "bugs in the works":
   - a plentiful supply of telephone quotation receipt pads? and are they accessible, not on the top shelf of a dimly lit storeroom?
   - paper in the adding–calculating machine?
   - staples in the stapling machine?
   - paper clips?
   - sharpened pencils?

Nearly all these items can be attended to before the actual bid day, and irritating as it may sound, that's the time to think about them!

11.3 The Bid Form

The checklist included a reminder about the signing of the bid form. There are a number of items pertaining to bid forms that could be completed ahead of time, or if that is not possible, at least some preliminary planning will be beneficial.

Bid forms vary in size and the information required. Some bid-calling authorities appear to have been indoctrinated into the belief that a bid is not bona fide unless the weight of the paper is equal to the weight of the intended structure! Others are quite satisfied with a single sheet that tells the owner in simple terms the sum of money for which the contractor will construct the building in accordance with the bid documents, which is really the "bottom line" in which the owner is most interested.

The following are some items included in the average bid proposal form:

1. *Addenda:* There is usually a requirement to confirm the numbers and dates of all addenda issued during the bidding period. This can be attended to at

least the day before the bid, unless one is dealing with an architect notorious for issuing bulletins up to an hour before bid closing!

2. *Unit prices:* Most bid forms include a schedule of unit prices to be used for changes to the contract, either as additions or deletions. These are usually confined to excavation, backfill, and concrete work; however, some bid-calling authorities request unit prices for nearly all trades. Estimators should note which unit prices pertain to general contractor's work and which to work by subcontractors. As subcontractors rarely see the general contractor's bid form, they will probably not be aware what unit prices are required; it will be advisable to contact them in advance and alert them to this requirement. Unit prices for general contractor's work can be established any time after the pricing of the pertinent trades is completed. This subject is further discussed in Section 11.10.

3. *Alternate prices:* Bid forms often require information regarding cost adjustments for alternative materials and methods, and these will refer to either *specified* alternate prices or alternates *volunteered* by the general contractor. For the specified alternates, the estimator is advised to prepare estimate sheets ahead of time noting all the pertinent items to be adjusted. For general contractor's trades, these could be priced and dispensed with very early, but the greater percentage of these alternates will most likely require input information from the subtrades. If appropriate analysis sheets are prepared in advance, all that needs to be done is insert the monetary amounts when they are known, and do the arithmetic to verify the adjustment amount.

   Figure 11.1 shows an example of an estimate sheet prepared in advance to determine the cost difference for an exterior wall to be finished in face brick in lieu of a base bid requirement for precast concrete. The face brick quantities have been measured and priced, with all labor burdens added; the only item not yet included is the quotation from the precast concrete contractor, which will clarify whether this alternate will increase or decrease the contract sum.

   Some alternate prices concern items of work that are included in the main bid but that the owner may decide to abandon if the bid amount is excessively higher than the owner's budget, and for which it is important to know the estimated cost immediately. These can vary from simple items like the anticipated deletion of a sauna for example, or they can be very complex like a complete floor of a hospital or a wing to a school.

   Many owners and architects encourage contractors to provide on the bid form any proposed alternate methods, materials, or systems based on previous experience on similar projects. Sometimes these unsolicited alternates originate as suggestions by subcontractors to be passed on by the general contractor.

4. *Separate prices:* These usually refer to items of work that are *excluded* from the main bid but that the owner is contemplating adding into the contract depending on the estimated cost. Like alternate prices, these could be very modest requirements or very costly ones. (The contractor should pay attention to these well in advance to ascertain the effect their inclusion might have on the scheduled duration of the project.) Sometimes the title "sepa-

PAGE 1 OF 1

GENERAL ESTIMATE

PROJECT Research Centre LABOUR RATES ______ QUANTITIES ______
ESTIMATE № 27/82 ______ EXTENSIONS ______ CHECKED ______
TRADE SECTION Bid Form Alternate DATE ______ PRICED ______

DESCRIPTION	QUANTITY	UNIT	MATERIAL U.P.	MATERIAL TOTAL	LABOUR U.P.	LABOUR TOTAL	TOTAL
Alternate No. 1 = Precast Conc. Wall Panels in lieu of Facing Brick.							
a) Delete:							
Facing Brick	29	MPcs	190 00	7410	293.00	11427	18837
Mortar	11.6	C.Y.	44 55	518		—	518
Clean Down Brick	3936	S.F.	0.03	118	0.07	276	394
Dovetail Anchors	1400	Pcs	0.12	168		—	168
				8214		11703	19917
Add: Labor Charges 27%						3160	3160
							23077
b) Add							
Quotation – P.C. Conc. Subcontractor →							
					Difference:		$
(Note: No adjustment made for Masonry Equip. Items – Still Requ'd for Back-up Materials)							

Figure 11.1.

rate price" will be given to items already discussed in "alternate prices," which have reference to items that the owner may wish to *deduct* from the contract.

5. *Itemized prices:* These normally refer to items *included in the main bid,* but of which the owner wishes to know the cost. It is important for contractors to check with the architects if there is any doubt about the true intent of this request for information. It is usually required as information relating to taxation or cost-sharing matters.
6. *Names of subcontractors:* Most bid forms require the general contractor to list the names of subcontractors whose quotations were included in the bid. Some bid-calling authorities restrict these lists to the major subtrades; others thirst for all the information available, sometimes not only the name of the masonry subcontractor but also who is going to supply and mix the mortar! The usual directive regarding work that the contractor does not intend to subcontract is to write the words "by own forces" in the appropriate space on the bid form.
7. *Cost breakdown of bid:* This is sometimes requested to be submitted with the bid. There are already enough things to keep estimators busy while trying to arrive at the final bid total, and this requirement adds a further irritant factor to the process. Attendance to this request usually means something else has to be neglected, and that could include the recording and processing of all the late subtrade quotations, (usually the most aggressively competitive prices), all of which are to the owner's advantage if reflected in the bid total. If such a breakdown is requested for submission at the time of the bid, the architects should be approached for permission to have it submitted at least 24 hours later. The normal procedure is for these kind of breakdowns to be submitted after, or at the time of, the contract award, when they are required for payment purposes.
8. *Completion dates:* Bid documents usually require contractors to make some statement regarding the anticipated duration and completion date of the project. Once the schedule has been agreed upon and finalized, this information can be entered on the bid form.

Some bid forms will include all the types of items just reviewed; others will be satisfied with half or less; while some bid-calling authorities will require double those items! These portend more bid-closing headaches for estimators, because most of them cannot usually be processed beforehand. However, advance knowledge and clear understanding of such requirements are still more desirable than only becoming aware of them on the last day. At least some methods and strategy can be planned to handle these items as efficiently as possible at the appropriate time.

11.4 Telephone Bids

With the exception of a few subcontractors who will submit their quotations in letter form, and also those areas where a large percentage of the subtrade

GELLEM CONSTRUCTION Co.

TELEPHONE QUOTATION

PROJECT	RESEARCH CENTRE	DATE	MAY 27/82
COMPANY	BEECH & ACORN LTD.	ESTIMATE №	27/82
ADDRESS	CENTREVILLE	TELEPHONE	418-2929
TRADE DIVISION	09250 — GYPSUM WALLBOARD	ADDENDA	1 to 4

SCOPE OF WORK	AMOUNT
(a) WORK INCLUDED	
ALL AS PER DRGS + SPECS	$106,400.00
(b) WORK EXCLUDED	
ACOUSTIC CEILINGS (SPECIFIED SECTION 09500)	
(c) ALTERNATE OR SEPARATE PRICES	

TAXES	INCLUDED	EXCLUDED		
FEDERAL	✓		QUOTATION GIVEN BY	BILL GREEN
PROVINCIAL	✓		RECEIVED BY	B.E.W.
OTHERS (DESCRIBE)				

Figure 11.2.

contractors bid the general contractors through the offices of a bid depository, most of the subtrade bids are telephoned in on the closing day.

Figure 11.2 shows an example of a typical form used by a general contractor to record bids received by telephone. Although these verbally transmitted quotations do not possess the legality of written quotations, estimators should attempt to have them recorded in such a manner that, except for the lack of a signature, they represent a formal communication.

The printed information requirements are useful to remind estimators about the pertinent items to be checked when the subcontractor calls. This will save calling back and asking questions like: "Did you include sales taxes?" or "What addenda have you included?" It is important also to ask the name of the bid caller; this saves time if a return call is necessary to query an item. (Contact can be quickly re-established with, "Can I speak to Bill Green, please," rather than, "I was just talking to someone in your office about so-and-so job . . .!")

The need to write legibly is an obvious statement. Everyone's handwriting is different and where there might be problems *printing* should be suggested (tactfully!). Of course, even the neatest handwriting can suffer when quotations are telephoned in during the pressures of the final 15 minutes! At this time estimators recording telephone bids should concentrate on getting three things down clearly and accurately:

1. The *name* of the company calling.
2. The *trade division* being quoted.
3. The *price*.

Badly transcribed figures can cause many more problems than words. The digits 4 and 7 are vexsome, and the European 7 is strongly recommended. A missing zero can be disastrous if not spotted in time ($40,000 written as $4000, for example).

The format of the telephone bid form can also be used to guide long-winded or inarticulate bid callers into more precise and factual statements about their quotations. Interrogatory questions like, "Are you quoting in accordance with the drawings and specifications?" will direct such bid callers into the right track. The specification section numbers should also be checked and confirmed. For example, Masterformat states the following trade divisions: 09300 Tile and 09400 Terrazzo. A telephone communication might start along the lines of: "I want to give you a price on the ceramic tile in the washrooms, and I'm also including the quarry tile to the lobby and the terrazzo; and also those brass expansion strips shown on the drawings. . . ."

The statement about the ceramic tile being located in the washrooms and the quarry tile in the lobby might be perfectly correct, but the estimator is not usually sitting at the telephone with a floor finish schedule facing him, and time is running too short for all this to be checked out. The estimator wants the satisfaction of knowing that the subcontractor's quotation includes all ceramic tile, quarry tile, divider strips, *everything* that is called for in those specific trade divisions. Subcontractors should be encouraged to first state the numbers and titles of the division on which they are quoting, and then proceed with their lists of qualifications or exclusions. This would assist in avoiding any misunderstanding at the time and reduce the chances of future confrontations.

11.5 Bid Depository Quotations

The bid depository system of processing subtrade quotations to general contractors exists in many regions, towns, and cities. The rules and procedures tend to vary in each locality, and also the number and classification of trades participating in the system; but most or all of the following basic principles seem to apply universally:

> To quote from the Ontario Bid Depository Standard Rules and Regulations: "The Bid Depository provides for the reception of sealed Tenders from Trade Contractors whereby the sanctity of the Bidding is protected and those receiving their Tenders obtain firm quotations in writing."

(This definition displays an interesting combination of Canadian and American terminology: *"tenders"* are submitted to the *"Bid"* depository!)

As already stated the number of trades who participate in the bid depository system differs across the North American continent. In Western Canada, for example, a greater percentage of trades make use of this service than in Ontario; in Toronto its use is currently confined to a few major trades such as mechanical, electrical, sprinklers, and, sometimes, structural steelwork.

Some fairly standard conditions regarding bid depositories are:

1. They are usually managed and supervised by local or regional construction association offices ("Builder's Exchange" is a time-honored appellation).
2. The time at which bids must be submitted to the designated depository offices is usually *24 or 48 hours prior to the general bid closing time*.
3. The bids must be submitted on official bid depository forms (white, pink, yellow, etc.) and in official envelopes, addressed to the various general contractors known to be bidding the project.
4. The general contractors will pick up their bids at the prescribed time.

Most bid depositories have many more rules and procedures than the few basic ones just outlined, which illustrated the methods for the submission and receipt of the bids.

The most significant and seemingly advantageous aspect of bid depository quotations to estimators are:

1. They are received well ahead of the general bid closing, thus providing reasonable time for proper analysis and also for checking out the proposed duration schedule with the low bidders to ascertain if it is realistic in regard to their trades; this would apply particularly to the delivery dates of major equipment items.
2. It is the accepted rule in most bid depository systems that the subcontractors' bids must include *everything* contained in the bid documents applicable to their trades, so all subcontractors are bidding on the same basis, "apples with apples."

The last two statements infer some bid closing alleviations for the estimators; to an extent it places the quotations in the same category as formal written quotations; however, sometimes and in certain localities a number of things can happen that detract from these advantages. For example, most bid depository systems allow for trade contractors to withdraw their bids up to 3 hours before the general bid closing. The usual reason for a withdrawal would be the discovery of an error in the bid or the suspicion of an error if the bid amount was extremely low. ("Too much left on the table!")

The withdrawal of a bid cancels out some of the advantages stated in item 1. The general contractor may suddenly have to start talking to another company (usually the second bidder) regarding schedules and other matters, with possibly only 3 hours before the bid deadline (although most estimators would prefer 3 *hours* to 3 *minutes,* which might be the case with telephoned quotations!).

Item 2 does not always hold absolutely true. In some cities or regions the subcontractors may use the weight of their trade associations and mutually agree to formally exclude certain work, which, although called for in the specification for their trade, they do not agree as being applicable to their operations. Their bids will have uniformity in respect to all other items, but the general contractor is still left with the problem of establishing or obtaining cost estimates for the excluded work. Excavation, backfill, concrete, and miscellaneous metal and steelwork are some of the items often falling in this category. However, the point must be conceded that if estimators are knowledgeable about these standard qualifications, they will automatically prepare prebid estimates of the cost of these items for inclusion in the bid, in the same way as they would with prebid proposals discussed in section 11.6.

11.6 Prebid Subtrade Proposals

The general contractor will often receive "lead" letters from trade contractors in advance of the bid-closing day, outlining the terms and conditions of the quotations they intend to submit. This is a commendable practice, particularly where the subcontractors may be only interested in performing certain portions of the work included in the specifications for their trade divisions. Formwork subcontractors, as an example, may only be interested in quoting on the principal structural elements in a project where they can be assured of a continuity of work for their labor force; it would not be economical for them to make intermittent return trips to the site to perform miscellaneous work to equipment bases and curbs, exterior landscaping, and similar items. The same could probably hold true for excavation contractors, who are often only inter-

AGGRESTONE PRECAST ENTERPRISES LTD.

May 23, 1982

Re: Research Building, Centreville

We are preparing a quotation for the precast concrete work as detailed in Division 03400 of the specifications. Please note our quotation will include the following items:

a) Supply and erection of the precast concrete wall panels.

b) Supply only of the precast concrete paving slabs and planters.

Our quotation is to be based on the general contractor providing all hoisting facilities. If the use of our mobile crane is required, there will be an additional charge of $5,000.00.

All taxes included. Quotation open for acceptance within 60 days.

Our price will be telephoned to you prior to the closing time.

Yours truly,

AGGRESTONE PRECAST ENTERPRISES LTD.

Figure 11.3.

ested in the main items of earthwork in the structure, which can be performed in one period of time.

The proposal letters are beneficial to estimators. Prebid arrangements can be made to simplify the necessary analysis of the actual quotations when they are received.

The following examples illustrate how this prebid information can be used in the formats set up to properly analyze the subtrade bids when they are received.

Example 1: Figure 11.3 shows a letter sent to all general contractors from a precast concrete company outlining the work and items that will form the basis of the quotation they intend to telephone out to the contractors on the day of the bid.

Figure 11.4 shows a second prebid proposal from another precast concrete company. This one has been received verbally and is recorded on a telephone bid form. The basis of this quotation is different from the first example and another analysis sheet should be prepared.

With the information provided on these two prebid proposals, the estimator can prepare analysis formats for purposes of quick comparison between the quotations when they are received. The items that will be excluded from the quotations will be measured and priced, and only the actual quotation amounts would then be required to obtain a true comparison between these two quotations, or any others that might be received.

The necessary quantities and prices shown in the following examples should in practice be written on formal estimate sheets (not on the backs of quotations or pieces of scratch paper!).

(a) Aggrestone Precast Enterprises Ltd.

Installation of P.C. pavers: 6861 ft.^{2} at $0.90	=	$ 6,175.00
Installation of P.C. planters: 15 each at $35	=	525.00
Labor burdens (31% × $6700)	=	2,077.00
Additional cost for mobile crane	=	5,000.00
		$13,777.00
Quotation		?
Projected total:		$?

(b) Mold-cast Products Ltd.

Installation of P.C. pavers: 6861 ft.^{2} at $0.90	=	$ 6,175.00
Labor burdens (31% × $6175)	=	1,914.00
		$ 8,089.00
Quotation		?
Projected total:		$?

GELLEM CONSTRUCTION Co.

TELEPHONE QUOTATION

PROJECT	RESEARCH CENTRE	DATE	MAY 24/82
COMPANY	MOLD-CAST PRODUCTS LTD.	ESTIMATE No	27/82
ADDRESS		TELEPHONE	246-8264
TRADE DIVISION	03400 – P.C. CONCRETE	ADDENDA	1 to 4

SCOPE OF WORK — PRE-BID INFO	AMOUNT
(a) WORK INCLUDED	
ALL AS PER DRGS & SPECS (EXCL. AS BELOW)	
(INCL. SUPPLY & INSTALLATION OF P.C. PLANTERS)	
(PRICE TO BE PHONED IN)	
NOTE: WILL PROVIDE OWN MOBILE CRANE –	
INCLUDED IN BID AMOUNT.	
(b) WORK EXCLUDED	
INSTALLATION OF P.C. PAVERS	
(c) ALTERNATE OR SEPARATE PRICES	

TAXES	INCLUDED	EXCLUDED		
FEDERAL	✓		QUOTATION GIVEN BY	AL JONES
PROVINCIAL	✓		RECEIVED BY	B.E.W.
OTHERS (DESCRIBE)				

Figure 11.4.

Example 2: Prebid proposals are received by telephone from two formwork subcontractors, A and B.

The basis of contractor A's intended quotation is that only the following items will be included:

Formwork to foundation and superstructure walls, columns, beams, suspended slabs and stairs
Formwork to all other items (including footings) is *not included*
Other exclusions: waterstops, expansion joints, setting of screeds, anchor bolts and other embedded items, bulkheads and keys
Hoisting to be provided by the general contractor.

Contractor B's proposal is somewhat different:

Formwork to *all* items excluding equipment bases and curbs, bulkheads, keys and setting of screeds.
Installation only: waterstops, expansion joints, anchor bolts, embedded items *(materials to be provided by general contractor)*
Separate price to be quoted for placing of concrete to *all above items only,* excluding the finishing of exposed concrete surfaces after forms are stripped
Additional cost of mobile crane for hoisting of *own work only:* $10,000.

The analysis sheets prepared for these quotations will include the estimated costs of the numerous items noted for exclusion from the quotations. The source of the quantities and costs for these items will be the general contractor's own estimates for concrete and formwork. The detailed analysis sheets for both quotations are demonstrated in Section 11.7 of this chapter.

These examples illustrate the "apples and oranges" syndrome of some quotations. Obviously, the basic quotation amounts from each subcontractor will be meaningless until the analysis process reduces them all to common denominators. This will have to be done as speedily as possible after the quotation amount is received.

The estimator now has advance knowledge of how some trade contractors intend to quote; but how about the other contractors who have not made known their intentions? Aggressive telephone canvassing is probably the only method by which an estimator might succeed in "flushing out" the prebid information. However, trade contractors cannot always make these decisions until they have gained sufficient knowledge about the project. Most of these contractors will cooperate with the general contractor by giving him the information as soon as it is known.

Estimators are also conditioned to the additional irritant of the subcontractor who suddenly decides to revise the conditions on the prebid proposal; and sometimes these changes are not announced until the time when the price is telephoned in by the subcontractor (probably 20 minutes to zero hour!).

Over a period of time estimators are able to recognize that certain trade contractors are consistent in their bid conditions and have certain standard exclusions or are members of trade organizations who impose these conditions. Thus when these contractors are known to be bidding, the format of the analysis can be visualized ahead of time; but estimators should always brace themselves for some surprises!

11.7 Subtrade Quotation Analysis

The following are some examples of the various items to be considered when analyzing subcontractors' quotations, particularly those where only part of the specified work will be included.

Formwork

Referring back to Section 11.6, which illustrated the prebid proposals from formwork subcontractors, if the analysis sheets had been prepared in advance, then as the quotations were received each analysis could be completed. Figure 11.5 illustrates the analysis, and the result indicates subcontractor B as having a low bid, but *only when the separate price for* concrete placing is taken into account.

However, although the analysis process revealed the bid from B as being more favorable than the one from A, the situation might exist where the general contractor's own estimate for this work was lower than all the subbids received. If the amount of difference was small, the contractor might still favor subcontracting the work, particularly to a reliable company. This would reduce the contractor's risk factor on direct labor.

It will be noticed in the examples shown that only one subcontractor intended to provide a mobile crane, but as the quotation stated specifically that this cost applied only to hoisting operations for the concrete and formwork, allowance should have been made on the analysis to cover the cost of the additional use of this crane for the unloading and handling of reinforcing steel. It should also be observed that the subcontractor would take no responsibility for the finishing of formed surfaces after the formwork had been stripped.

Analysis of Formwork Quotations

Subcontractor A			
Quotation:			$126,000
Add:	Value of exclusions		22,847
	*Labor Charges (on exclusions)		3,455
	Contractor's estimate conc. labor		15,411
	Labor charges on last		4,161
	Contractor's crane cost		13,000
			$184,874
	* 27% of $12,795		
Subcontractor B			
Quotation:			$134,300
	Separate price conc. placing		17,000
	Separate price, mobile crane		10,000
Add:	Value of exclusions (conc. & forms)		13,060
	*Labor charges on exclusions		2,446
			$176,806
	* 27% of $9,059.00		
Contractor's Estimate (for comparison and adjustment)			
	Total cost, formwork		$140,412
	Labor costs, concrete		15,411
	Labor burdens (on concrete & forms): 27% of $117,590		31,749
	Mobile crane, rental		13,000
			$200,572
		Less:	176,806
			$ 23,766

Figure 11.5.

This work could be very costly, especially if the architect demanded a high-class finish on the concrete and the contractor was faced with *repair* work rather than *finishing* because of faulty formwork.

Precast Concrete

Section 11.6 demonstrated the analysis sheets prepared in accordance with the prebid proposals received from two precast concrete subcontractors. The following shows the final projection of these analyzed quotations:

	(a)	(b)
Quotation:	86,400	90,511
Exclusions:	13,777	8,089
	$100,177	$98,600

The quotation for (b) is the most favorable. It provides a lesser amount plus the advantage of a lower risk in the direct labor estimate.

Miscellaneous Trade Analysis

The following are some trade examples picked at random where problems could arise if no analysis were made or the terms of the quotation were not fully read or understood.

1. *Structural steel:* The quotation might refer to the inclusion of "field painting as specified," which could be misinterpreted if the specification only referred to "field touch-up," with the actual field painting to be done by the painter.
2. *Glass cleaning:* The subcontractor for windows or curtain wall might state that all cleaning of glass is included in the quotation. However, careful reading of the specification could reveal a requirement for this subcontractor to clean the glass at the *completion of his work,* while the general conditions would still require final glass cleaning at the *end of the project*.

11.8 Sales Tax

Quotations should be checked carefully regarding the inclusion or exclusion of applicable sales taxes: state, provincial, federal, or others. This applies particularly to bids received by telephone; with time running short and other expediencies to be handled, a quick and clear understanding is vital about the status of these taxes in a quotation. There could be considerable sums of money involved, which could be financially harmful if omitted from the total bid or could impair the competitiveness of that bid if included unnecessarily.

Very often subcontractors and suppliers are not absolutely certain about the sales tax applications to specific projects, and it is not uncommon for the quotation amount to be given followed by the statement: "Amount of sales tax applicable is $15,000." In most instances this could be taken to mean that the amount of $15,000 was to be *added* if sales taxes were to be included; it could, however, mean that this was already *included* in the quotation amount, and it was left to the contractor to make the adjustment if this amount could be omitted. Persons recording telephoned bids should clarify and properly record this information before passing the quotation on to another person to analyze.

A further complication can occur when a subcontractor quotes on the *supply and installation* of a specified item and merely states the official percentage to be added for sales tax. The problem here is that the sales taxes are usually only applicable to the *cost of the material*, and do not apply to the transportation or installation charges, and those amounts need to be known for the correct tax adjustment to be made.

Example:	Total amount of quotation:	$175,000
	Less: Installation	45,000
	Less: Freight	1,000
	Amount subject to sales tax	$129,000

As can be readily calculated, a 7 percent tax on $175,000 and the same percentage applied to $129,000 produces a difference of $3920, not a large sum but still a contribution to a low bid.

Estimators should familiarize themselves with regional sales tax regulations. Certain materials might only have tax exemptions applied to the *parts* and not to the *whole* (e.g., concrete or concrete masonry units).

11.9 Main Estimate Summary

Figure 11.6 shows a (completed) format for a bid summary sheet including all the amounts and adjustments to arrive at a final bid total. All construction companies will differ (some slightly, some widely) on the format of a main estimate summary sheet necessary for determining the final bid total. The example shown provides for all the direct trade estimate amounts and the subtrade amounts to be entered in the applicable columns. These amounts should be totaled as shown, preferably not less than 1 hour before the bid closes. This allows time to make the necessary calculations regarding labor burdens, insurances, bonds, and permits and for a total sum to be established.

However, as subtrade bids might still be pouring in by telephone, only easing off probably in the last 10 minutes, it will be necessary to allow for late *price adjustments*. These adjustments are shown in the appropriate column and represent the differences between the amounts already entered and the revised amounts, whether more or less. Often a subcontractor will *raise* his price if he has discovered an error (or considers the possibility of an error if he has been informed his bid is uncomfortably low!). The total of these adjustments will either decrease or increase the final bid amount.

The percentage for head office overhead and profit (usually combined) will be added to the total at this stage. The percentage of desired profit will have been considered earlier by senior management, but very often the final decision is not made until the adjusted summary total is known. The total labor content will have some influence on this margin. As stated in Chapter 8, this provides the biggest risk to a contractor. Also the caliber of some of the sub-

BID SUMMARY SHEET

ESTIMATE NUMBER: 27/81 DATE: May 27, 1982 PROJECT: RESEARCH CENTRE

	Div. No.	Trade Section	Material	Labour	Sub Quotation	Total	Adjustment
1	02200	Earthwork	45 276	1 376 2	✓	59 038	
2	02480	Landscaping	✓	✓	9 700	9 70 0	
3	02500	Paving & Surfacing	✓	✓	15 000	15 0 00	(15 00)
4	03100	Formwork	38 233	10217 9		140 4 12	(237 6 6)
5	03200	Reinf. Steel-Supply/Detail	✓	✓	10 700	10 7 00	
6		-Placing Mesh	✓	✓	✓	Incl. above	
7		-Wire Mesh	✓	✓	✓	Incl. above	
8	03300	Cast-in-Place Concrete	82 553	1541 1	✓	9 7964	
9		Conc. Floor Finishing	✓	✓	8 606	8606	
10	03400	Precast Conc.-Wall Panels	✓	✓	90511	9 0511	
11		-Paving	✓	617 5	Incl. above	6175	
12	04200	Unit Masonry	3 9882	4 449 1	✓	8 4373	
13	05300	Metal Decking	✓	✓	7800	7800	
14	05500	Metal Fabrications	✓	420 0	35000	3 9200	
15	06100	Rough Carpentry	862	3961	✓	4823	
16	06200	Finish Carpentry	1 00	693 9	16000	2 3039	
17	07100	Waterproofing	✓	✓	2 5000	2 5000	(20 00)
18	07500	Membrane Roofing	✓	✓	486 00	4 8600	
19	07900	Sealants	✓	✓	1 1000	1 1000	
20	08100	Metal Doors & Frames	100	168 1	10300	1 2081	
21	08200	Wood & Plastic Doors	✓	314 2	7875	1 1017	
22	08500	Metal Windows	✓	✓	47000	4 7000	(35 00)
23	08800	Glazing	✓	✓	✓	Incl. above	
24	09250	Gypsum Wallboard	✓	✓	1 06400	10 6400	(87 00)
25	09300	Tile	✓	✓	19750	1 9750	
26	09500	Acoustic Treatment	✓	✓	5 7400	5 74 00	
27	09650	Resilient Flooring	✓	✓	38600	3 8600	
28	09680	Carpeting	✓	✓	3600	3600	
29	09900	Painting	✓	✓	17800	1 7800	
30	10000	Specialties	4 50 0	620 0	32 000	4 27 00	
31	15000	Mechanical	✓	✓	350000	35 00 00	(60 00)
32	16000	Electrical	✓	✓	186500	18 6500	
33			211506	208141	1 155142	1574789	(454 66)
34		Site Overheads	53975	71652	✓	125627	
35			26 5481	2797 93	1 155142	170 0416	(454 66)
36				Labour Burdens		7 5544	
37						177 5960	
38				Office Overhead/Profit		9 0000	
39						186 5960	
40		BID: $1,820,500.00			Adjustments	(4 5466)	
					BID TOTAL	$182 0494	

© WILSON JONES COMPANY G7513 GREEN

Figure 11.6.

contractors who have provided the lowest quotations may be taken into consideration as other risk factors.

The example shown demonstrates the methods by which the adjustments resulting from the analysis of the formwork subcontractors' quotations previously discussed are recorded. The net adjustment includes an amount of $29,303 ($31,749 less $2,446) applicable to the labor burden charges already included in the summary total; also this reduction of the labor content alleviates the accompanying risk factor, and a modified percentage for margin can be considered.

11.10 Unit Prices

Item 2 in Section 11.3 dealt briefly with the requirement in most bid documents for unit prices to be used as contract adjustments. Estimators should be wary about units that very often cover certain operations *generally* rather than *specifically*, and consideration must be given to the price or rate to be applied against each unit. For example, a unit might be described very simply as "Supply, place, and finish 3,000 p.s.i. concrete, per cubic yard." The estimator will have no problem with the material cost of the concrete, which can be extracted from the priced estimate; but what about the placing and finishing costs? They vary considerably with different items—footings, walls, slabs and so on. Which category is most likely to be subject to any revisions, requiring more or less quantities? One way of dealing with the problem is to decide on the category most likely to fluctuate and then qualify the unit price accordingly, that is, revise the item to read "Supply, place, and finish 3,000 p.s.i. concrete *to foundation walls below grade*."

Markup for overhead and profit should be added to the unit prices for additional work; the deleted items can be quoted at "cost," although some contractors adjust these rates to provide some percentage for overhead.

Unit prices for excavation and backfill should be checked to see if the quantities are to be based on bank measure or if the measurements are to be kept within defined lines. This will mean that all allowances for side slopes, compaction, and similar factors, will have to be included in the unit rate. The same holds for rock overbreak.

11.11 Bid Delivery

It is the rule rather than the exception that in most cities and regions the bid has to be kept "alive" until at most the *final quarter of an hour*. This means that the estimators are kept "hopping" right up to the end taking quotations, adding up summary sheets, calculating adjustments, and so on. Because of this, usually some other person in the company (clerk, junior engineer, secretary) will be delegated to take the uncompleted bid form down to the official place of submission and telephone back to the main office for the final total, information, and bid total. (Item 5 in Section 11.2 already emphasized the need for prebid reconnaissance regarding telephones.)

When the final bid amount is known, it should be given out to the bid deliverer as slowly and clearly as possible during those closing moments of tension; and have him or her repeat it back immediately. Most bid forms require that the bid amounts be stated in both figures and words. Always ask the courier to write down the figures first, and then to repeat the amount back slowly in words both *before* and *after* writing *the words* on the bid form. If two people have been assigned to deliver the bid, both should check and agree that the amounts expressed in figures agree with those in words. (Remember, the words will take precedence over the digits, and $2,760,000 worded erroneously as "Two million, six hundred and seventy thousand dollars" will be the cause of much grief!)

The bid delivery person should always check the correct time at the desk, table, or whatever, where the bid is to be accepted. This could be a wall or desk clock or a receptionist's watch; but this will undoubtedly be the official time-recorder! Never rely on a personal wristwatch!

If the bid is for a publicly owned project (school, hospital, government building, etc.), the bids will be opened and announced publicly; for private bids the estimators and contractors may have to "sweat it out" for a week, a month, or even longer. (During that period they will be subject to almost daily rumors and snatches of gossip, some encouraging, some discouraging, never anything factual!)

11.12 Brief "Recap"

Everything stated in this chapter would suggest that contractors, by merely following the recommended procedures, will be ensured of an orderly, problem-free bid-closing session; this is not necessarily so! Even in circumstances where all (or nearly all) of the subtrade quotations are delivered in advance and in writing (or through the facilities of a local bid depository) there will still be tension plus an awareness of the approaching deadline, all of which can affect the work habits of the most seasoned and stabilized estimator. Everyone is too well aware that a contracting company has to secure work and therefore the goal is to be competitive; everyone is equally aware that a contracting company has to show a profit, which will be exceedingly difficult, if not downright impossible, with a serious error made in the bid!

It is walking along the thin line between these two alternatives that creates the tensions. However, most veterans of a thousand nerve-wracking bid-day tensions would agree that a few drops of prevention here and there would never aggravate the problems, and might assist in alleviating them.

Also, if and when mishaps do occur, then the causes of these mishaps should be investigated with the view to preventing recurrence on the next bid. When something goes wrong the leading statement should always be: "Let's check to see how this happened and let's make sure it doesn't happen twice!" Experienced construction people hold "Murphy's Law" in great respect: "If anything **can** go wrong, it will!"

Appendix
Et Alia

Postbid Activities

With the bid duly delivered to the building owner there is usually a sigh of relief from the estimators as the tension recedes, apart from the natural anxiety while waiting to learn the results of the bid. With public work, this information is usually available almost immediately; with private projects it may be a few days, even weeks, before the results are made known. During that period the local construction "grapevine" will be in full operation, with "A" predicted as low bidder today and "B" a successful bidder tomorrow, and so on; the rumors alternating between the discouraging "lows" and exciting "highs," very little of which is factual!

If the bid is unsuccessful, then—apart from making the normal predictions about the low bidder's imminent bankruptcy due to such a low bid!—the normal task for the estimator is to gather together all the bid documents and return them to the bid-calling authority and ensure the return of the monetary deposit, if applicable. On the other hand, if the bid is successful, then—following the initial self-congratulatory demonstrations of joy at producing such an excellent and realistic estimate!—the estimator should still gather together all the documents but this time with the more congenial objective of labeling or tagging them with the title 'Original Bid Copy,' or similar wording.

It is wise to do this as eventually a set of drawings and specifications will be issued for formal contract execution by both parties—owner and contractor—and it will be necessary to check that these contract documents correspond exactly with the bid documents.

Bid Analysis

Whether the bid is successful or unsuccessful an analysis of the bid should be prepared on a trade by trade basis. This analysis should show the amount for each specification or trade division along with the applicable cost per square

Bid Analysis

Project: Research Center, Jackson University Date: May 27, 1982
Estimate No.: 27/82 Gross Floor Area: 31,485 s.f.

Section	Amount	Cost per SF/GFA	% of Total
Earthwork	62,753	1.99	3.45
Landscaping & Paving	23,200	0.73	1.27
Formwork	144,234	4.58	7.92
Reinforcing Steel	10,700	0.34	0.59
Cast-in-Place Concrete	97,964	3.11	5.38
Concrete Floor Finishing	12,767	0.41	0.70
P.C. Concrete-Wall Panels & Paving	98,353	3.12	5.40
Unit Masonry	96,386	3.06	5.29
Metal Deck	7,800	0.25	0.43
Metal Fabrications	40,334	1.29	2.22
Rough & Finished Carpentry	35,204	1.12	1.91
Waterproofing	23,000	0.73	1.26
Roofing	48,600	1.55	2.67
Sealants	11,000	0.35	0.60
Metal Doors & Frames	12,534	0.40	0.69
Wood & Plastic Doors	13,143	0.42	0.72
Metal Windows & Glazing	43,500	1.39	2.39
Gypsum Wallboard	97,700	3.10	5.37
Tile	19,750	0.62	1.08
Acoustic Treatment	57,400	1.81	3.15
Resilient Flooring & Carpet	42,200	1.34	2.32
Painting	17,800	0.57	0.98
Specialities	44,374	1.42	2.44
Mechanical	344,000	10.92	18.90
Electrical	186,500	5.92	10.25
	1,591,196	50.54	87.38
Overheads & Profit	229,304	7.28	12.62
	$1,820,500	$57.82	100.00

NOTE: Labor Burden Total ($75,544) is re-allocated to the pertinent trade divisions.

foot of gross floor area. These square foot costs are valuable aids to the development of an estimator's expertise and to the understanding of the cost factors applicable to the various building elements and trade divisions.

Figure A shows a suggested format of a bid analysis sheet, in this case pertaining to the Research Center estimate. Some estimators might prefer to show the costs per cubic foot in addition to (or in lieu of) the square foot costs. A column is also provided to show the status of each trade division expressed as a percentage of the total amount.

Other information that could be incorporated into the bid analysis would include:

1. The *structural frame* cost per square foot, which in the sample for the Research Center would be the aggregate of the square foot costs for concrete, formwork, reinforcing steel, structural steel, and metal deck (= $14.32 per square foot).
2. A functional unit cost—e.g., the cost per apartment or hotel suite, per hospital bed, and so on.
3. Data regarding the ratio of *unfinished* areas (e.g., parking and basement areas, etc.) to the *finished* areas (offices, suites, lobbies, corridors, public areas, washrooms, etc.).
4. Comments regarding the possible impact on cost by the shape and size of the building, and the ratio of perimeter to floor area. This greatly influences the cost of exterior 'cladding' or 'skin'—brick, stone, precast, aluminum, glass and glazing, metal siding, and so on.
5. Average unit costs of formwork (per s.f.), concrete (per cu. yd.), reinforcing steel (per ton), excavation (per cu. yd.) and so on.

This information will prove invaluable for preparing preliminary estimates where only sketch drawings are available and the building owner is considering negotiating a contract with a specific contractor and desires some early cost budgets. It will, of course, be necessary to continually update these analyses to allow for current material and labor price.

This data should be prepared as soon as possible after the bid has been submitted, and in the case of an unsuccessful bid, before the drawings and specifications are returned.

Mechanical and Electrical Trades

These trades were not discussed in the main chapters of this book. Although these are specialist trades for which general contractors usually receive firm price bids from mechanical and electrical contractors, the drawings and specifications for these trades should still be examined by the contractor's estimators to ascertain all pertinent information, including but not limited to the following items:

1. Work specified to be performed by the general contractor—excavation, backfill, concrete, equipment bases, etc.
2. Miscellaneous items which often only appear on the mechanical and electrical drawings with the ominous notation "by the general contractor"!
3. Items which have impact on scheduling and site overhead cost:
   a. Complexity and location of ductwork.
   b. Size and location of mechanical rooms—in the basement, on the roof, intermediate floor? Also location of cooling tower.
   c. Type and location of equipment items. Are they spread throughout the building, or concentrated in certain areas? Any delivery problems?
   d. Size of equipment. Will there be hoisting problems? Will openings have to be left in walls or floors?
   e. The method of heating and possible impact on temporary heating costs.
   f. Electrical equipment deliveries, and their impact on temporary power, lighting, operation of elevators and mechanical equipment items.
   g. Convector units and similar items—how they interface with other trades; do the details correspond with the architectural detail drawings?

Many of the above items (delivery problems, for example) will require checking with mechanical and electrical contractors known to be preparing quotations. Anything noted in the documents for these trades which is not clear and which could have an impact on the contractor's estimate of cost should be pursued and clarified before the bid is finalized. It will be too late if only brought to light afterwards!

Index

A

Acceptance period, bid, 5
Access flooring, 135
Accessories, formwork, 85, 174, 175
Accountant, project, 193
Addenda
  acknowledgement of, 34
  contractural status, 34
  definition, 34
  recording, 8, 9
  query on, 35
  sample of, 35
Advertisement
  public bid call, 4, 5
  for subtrade bids, 17
AIA (*see* American Institute of Architects)
Air tools, 212
Alternate Prices, 218, 219
Aluminum Joists and Trusses, 173
Aluminum Windows, 28, 29
Ambiguities, in bid documents, 22, 33, 36
American Institute of Architects, 20
Analysis
  bid, 238
  subtrade bid, 226–231
Anchors, dovetail, 105, 116, 120, 181
Anchor slots, 89, 104, 116, 120, 173, 174
Architect
  "Approved Equal" clause, 30, 31
  interpreter of contract, 33
Architect *(Contd.)*
  "invitation to bid" from, 4, 6
  queries to, 31–34
Architectural Concrete, 78, 84, 173
Area
  contact, formwork, 83
  gross floor, 13, 14, 239
Asphalt Paving, 135

B

Back-charges, 204
Backfill
  compaction, 42, 57, 61, 62, 72, 73, 161
  fill to grade, 62
  items and measurements, 62, 63
  manholes and catchbasins, 62
  manhour factors, 160, 161
  for mechanical and esectrical trades, 62
  perimeter foundations, 62
  pricing, 160, 161, 164, 165
  to pits, 62
  to spread footings, 62, 164
  take off, 68, 73, 75
  using excavated materials, 61
Backhoe, 56
Balustrades, concrete, 88
"Bank Measure," 55, 58

"Bar Chart" Schedule, 189, 190
Beams
  concrete
    formwork, 86, 87, 93, 172, 173
    placing, 80, 90, 93
Berm, excavation of, 64
Bid
  acceptance period, 5
  analysis, 238, 239
  bonds, 13
  call, 4, 5, 6
  check list for closing, 216, 217
  cost breakdown of, 220
  delivery, 217, 234, 235
  depository, 222, 223, 224
  documents
    checking, 8, 10
    misinterpretations in, 20, 21
    recording, 6, 7, 8, 9, 10, 11
  form, 217, 218, 220
  info reports, 12, 13, 14
  invitation to, 4, 5, 6
  public, 4
  public, advertisement for, 5
  security, 13
  subtrade, 14, 15, 16, 17, 18
  telephone, 220–223
Bidders, instructions to, 12
Bidding, function, 2
Block, concrete
  estimating quantities, 108, 109
  items and measurements, 103
  manhour factors, 179
  pricing, 181, 182
  take-off, 115, 117, 120
Boarding, 125
Bonds
  bid, 13
  performance, 13, 213
  performance, subcontractor's, 213
Boom, Chicago, 211
Boxings, formwork to, 84, 88, 172
Broken glass, 206
Budgets, preliminary, 14, 239
Buggies
  brick, 181
  concrete, 169, 212
Builder's Risk (*see* Insurance)
Buildings, temporary, 194, 195
Bulking factor, excavation, 55
Bulkheads, formwork to, 88, 172, 174
Bulldozer
  placing backfill, 165, 166
  rental rate, 164
Bulletins (*see* Addenda)
Building permits, 191

C

Caisson cap
  formwork, 85, 171
  place concrete, 79, 166
Calcium chloride, 79
Camera, for site visit, 191
Canadian Construction Association, 5, 20
Canadian Institute of Quantity Surveyors, 14, 40
Cards, soliciting subcontractor's bids, 16
Carpenter
  composite rate, 149, 150, 158
  hourly rates, 157
  output
    formwork, 171–173
    doors and frames, 184
    rough carpentry, 179–180
Carpentry, Finish
  benches, 128
  capping, 128
  ceiling strips, 128, 183, 186
  counters, 127, 128, 183, 186
  cupboards, 128, 183
  definition, 126
  handrail, 129, 183, 186
  items and measurements, 128, 129
  manhour factors, 183
  mop rails, 129
  paneling, 128, 183, 186
  priced estimate, 186
  shelving, 129
  sills, 129
  stairs, 128
  take-off
    basic principles, 126–128
    examples, 137, 138
  trim, 128, 183

Carpentry, Finish *(Contd.)*
valance, 129
window stools, 129, 183
Carpentry, Rough
blocking, 122, 123, 124, 125, 182, 185
building paper, 125
cant strips, 121, 122, 124, 182, 185
framing, floor and ceiling, 125
furring, 124
items and measurements, 124, 125
manhour factors, 182
nailing strips, 122, 182
priced estimate, 185
roof framing, 125
roofing felt, 125
rough hardware, 126
take-off
example, 137, 138
principles, 123, 124
vapour barrier, 126
wallboards, 125
walls and partitions, 125
Caulking (*see* Sealants)
Cavity wall
insulation, 105, 180, 181
productivity, 180
CCDC No. 12, 1979, 20, 22
Center Line Measurement, 90
Chalkboards, 135
Chamfers, formwork, 88, 172
Chases, formwork, 88
Check List of Trades, 10, 11, 12
Chicago boom, 211
CIQS (*see* Canadian Institute of Quantity Surveyors)
Cladding wall, exterior, 13, 239
Clay tile, structural (*see* Structural Clay Tile)
Cleaning
during construction, 204
glass and aluminum, 205
final, 204, 205
Clerk of Works, 202
Climatic conditions, 145
Columns and Piers
formwork, 86, 172, 174, 177
placing concrete, 80, 166, 169
Column capitals, 87
Column footing, (*see* Spread footing)
Completion date, 220
Compressors, 212
Concrete
admixtures, 79
calcium chloride, 79
embedded items in, 82, 83
finishing formed surfaces, 82, 167, 169
floor finishes, 83, 170
heating and protection, 200, 207
items and measurements, 78, 79, 80, 81, 82, 83
precast, 12, 28, 136, 225–227, 230
ready-mix, 76–79, 143, 179
specification notes, example, 24, 25
caisson caps, 79, 166
columns and piers, 80, 166, 169
core walls, 79, 167
curbs, 81, 167
duct banks, 81
dwarf walls, 80
equipment for, 169, 152, 153, 171, 212
equipment bases, 81, 167
exterior slabs on grade, 81, 167
footings, 79, 166, 169
foundation walls, 79, 166, 169
grade beams, 79, 166, 169
light standard bases, 82
loading docks, 80
manholes and catchbasins, 81
manhour factors, 166–168
metal deck fill, 94, 167, 169
metal stair fill, 81, 169, 171
pile cap, 79, 166
pipe bed and surround, 81
pits, 80, 166
pricing, 166–171
ramps, 80
retaining wall, 80, 166
shear walls, 79, 167
skim slab, 80, 166
slabs on fiber tubes, 81
slabs on grade, 80, 166, 169
slab on membrane waterproofing, 80
slabs on pans, 81, 167
slabs on structural steel, 80
slabs on V-rib forms, 81, 167

Concrete *(Contd.)*
stair walls, 79
suspended beams and slab, 80, 166, 169
suspended flat plate slabs, 80, 166, 169
stairs, 81, 167, 169
steel fireproofing, 82, 167
steps, exterior, 81
topping, monolithic, 81, 167
topping, separate, 81, 167
trenches, 81
walls, 79, 80, 166, 169
winter delivery, 79
Concrete block, 43, 103, 115, 117, 181
Concrete block, glazed, 43, 104, 179
Construction Joints, 88, 96, 172, 174
Construction Safety Act, Ontario, 58
Contact area, formwork, 83
Contract
AIA—A.201, 20
CCDC 12, 20
documents, 7, 237
stipulated sum, 1, 20
types of, 1
Conversion factors, masonry, 106–111
Core walls
formwork, 86
place concrete, 79, 167
Corner guards, 135
Cost breakdown, of bid, 220
Cost feasibility studies, 1
Cost records, 40
Cost Reports, 144
Covers and frames, metal, 134
Covered way, 196, 197
Crane
climbing, 208, 209, 210
mobile, 153, 168, 169, 171, 208
tower, 209, 210
Crushed stone (*see* Underfloor Fill)
Curbs
formwork to, 87, 172, 173
place concrete to, 81, 167
Curing, to concrete floors, 83, 170
Cutting and Waste (*see* Wastage)

D

Dampproofing, 136
Debris, removal of, 60, 66, 68
Demolition
existing buildings, 66
exterior masonry, 67
general remarks, 66, 67
interior masonry, 67
items and measurements, 67, 68
manhour factors, 162, 163
Deposit, bid (*see* Bid Security)
Dewatering, 65, 66
Directories, manufactured, 135
Directory, Sub-trade, 15
Discrepancies, in bid documents, 22, 36
Disputes, avoidance of, 35, 36
Documents, bid
recording of, 6, 7, 8
understanding, 19–21
Documents, Contract
AIA No. 210, 20
CCDC 12, 1979, 20
Documents, prequalification, 5
Door frames
metal, 45, 133, 138, 184, 186
wood, 134
Door grilles, 26, 27, 135
Doors
bifold, 134, 184
folding, 135
items and measurements, 133, 134
lead-lined, 134, 184
metal, 45, 133, 138, 184, 186
plastic, 133, 138, 184, 186
sound-proofed, 134, 184
special purpose, 134
overhead, 135
vault, 135
wood, 133, 138, 184, 185
Drainage tile
bed and surround to, 63
pipe and fittings, 63
Drawings
checking numbers received, 8, 10
electrical, 239, 240
as instruments of communication, 19

Drawings *(Contd.)*
mechanical, 239, 240
recording, 6–8
revised, 8, 34
for "take-off" example, 46–53
as visual communication, 21
Drilling, line, 61
Drops, slab, formwork to, 87, 172
Dust screens, 67, 68, 191, 207
Dwarf walls
formwork, 86
place concrete, 80

E

Earth, categories of, 58
Earthwork (*see* Excavation)
Edges, formwork to (*see* Slab Edges)
Electric drills, 212
Electrical drawings (*see* Drawings, electrical)
Electrical service, temporary, 199, 200
Elephant trunk, 212
Elevators, temporary, 211
Enclosures, temporary, 206, 207
Equipment
concrete placing, 152, 153, 168, 169, 212
excavation, 56, 163, 165, 166
masonry, 106
miscellaneous, 212
office, 195
output, 152, 153
rentals, 152
Equipment bases
formwork, 87, 172, 174, 175
place concrete, 81, 167
Estimate
budget, 14, 239
for stipulated sum contract, 1, 20, 21
Estimating
function of, 2
text and reference books, 3
Estimator, professional obligation of, 2
Excavation
to basements, 60
computation of machine work, 163, 165
in earth, 58
equipment productivity, 165
equipment rentals, 163
foundation trenches, 60
by hand, 58, 61, 161
haulage time, 165
items and measurements, 59, 60, 61
manholes and catchbasins, 60
measuring, 54, 55
small quantity items, 59
mechanical and electrical trenches, 60
methods and equipment, influence of, 56
pits, 60
pricing, 163, 164, 165, 166
rock, 58, 61
side slope ratios, 59
spread footings, 60
side-casting, 59
stock-piling, 59
take-off example, 68–73
take-off, general principles, 54, 55
trenching, 60
tunnels, 60
working space, 54, 55, 56
Existing foundations, breaking up, 60
Existing structures, 189
Expansion joints
covers, 135
pricing, 169, 173
take-off for, 82, 95
Exterior cladding, 13, 239

F

Falsework, 85
Fill, (*see* Backfill)
Filler, liquid joint, 82
Fine grading, 161
Finish Carpentry (*see* Carpentry, Finish)
Fireproofing, concrete
formwork, 87
placing, 81
mesh wrapping to, 82
Fireproofing, masonry, 111

Flagpoles, 135
Float charges, 58, 160, 165
Floor Finishes, concrete
  sub-trade prices, 170
  take-off, 83, 97
Floor hardeners, concrete, 83
FOB, 142
Folding doors, 135
Folding partitions, 135
Footings
  formwork, 85, 91, 171, 174, 177
  place concrete, 79, 91, 166, 169
  stepped, 90, 91
Foreman, composite rate adjustment, 159
Forklift, 106
Form panels, metal, 173
Formed surfaces, finishing to, 82, 167, 169
Forms of agreement, contract, 20
Formwork
  accessories and hardware, 85
  balustrades, 88
  boxings, 88, 172
  bulkheads, 88, 172, 174
  caisson caps, 85, 171
  chamfers, drips, etc. 88, 172
  chases, 88
  columns, 86, 172, 174, 177
  column capitals, 87
  contact area, 83
  core walls, 86
  curbs, 87, 172, 173
  double-forms, 88, 98, 174
  dwarf walls, 86
  equipment bases, 87, 98, 100, 172, 174, 175
  fireproofing, concrete, 87, 172
  flying forms, 173
  foundation walls, 86, 171, 174, 176
  grade beams, 85
  items and measurements, 85–89
  light standard bases, 87
  loading docks, 86
  manhour factors, 171–173
  masonry shelves (*see* double forms)
  materials, 175–177
  metal pan joist, 89
  miscellaneous projections, 89
  oil, form 85
Formwork (*Contd.*)
  parapets, 88
  pedestals, 87
  pilasters, 86, 90, 92, 172, 174
  pile caps, 85, 171
  pits, 86, 172
  pricing, 171–178
  ramps, suspended, 86
  retaining walls, 86
  reuse, 175, 176
  shear walls, 86, 172
  slab drops, 87, 172
  slab edges, 88, 95, 172, 173, 174
  soffits, metal pan joists, 87
  spread footings, 85, 171, 174, 177
  stair walls, 86
  steps, exterior, 87
  subcontractor's quotations, 225, 228–230
  suspended beams, 86, 172, 174
  suspended slabs, 87, 172–174, 177, 178
  stairs and landings, 87, 172, 174
  take-off example, 91–100
  tile-joist floors, 89
  up-turned beams, 87, 172
  waffle pans, 89
  wall footings, 85, 90, 91, 171, 174, 177
Foundation walls
  formwork to, 86, 92, 171, 174, 176
  place concrete to, 79, 92, 166–169
Freight-on-board (*see* FOB)
Fuel
  for equipment, 152
  for temporary heating, 200
Function
  bidding, 2
  estimating, 2
Furniture, for project office, 194

G

Gang forms, 172, 173
General Conditions (*see also* Site Overhead Costs)
  definition, 23
  Masterformat sections, 23, 187
  making notes on, 23, 213

General Contractor's Work, 23, 44, 45
General Estimate summary sheet (*see* Pricing Examples)
General office overhead, 232
Generator, electric, 212
Glass Breakage, 206
Glazed concrete block, 104, 179
Glazed structural tile, 103, 179
Grade beam
  formwork to, 85
  place concrete, 79, 166, 169
Grade man, 161
Grading, fine, 161
Gratings and frames, 135
Grinders, concrete, 212
Gross Floor Area, 13, 14
Grouting baseplates, 82, 168, 169
Guardrails, 205
Guarantee, on doors, 27
Guaranteed Maximum Contract, 1
Gypsum, masonry, 104

H

Hardware
  finish, 130, 184
  formwork, 85
  rough, 126
Haulage, excavated materials
  computing cost of, 163, 165
  time cycles, 165
  truck rentals, 163
Heat, temporary
  to concrete, 200
  to enclosed building, 200, 201
Heaters (*see* Temporary Heat)
Hoardings, perimeter, 187, 196, 197
Hoist
  material, 210
  personnel, 211
Hoisting, materials and personnel, 208–211
Hollow Metal Work (*see* Metal Doors and Frames)
H-piling, to perimeter shoring, 64
Hose and cable, 212

I

Imperial measurements, 3
Indirect Costs, definition, 187, 188 (*see also* Site Overhead Costs)
Instructions to Bidders, 12
Instrument man, 193
Insulation
  cavity wall, 105, 180, 181
  material prices, 142
  roof, conflict in specification, 30
Insurance
  builder's risk, 212
  fire, 212
  labor (*see* Labor Charges)
  liability, 212
Isolated beam, 86
Itemized prices, 220
Items and Measurements, schedule of:
  carpentry
    finish, 128–129
    rough, 124–126
  concrete, 78–83
  demolition, 87, 88
  doors and frames, 133, 134
  excavation, 59–61
  fill and misc. earthwork items, 62, 63
  formwork, 85–89
  masonry, 102–105
  miscellaneous metals, 134, 135
  miscellaneous trades, 133
  specialties, manufactured, 135

J

Janitorial services, 195
Jet-eductor, 65
Joints, construction, 88, 96, 172, 174
Joints, expansion (*see* Expansion Joints)
Joint filler, liquid, 82
Joists
  concrete, metal pan, 89
  wood, 125

K

Keys, forming, 88, 91, 96, 172, 174

L

Labor
  charges, 151, 157, 230, 233, 234
  composite rates, 148, 149
  cost units, 143–151
  rate escalations, 143, 190
  insurances (*see* labor charges)
  premiums (*see* labor charges)
  productivity factors, 144–147, 150, 151
  rates, for pricing examples, 157
Land Surveyor, 203
Landscaping (*see* Sodding and Seeding)
Laps, 42, 43
Layout, 203
Lighting, temporary, 199, 200
Light standard base
  formwork, 87
  place concrete, 82
Line drilling, to rock, 61
Lines and Levels (*see* Layout)
Lintel
  masonry, 105, 117, 179, 181, 182
  precast concrete, 195
  steel, 105
Liquidated Damages, 13, 14
Loading Dock
  formwork, 86
  concrete placing, 80
Lockers, 135
Loose measure volume, 55
Louvres, 135
Lumber
  formwork, 175–177
  pressure treatment, 124
  rough carpentry, 123, 124
Lump Sum Contract (*see* Stipulated Sum)
Lunchroom facilities, on-site, 194

M

Machine excavation (*see* Excavation)
Machine trowel finish, 83
Main Estimate Summary, 232–234
Manholes, concrete, 81
Manhour Factors, principles, 148–151
Manhour Factors Tables
  concrete placing and finishing, 166–168
  demolition, 162, 163
  doors and frames, 184
  excavation and fill, 160, 161
  finish carpentry, 183
  formwork, 171–173
  masonry, 179, 180
  preparation of, 150, 151
  rough carpentry, 182
  shoring and underpinning, 162
Masonry
  anchorage materials, 105, 112, 116, 118
  bonding, 107–110
  concrete block, 108, 109
  brick factors, tables of, 109, 110
  brickwork, 102, 103, 107–110
  clay tile, structural, 103, 110, 111, 179, 180
  cleaning, 104, 114, 118, 180, 181
  conversion factors, 106–113
  dampcourses, 104, 113, 115
  equipment, 106
  face brick, 102, 107, 108–110, 113, 114, 179, 181, 182
  fireproofing, 111
  flashings, 104, 113, 116
  glazed block and tile, 103, 104, 111, 180
  gypsum, 104
  items and measurements, 102–105
  lintels, 105, 117, 118
  manhour factor table, 179, 180
  mortar, 104, 111–113, 119, 120, 181, 183
  pricing, 178–181
  reinforcement, 105
  take-off
    example, 113–120
    principles, 101–120
  wastage factors, 43, 102, 111, 112
Masonry shelves (*see* Formwork, double forms)
Masterformat, 16, 22, 23, 30, 66, 126, 129, 130
Material and Labour Bonds, 13
Material Hoists and Towers, 210, 211

Materials
  formwork, 175–177
  quotations, 141, 143
  pricing, principles of, 140–143
Measurement, methods of, 40, 41, 85
Mechanical drawings (*see* Drawings, mechanical)
Mechanical trade, 239, 240
Membrane curing, 25, 83, 170
Metal deck, concrete fill to, 94, 167, 169
Metal doors and frames, 45, 133, 138, 184, 186
Metal fabrications (*see* Miscellaneous Metals)
Metal form panels, 173
Metal pan slabs
  formwork, 89
  place concrete, 81, 167
Metal stairs, cement fill to, 81, 169, 171
Method of Measurement, CIQS, 40, 85
Metric Measurements
  clarification, 3
  conversion tables, xiii
Miscellaneous Contractor's Work, 132, 135, 136
Miscellaneous metals, 130, 131, 134, 135
Miscellaneous obstructions, removal of, 60
Misinterpretation, of documents, 20, 21
Mixes, concrete, 76, 77
Mobile crane, 153, 208, 209, 225, 228–230
Mortar, 104, 111–113, 119, 120, 181, 183
Mortar joints, rake out and point, 104
"Murphy's Law," 236

N

Normal trade practice (*see* Trade practice, normal)
Notes, on bid documents, 22–28

O

Offices and buildings, temporary, 194, 195
Office, site (*see* Site Office)
Ontario, Construction Safety Act, 58
Out-of-town projects, 191
Output
  per specific quantity, 149
  per time cycle, 149
Overbreak, in rock excavation, 42, 62
Overburden, stripping, 61
Overhead, general office, 232
Overhead costs, site (*see* Site Overhead Costs)
Overhead doors, 135
Overlapping (*see* Laps)

P

Paging Systems, 203
Parapets, formwork to, 88
Parking Areas, temporary, 198
Paving
  asphalt, 135
  precast, 11, 12, 136, 225–227
Pedestal, formwork to, 87
Permits, 212
Personnel Hoist, 211
Photographs
  progress, 207
  site visit, 191
Pilaster, formwork to, 86, 172, 174
Pile cap
  formwork, 85, 171
  place concrete, 179, 166
Piling, perimeter, 63, 64
Pipe bedding, concrete, 81
Pits
  formwork, 86, 99, 172
  place concrete, 80, 99, 166
Plot plan, 46
Plywood
  formwork, 175–177
  rough carpentry, 124, 125
Power, temporary electrical, 199, 200
Prebid proposals, subtrade, 224–229
Prebid Site Visit Report, 192
Precast concrete
  alternate to face brick, 219
  analysis of subtrade bids, 225–227, 230, 231
  anchors for, 98

Precast concrete *(Contd.)*
- paving, 11, 12, 136, 225–227
- pre-bid proposals, 225–227

Prefabricated partitions, 135
Prequalification documents, 5
Pressure treatment, lumber, 124
Pricing
- carpentry, finish, 183, 186
- carpentry, rough, 182–183, 185
- composite labor rates, 148–151
- concrete placing, 166–171
- doors, frames, and screens, 184, 186
- examples, 156–186
- formwork, 171–178
- general categories, 140–141
- labor, 140, 141, 143–151
- manhour factors, principles, 144–148
- manhour factors, tables (*see* Manhour factor tables)
- masonry, 178–182
- materials, 141–143
- on-site observations, 147, 148
- productivity factors, 144–146
- subcontractor's unit prices, 153, 154

Proctor test, for compaction, 62
Productivity Factors
- climatic conditions, 145
- labor conditions, 145
- relative to tradesmen, 158
- repetitive work, 145, 168, 173
- supervision, 145

Profit margin, 232
Project Engineer, 193
Project Estimator, 193
Project Manager, 194
Project office (*see* Site Office)
Project superintendent, 145, 146, 188, 193
Protection
- of existing trees, 59, 197
- of finished floors, 197
- of public, 196

Public Address Systems, 203
Pumping equipment, 212
Pump mix, concrete, 18
Purchasing and expediting, 193

Q

Quantity Surveyors, Canadian Institute of, 40
Quantity take-off
- basic principles, 37–39
- deductions or voids, 37
- dimensions, figured, 37
- dimensions, sequence of, 37
- example
  - concrete and formwork, 90–100
  - earthwork, 68–76
  - masonry, 113–120
  - rough and finished Carpentry, 136–139
- identifying locations, 38
- marking items taken-off, 38
- "net-in-place", 37
- net and gross quantities, 41–43
- posting to estimate sheet, 38
- sheets, 39, 44
- studying drawings, 38
- systematic order of measuring, 37
- "timesing," 38
- waste, adjustments for, 37, 41–43

Queries, making and recording, 31–33, 36
Quotations
- materials, 141–143
- subcontractors', 220–232

R

Radial saw, 212
Rakers, for perimeter shoring, 64
Ramps
- formwork to, 86
- place concrete, 80

Ratio
- finished/unfinished areas, 239
- perimeter to floor area, 239

Reading specifications, 22–26
Ready-mix concrete (*see* Concrete)
Recording Bid Documents, 6–9
Reinforcing steel, 11, 12
Reference books, list of, 3
Removal, of rubble or debris, 60, 66, 68

Research Center
  drawings
    building section, 51
    east elevation, 50
    foundation plan, 52
    ground floor plan, 47
    north elevation, 49
    plot plan, 46
    second and third floor plans, 48
    south elevation, 50
    structural floor plans, 53
    west elevation, 49
  specification notes
    carpentry, 136
    concrete, 90
    excavation, 68
    masonry, 113
Retaining walls
  formwork to, 86
  place concrete, 80, 166
Revised drawings, 34
Risk, in pricing, 140, 141, 143
Roads, temporary, 195
Rock, classification, 58
Rock surfaces
  cleaning, 59
  line drilling, 61
Rodmen, 203
Roof hatches, 135
Roof insulation (*see* Insulation)
Rough carpentry (*see* Carpentry, rough)
Rubbish chute, 66
Rubble, removal of, 60, 66, 68

S

Safety Act, Construction, 58
Safety requirements, 205
Safety supervisors, 193
Sales taxes, 142, 231, 232
Sand and gravel, compaction factor, 57
Sand blinding, 63
Sanitary facilities, temporary, 201, 202
Saw cuts, in concrete, 83
Saw, masonry, 106, 181
Scaffold
  frames, erection and dismantling, 106, 181
  hanging, 106
  plank, 181
  rental, 106, 181
Schedule, project, 189, 190
Scheduling costs, 207
Screeds, 83, 94, 95, 97, 100, 173, 174
Screed finish, to concrete, 83
Sealants, 28
Secretarial supplies and equipment, 195
Security services, 198, 214
Seeding, 136
Seepage, concrete, into ground, 42
Separate prices, 218
Shale, classification, 58
Shear walls
  formwork to, 86, 172
  place concrete, 79, 167
Sheathing (*see* Boarding)
Shelving units, 135
Shoring, perimeter, 63, 64
Shovel, excavating
  output, 163, 165
  rental rates, 163
SI (*see* Metric Measurements)
Sills
  metal, 134
  wood, 129
Site, access to, 191, 192, 196
Site office
  for architect's representative, 194
  for contractor, 194, 195
  furniture, 194
  janitorial services, 195
  secretarial supplies and equipment, 195
Site Overhead Costs
  categorizing, 191–193
  checklist, 213
  definition, 187, 188
  managerial input, 188
Site plan (*see* Plot plan)
Site visit, 189, 191, 192
Sitework, general comments, 54–56 (*see also* Excavation)
Skilsaws, 212

Slabs, concrete
  formwork to, 87, 100, 172, 173, 174, 177, 178
  placing, 80, 81, 166, 167, 168, 169, 171
  pricing, 66 to 170, 172–174, 177, 178
  take-off example, 90 to 100
Slab edges, formwork to, 88, 95, 172–174
Sleeves, set in masonry, 104
Slots, anchor, 89, 194, 112, 113, 116, 120, 173, 174
Small tools and equipment, 211, 212
Snow and ice, removal of, 205, 206
Sodding, 136
Soffits, concrete slabs
  finishing to, 82, 97, 169
  formwork to, 87, 94, 172, 173, 174
Soil
  classifications, 58
  compaction, 57
  report, 56, 57
  swelling, 55
Specialties, manufactured, 132, 135
Specification
  allocation of trades, 29
  "approved equal" clause, 31
  approved subcontractors or manufacturers, 30, 31
  check pages of, 10
  concrete, sample of, 24
  contractural status of, 22
  definition of, 22
  as instrument of communication, 19
  Masterformat sections (*see* Masterformat)
  normal trade practice items, 29, 30
  note-making methods, 22, 23, 24, 25
  for plastic doors, 26, 27
  queries, 31, 32, 33
  reading, 22 to 28
  receipt and distribution, 6–9
  subtrades, relative to, 26 to 31
  "work by others" clause, 28, 29
  writing, 22
Spread footings
  formwork, 85, 171, 174, 177
  place concrete, 79, 90, 91, 166, 169
Stairs and ladders, temporary, 197
Stairs and landings, concrete
  finishes to, 83, 170
  formwork to, 87, 96, 172, 174
  place to, 81, 96, 167, 169
Stair nosings, 83
Stairway walls, concrete
  formwork, 86
  place to, 79
Statutory declaration, 216
Steel, fireproofing to
  concrete, 81, 82, 167, 172
  masonry, 111
Steel trowel finish, 83
Steps, exterior
  formwork to, 87
  place concrete, 81
Stipulated sum, 1, 20
Stone, crushed (*see* Underfloor Fill)
Stools
  metal, 134
  wood, 129, 183
Storage space, availability, 191
Structural clay tile, 103, 110, 111, 179, 180
Structural Frame Cost, 239
Subcontractors
  analysis of quotations, 226, 227, 228, 229, 230, 231
  approved, 27, 30, 31
  bid depository, 223, 224
  directory of, 15, 16
  misinterpretation of documents, 20, 21
  naming on bid form, 220
  prebid proposals from, 131, 224–229
  soliciting bids from, 14–17
  telephone bids from, 220–223
Subtrades (*see* Subcontractors)
Summary, main estimate, 232, 233, 234
Superintendent (*see* Project Superintendent)
Supervision, project, 145, 146, 188, 193
Surety company, 213
Surveyor's Level, 54
Surveys, 203
Surveying instruments, 203
Suspended beam, concrete:
  formwork to, 86, 172–174, 177, 178

Suspended beam, concrete: *(Contd.)*
placing, 80, 166–169, 171
Système Internationale (*see* Metric Measurements)

T

Tackboards, 135
Take-off (*see* Quantity Take-Off)
Tampers, compaction, 212
Tarpaulins, 206, 207
Technologym construction, 2
Telegrams, 202
Telephone service, temporary, 202
Telephone Bid Form, 220–223
Telex, 202
Temporary doors (*see* Temporary Enclosures)
Temporary electrical work, 199–200
Temporary elevators, 211
Temporary enclosures, 206, 207
Temporary heat, 200, 201
Temporary offices and buildings, 194–195
Temporary parking areas, 198
Temporary roads, 195
Temporary sanitary facilities, 201, 202
Temporary telephone service, 202
Temporary toilets (*see* Temporary sanitary facilities)
Temporary utilities, 198–203
Temporary water supply, 199
Temporary windows (*see* Temporary Enclosures)
Thresholds, metal, 134
Tile-joist floor, 89
Timber lagging, 64
Timber sheeting
to excavation, 63
to underpinning, 65
Timekeepers, project, 193
Toilet partitions, 135
Toilets, temporary (*see* Temporary Sanitary Facilities)
Topping, concrete, 81, 167
Topsoil, stripping, 60, 74, 164
Trade practice, items, normal, 29, 30
Trades, check list of, 10, 11, 12
Trailer, office, 194
Trees
protection of, 59, 197
removal of, 59
Trench excavation
pricing, 164, 165
take-off, 60, 61, 71, 73, 74, 75
Trenches, place concrete to, 81
Trimming, hand, to excavation, 58, 61, 70, 71
Trowels, machine, 212
Trucking, for excavation, 163, 165
Trucking, general, 204

U

Underfloor fill
pricing, 161, 164
take-off, 63, 73
Underload charges, ready-mix concrete, 78, 143
Underpinning, 64, 65
Unions, labor, 157, 158
Unit costs
functional, 239
labor, 143–151
material, 141–143
Unit Price Contracts, 1
Unit Prices
on bid form, 218, 234
from subcontractors, 153–154
Up-turned beam, 87, 172
Utilities, temporary, 198–203

V

Vault doors, 135
Vibrators, concrete, 212
Vibrating plates, compaction, 212
V-rib forms, 81

W

Waffle (dome) forms, 89
Walls, concrete
  formwork, 86, 92, 171, 172, 174
  placing, 79, 80, 166, 169
Walls, masonry, 102–104, 114, 115, 117, 120, 179–181
Walls, wood-framed, 122, 123, 125
Washroom accessories, 135
Wastage
  of materials, 41, 42, 43
  factors, 43
Water, temporary, 199
Watchman (*see* Security services)
Weep hole plugs, 105
Weeping tile (*see* Drainage tile)
Well-point System, 65
Wells, relief, 65, 66
Winter delivery, of ready-mix concrete, 79, 143, 168, 169
Winter heat and protection
  to concrete, 200, 206, 207
  to masonry, 106, 206, 207
Wood doors and frames, 133, 134, 138, 184, 185
Wood float finish, to concrete, 83
Wood sheathing, T and G, 43, 125
"Work by Others," clauses, 28, 29
Working space, 54, 55, 58